CATECHISMS AND WC
SEVENTEENTH-CEN

Catechisms and Women's Writing in Seventeenth-Century England is a study of early modern women's literary use of catechizing. Paula McQuade examines original works composed by women – both in manuscript and print, as well as women's copying and redacting of catechisms – and the construction of these materials from other sources. By studying female catechists, McQuade shows how early modern women used the power and authority granted to them as mothers to teach religious doctrine, to demonstrate their linguistic skills, to engage sympathetically with Catholic devotional texts, and to comment on matters of contemporary religious and political import – activities that many scholars have considered the sole prerogative of clergymen. This book addresses the question of women's literary production in early modern England, demonstrating that the reading and writing of catechisms were crucial sites of women's literary engagements during this time.

PAULA MCQUADE received her Ph.D. from the University of Chicago in 1998. The recipient of a 1996 Charlotte Newcombe Fellowship, McQuade is the author of multiple articles on early modern women and gender. Her article on the female catechist Dorothy Burch was selected as the best article published in 2010 by the Society for the Study of Early Modern Women Writers. She is also the recipient of an Excellence in Teaching Award from DePaul University.

CATECHISMS AND WOMEN'S WRITING IN SEVENTEENTH-CENTURY ENGLAND

PAULA MCQUADE

DePaul University

CAMBRIDGE
UNIVERSITY PRESS

University Printing House, Cambridge CB2 8BS, United Kingdom

One Liberty Plaza, 20th Floor, New York, NY 10006, USA

477 Williamstown Road, Port Melbourne, VIC 3207, Australia

314-321, 3rd Floor, Plot 3, Splendor Forum, Jasola District Centre, New Delhi - 110025, India

79 Anson Road, #06-04/06, Singapore 079906

Cambridge University Press is part of the University of Cambridge.

It furthers the University's mission by disseminating knowledge in the pursuit of education, learning and research at the highest international levels of excellence.

www.cambridge.org
Information on this title: www.cambridge.org/9781316648087
DOI: 10.1017/9781108182232

© Paula McQuade 2017

This publication is in copyright. Subject to statutory exception and to the provisions of relevant collective licensing agreements, no reproduction of any part may take place without the written permission of Cambridge University Press.

First published 2017
First paperback edition 2021

A catalogue record for this publication is available from the British Library

ISBN 978-1-107-19825-8 Hardback
ISBN 978-1-316-64808-7 Paperback

Cambridge University Press has no responsibility for the persistence or accuracy of URLs for external or third-party internet websites referred to in this publication, and does not guarantee that any content on such websites is, or will remain, accurate or appropriate.

This book is dedicated to Patrick, Peter, Henry, and Jim Navarre, with love and gratitude.

Contents

Acknowledgments	*page* ix
Notes on Transcription and Citation	xi
Introduction: "Milk for Babes": Catechisms and Female Authorship in Early Modern England	1

PART I DOMESTIC CATECHESIS AND FEMALE AUTHORSHIP — 17

1 "Mother Bare Me": Catechisms and Maternity in Early Modern England — 19

2 "A Tender Mother": Domestic Catechesis in the Household Devotional of Katherine Fitzwilliam (b. 1579) — 56

PART II FEMALE WITNESS AND INTER-CONFESSIONAL DIALOGUE — 89

3 "At Magdalin's House": Maternal Catechesis and Female Witness in the Manuscript Miscellany of Katherine Thomas (b. 1637) — 91

4 Catholicism, Catechesis, and Coterie Circulation: The Manuscript of Barbara Slingsby Talbot (b. 1633) — 117

PART III PRINT AND POLEMIC — 139

5 "A Knowing People": Catechesis and Community in Dorothy Burch's *A Catechisme of the Severall Heads of the Christian Religion* (1646) — 141

6 Prophecy, Catechesis, and Community in Mary Cary's
  The Resurrection of the Witnesses (1653) 162

  Epilogue: Catechisms and the History of Women's Writing 182

Select Bibliography 188
Index 204

Acknowledgments

First, I'd like to thank scholars and friends working on early modern women's writing – Vicky Burke, Michelle Dowd, Jaime Goodrich, Kate Narveson, and Micheline White – for their insights and support. Kate Narveson deserves special thanks for alerting me to the manuscript catechisms of Lady Fitzwilliam and Lady Montagu. Alec Ryrie enthusiastically supported the project from its inception, and Dennis Danielson generously shared with me his unpublished manuscript on catechisms and catechizing. I appreciate Ray Ryan's support of this project. I'd also like to thank Erica Longfellow, as well as an anonymous reader for Cambridge University Press, for very helpful suggestions. Colleagues at DePaul University read multiple drafts: Rebecca Cameron, June Chung, Jenny Conary, Billy Johnson-Gonzalez, Helen Marlborough, Lucy Rinehart, John Shanahan, Richard Squibbs, and Eric Selinger. Megan Heffernan offered careful readings of Chapters 3 and 4. James Murphy provided a crucial final "push." Genny Costanzo and Brenda Wegmann read and commented upon Chapter 5. Nina Wedell fielded my questions about Ewyas Lacy. Catharina Clement answered my inquiries about Strood. Mallory Gevaert, Jaclyn Leonard, and Alex Anderl provided top-notch research assistance. Karen and Jackie Navarre graciously proofread an early draft.

DePaul University provided multiple grants and a research leave. Special thanks are due to DePaul's Vincentian Endowment Fund for supporting a research trip to the Huntington Library in 2014. I'd also like to thank DePaul University's Catholic Studies Department for inviting me to present an early version of Chapter 4 and for their helpful suggestions concerning cross-confessional toleration.

I presented papers based upon my work in progress to the Renaissance Society of America, the Sixteenth-Century Studies Conference, the Bible in the Seventeenth Century Conference (2011) at the University of York, where I benefited from the comments of Ian M. Green, and the What

Is Early Modern Catholicism Conference (2013) at Durham University. I also presented a version of Chapter 3 to the University of Chicago's Renaissance Workshop, where David Bevington, Kasia Fowler, Phillip Goldfarb, Bonnie Gunzenhauser, Sarah Kunjammen, and Richard Strier provided helpful suggestions. Ada Palmer alerted me to Renaissance images depicting Mary Magdalene as a resurrection witness. I'd like to thank the Charlotte W. Newcombe Foundation for generously supporting my dissertation research. The Society for the Study of Early Modern Women Writers provided a vital endorsement of the project at an early stage by selecting my essay on Dorothy Burch (Chapter 5) as the best essay published on a woman writer in 2010.

A version of Chapter 5 appeared as "A Knowing People: Early Modern Motherhood, Female Authorship, and Working-Class Community in Dorothy Burch's *A Catechisme of the Severall Heads of the Christian Religion*" in *Prose Studies* 32, No. 3 (2010): 167–76. I am grateful to Taylor & Francis for permission to reprint. Many thanks are due to librarians at the Huntington Library, the Folger Library, the Newberry Library, the University of Illinois-Urbana Champaign Rare Books Library, the Houghton Library, the Williams Andrew Clark Library, Chetham's Library, and the Northamptonshire Record Office.

Janel Mueller deserves special thanks for reading the entire manuscript during a snowy Chicago week in February 2015 and for offering invaluable suggestions concerning early modern women, paleography, and scripturalism.

Finally, I'd like to thank Joshua Scodel, who graciously read and commented upon multiple drafts of every chapter, always offering concrete suggestions for improvement. This book is a great deal better thanks to his erudition and intelligence.

Notes on Transcription and Citation

Original spelling and capitalization have been retained in quotes from manuscripts and printed texts, although contractions have silently been expanded. I have modernized conventions such as long "s" and archaic uses of "i," "j," "u," and "v." Thorns are rendered "th" and yoghs "y." I have regularized the spelling of Biblical books and modernized the names of Biblical places.

I have retained original punctuation, except in cases where it poses a difficulty in understanding a sentence's structure or meaning. I have not reproduced italicization when it is used in printed texts for emphasis or to set apart a block of text. I reproduce textual insertions within manuscripts by designating them with a ^ and formatting them in superscript. The occasional editorial interpolation is indicated by a square bracket. I follow contemporary practice in the capitalization of titles.

When I quote from an early modern work obtained from Early English Books Online, Eighteenth-Century Collections Online, or Early American Imprints Online, I indicate this and provide its reel position number. I do not provide printers for works published before 1900.

All quotations are from the Geneva Bible, unless otherwise noted. I provide a more detailed discussion of this choice in my Introduction, footnote 9.

Introduction
"Milk for Babes": Catechisms and Female Authorship in Early Modern England

Q. What is the mother's duty?
A. To nourish her children and to instruct them. 1 Timothy 5.10
Samuel Hieron, *The Doctrine of the Beginning of Christ* (1620)[1]

A number of accounts confirm the importance of maternal catechesis to early modern women's reading and writing practices.[2] But literary scholars have been reluctant to acknowledge the centrality of the catechism, a work written in question-and-answer form on a religious subject, to early modern women's textual production. This reluctance stems in part from the genre's association with rote memorization, an association that developed during the first part of the twentieth century and still colors modern perceptions.[3] But it also reflects unacknowledged biases that influence which early modern women writers get recognized. Trained to value linguistic complexity, ambiguity, playfulness, and lyric expression, we anthologize early modern women who wrote psalm translations and sonnets; alternatively, we seek out women writers whose scripturally inspired texts subvert norms of gender or class. Catechisms, with their question-and-answer formats and their focus on religious orthodoxy, get ignored. But as Debora Shuger argued more than twenty years ago, "If no unchanging human nature exists, and what 'man' is cannot be separated from his culture, then we cannot approach a given period or its texts by disregarding the self-interpretation of that period."[4] If we are interested in early modern women's authorship in all its forms, as well as its cultural function and importance, we need to acknowledge that the catechism, associated with domestic piety, was a genre unusually open to early modern women writers – regardless of whether we find it appealing.[5]

Catechisms and Women's Writing in Seventeenth-Century England argues that the reading and writing of catechisms were crucial sites of women's literary engagements in early modern England. By studying female catechists, we learn how early modern women used the power and authority granted to them as mothers and domestic catechists to teach religious doctrine, to demonstrate their linguistic skills, and to comment on matters of contemporary religious and political import – activities that many scholars have considered the sole prerogative of clergymen. I draw upon recent work that asserts the importance of manuscript circulation in early modern England and introduce the catechetical compositions of six (largely) unremarked seventeenth-century Protestant women writers of diverse social classes: Katherine Fitzwilliam (b. 1579), Ann Montagu (b. 1573), Katherine Thomas (b. 1637), Barbara Slingsby Talbot (b. 1633), Dorothy Burch (fl. 1646), and Mary Cary (b. 1621).[6] These women were evangelical Protestants and Church of England loyalists. They wrote original catechisms in manuscript for use within the home, tailoring their compositions to the age and abilities of their children. They used their knowledge of the catechetical form to redact compendious Protestant devotional treatises in manuscript for their households, emulating godly ministers who performed similar redactions for their congregations. They transcribed catechisms alongside didactic poems of their own composition in loose papers dedicated to their children. Two of the six female catechists that I discuss use the catechetical form to redact Catholic devotional treatises. One of these women circulated her catechism in manuscript. These compilations provide concrete examples of sympathetic inter-confessional devotional reading in early modern England and thus challenge the current scholarly emphasis on inter-confessional conflict.[7] During the English Civil War, women published catechisms in order to comment on politics, using the cultural authority of maternal and domestic catechesis to legitimize their participation in contemporary religious and political controversies.

Female-authored catechisms can teach us a great deal about the power and authority accorded to women as mothers in early modern England and its effect of authorizing their textual compositions in both print and manuscript. As Kimberly Ann Coles has remarked, "The terms of religion both empowered and controlled the conditions of female authorship" in early modern England.[8] Nearly all Protestant churches forbade women from "speaking" in Church – that is, teaching religious doctrine, interpreting scripture, or pronouncing on church polity. Protestant ministers defended this prohibition by reference to Paul's advice to the Corinthian community: "Let your women keepe silence in the churches; for it is not permitted unto them to speake" (1 Corinthians 14:34).[9] Some early modern women objected to this prohibition on the grounds that it impeded their spiritual freedom, but ministers insisted it was necessary to ensure women's social subordination.[10] However, while ministers prohibited women from teaching religious doctrine or sermonizing in church, they urged mothers to instruct their children and servants within the home. By so doing, they (perhaps unwittingly) encouraged mothers to assume such traditionally ministerial roles as the explanation of religious doctrine, the explication of scriptural passages, and the interpretation of complex devotional treatises.

This study of women's catechetical composition thus contributes to a current move to complicate and supplement earlier studies of early modern maternity. Drawing in part on Virginia Woolf's representation of the death of Shakespeare's sister in childbirth in *A Room of One's Own*, early feminist scholarship associated early modern motherhood with maternal and infant death. Influential works by Janet Adelman, Coppelia Kahn, and Frances Dolan examined dramatic representations of "suffocating," "absent," and "dangerous" maternity on the early modern stage.[11] But recent scholarship has shifted its focus to explore the multiple ways women used genres associated with childbirth and motherhood to engage in what Michelle Dowd has characterized as "a vibrant historical conversation about maternal authority."[12] *Catechisms and Women's Writing* seeks to join in this ongoing conversation about women, maternity, and authorship by demonstrating that maternal catechesis was a culturally sanctioned source of female intellectual activity, textual production, and political engagement in early modern England.

Milk for Babes

Aware of Martin Luther's use of catechisms in the German Reformation, English Protestant reformers developed the English catechism in the mid-sixteenth century as a means of promulgating the Reformed faith in England. Drawing on 1 Corinthians 3:2 ("I gave you milke to drinke, and not meat: for yee were not yet able to bear it"), catechists describe catechisms as providing scriptural and doctrinal truths in an easily digestible form for the young or unlearned (milk for babes). Only after they have digested these basic doctrinal truths are they able to sample more advanced religious instruction, such as sermons, which are "meate for men."[13] English catechisms served diverse functions. Many catechisms were designed for the instruction of very young children within the home, but as the Reformation took hold, Protestant ministers became aware of the need for advanced religious instruction, perhaps, as Eamon Duffy has suggested, to "arouse to faith" the spiritually tepid believer.[14] Catechisms were developed for children of various ages and abilities; some of them, intended to be read silently, not orally rehearsed, offered theological instruction and introduced high-level literary interpretation to students who lacked university training. More broadly, seventeenth-century Protestant ministers recast lengthy Protestant devotional treatises into catechetical form for parishioners who lacked the time or inclination to read them or money to purchase them. Print catechisms became ubiquitous in seventeenth-century England. Ian Green estimates that English printers produced more than 250,000 catechisms between 1540 and 1640; "one of a half to three quarters of a million is not beyond possibility."[15]

Catechisms played a central role in the literary activities of early modern English women throughout their lives.[16] As children, they learned to read by rehearsing the catechism with their mothers; as mothers, they used print catechisms and composed original catechisms to teach their households; as mature women, they might read or compose catechetical redactions of devotional works as part of their domestic religious meditation or for circulation among friends and co-religionists. Grandmothers catechized their grandchildren, a practice that catechists lauded as following the scriptural example of Lois, grandmother and teacher of Paul's disciple Timothy (2 Timothy 1:5). The duty of maternal catechesis applied to women of all social classes and confessional affiliations. Many catechisms, like Robert Abbot's *Milk For Babes*, acknowledge noble women patrons and emphasize their active role in the domestic catechesis of young children. Other catechisms were designed for (and, as we will see in Chapter 5, composed by) working-class mothers. Because catechisms were typically designed to provide an introduction to the Protestant faith, they generally avoided theological controversy and so were used by persons of various confessional affiliations – evangelical Protestants, Church of England loyalists, and separatists.[17]

Immersion in maternal catechesis enabled early modern women to move from being readers to writers: it provided them with the textual skills, authorial confidence, and linguistic prowess necessary for original composition in both manuscript and print. In making this claim, I draw upon and extend the work of Janel Mueller, Margaret Hannay, Erica Longfellow, Katherine Narveson, and Femke Molekamp on the importance of the English Bible to early modern women's reading and writing practices.[18] The process by which a person masters a genre is admittedly complex, but genre theorists identify repeated exposure to its defining features as a key component. Alistair Fowler suggestively compares genre acquisition to learning a language.[19] *Catechisms and Women's Writing* argues that by catechizing their children (and being catechized as children), early modern women gained an appreciation of the genre's features: its use of a question-and-answer format and its frequent reliance on complex patterns of scriptural citation. They also increased their knowledge of religious doctrine and developed their sense of audience. Perhaps most significantly, they gained confidence in their ability to teach religious truth.

As we will see, maternal catechists emulated their ministerial counterparts by composing catechisms, but the scope of their activity in both manuscript and print extended beyond the household walls. Women circulated catechisms in manuscript among friends and family, adapting the genre to their unique concerns. Some of these women recast prohibited Catholic devotional texts and thereby intervened in late seventeenth-century political debates concerning the status of English Catholics, while others published original catechisms that engage in the religious and political debates of England's Civil War. Such interventions improve our understanding of the depth and complexity of women's religious and political agency, confirming Julie Crawford's claim that the early modern household could be a "headquarters for religious and political activism at both the national and international level."[20]

Methodology

Catechisms and Women's Writing can be broadly described as a feminist genre study. Sarah Ross has recently remarked that "the radical differences between the cultural capital of women and men in early modern England, and women's concomitantly particular position in relation to high literary genres, means that continued exploration of genre as an apparatus of authorship is essential."[21] My understanding of genre is indebted to Alistair Fowler's claim that genres are like families: a member of a genre may "inherit" certain characteristics from its parent, like a child inherits blue eyes. But not all generic traits are displayed within a single offspring; it is only by looking at the extended family that one can get a sense of the inherited traits that constitute a family resemblance. "What produces generic resemblances . . . " says Fowler, "is tradition: a sequence of influence and imitation and inherited codes connect works in the genre . . . Poems are made in part from older poems; each is the child . . . of an early representative of the genre and may yet be the mother of a subsequent representative."[22] Generic "family resemblance" is both synchronic and diachronic; it accounts for continuity and discontinuity within a particular historical moment and across generations. Throughout *Catechisms and Women's Writing*, I attempt to respect the form and the content of individual catechisms, while simultaneously paying attention to patterns across works. I also consider the multiple functions of ministerial catechisms in seventeenth-century England and the ways in which women's catechetical compositions draw upon and extend this diversity. By focusing on genre, I account for the uniqueness of each woman's composition, while at the same time I acknowledge women's shared experiences.

Drawing on recent work on the materiality of textual practices, I consider the material form of each text and how its materiality shaped its composition.[23] Victoria Burke, Margaret Ezell, Harold Love, and Arthur Marotti have convincingly demonstrated that in seventeenth-century England, manuscript and print were competing for cultural prominence.[24] Trained from birth to avoid public notice, women often composed and circulated their works in manuscript; like coterie male authors, they limited their readers and used writing to reinforce a sense of community. Margaret Ezell asserts that the scholarly focus on print publication has caused us to underestimate early modern women's writing practices.[25] By considering manuscript catechetical composition as a form of authorship, *Catechisms and Women's Writing* adds six authors to the emerging canon of early modern English women writers. Some women's manuscript compositions were designed exclusively for household use, while others resemble male-authored publications. By attending to the material features of the manuscript text – its length, its form, its orthography, and its handwriting – we gain valuable insights into its composition and purpose.

Studying women's manuscript catechisms also provides insights into women's print catechisms. Of the six women catechists I discuss at length in the present study, only two saw their texts into print. This ratio of print and manuscript circulation accords with what historians have ascertained concerning women's compositional practices in seventeenth-century England. While it may not have been remarkable for an early modern Englishwoman to compose a catechism, it was unusual for her to publish it. Micheline White proposes that when an early modern woman published a catechism, she probably did so for political reasons: she wanted to contribute to contemporary religio-political discussion and debate.[26] I argue that it is not only the content of the catechism that contributes to contemporary political debates; it is also the female knowledge and authority that it demonstrates. By publishing catechisms, women were exhibiting their knowledge of religious doctrine and their ability to teach this knowledge to others – and in the process, implicitly challenging ministerial authority. Yet, as we will see, some women likewise composed manuscript catechisms and circulated them selectively among readers in order to intervene in contemporary politics, so we cannot assume that print publication was "subversive" and "political" and that manuscript composition was "conservative" and "private." Print and manuscript are two different forms of dissemination: each has its own function and intended audience; neither is inherently more radical or political than the other.

In this study I have applied the methodology of local history – that is, I situate each author within her regional and kinship networks while simultaneously noting her engagement with larger historical and political developments. Micheline White has asserted that "prioritizing geographical locality and seeking to excavate a region's literary, religious, and kinship networks can yield surprising results about women writers' engagements with local culture, their relation to other female writers, and their representation by their male peers." Such analysis requires literary critics to examine archival documentary sources in order to gain a sense of "the intellectual circles in which these works were produced and read."[27] In what follows, I draw upon such diverse sources as county histories, public records, taxation lists, and churchwardens' accounts in an attempt to reconstruct the religious, literary, and family communities that supported the composition of these catechisms. By placing each author within her local context, while at the same time exploring how she emulated and adapted the generic features of other catechisms, I attend to both the material and the formal aspects of early modern women's textual production.

Range of Chapters

The following study is divided in three parts, with two chapters each. Part I, "Domestic Catechesis and Female Authorship," surveys print and manuscript catechisms to demonstrate both that these works provide insight into relations between mothers and children in early modern England and that the practice of maternal catechesis contributed to female textual production. Replacing the concept of catechesis as exclusively rote memorization, I demonstrate in Chapter 1 that catechesis was also an interactive performance between two people, often, but not exclusively, a mother and her child. Its practice more closely resembled a play rehearsal than an oral examination. Published catechisms were geared to the interest and abilities of children. Both children and adults describe catechesis as an exercise in which they most fully experienced maternal love. Chapter 1 concludes by looking at two manuscript examples of maternal catechesis. Katherine

Thomas' historical catechism is designed for children between the ages of seven and eleven years old. With its focus upon the sensational and the amusing, this catechism exemplifies how catechesis could be enjoyable and educational. Lady Ann Montagu includes a carefully copied version of Joseph Hall's catechism alongside her original didactic poem. Hall's work and hers cohere in the representation of literate, pious maternity and thereby facilitate Montagu's participation in manuscript culture.

I next consider the range of writing that a mother might undertake when composing household catechisms. Chapter 2 focuses upon the four original catechisms contained in FH 246, a manuscript devotional manual by Lady Katherine Fitzwilliam. The first two catechisms are tailored to the ages and abilities of her children and demonstrate Fitzwilliam's authorial sense of audience. The third catechism is Fitzwilliam's redaction of Richard Rogers' *Seven Treatises* (1603). In 1618, the godly minister Stephen Egerton published a catechism based upon Rogers' text, so Lady Fitzwilliam's maternal catechesis demonstrated textual and linguistic skills that rivaled ministerial authority. Her fourth catechism invites a detailed discussion of the theological problems posed by "affliction," a topic of central concern to Calvinists in the late sixteenth and early seventeenth centuries. Here Fitzwilliam draws upon her experience as a mother, imaging God as a "tender mother" who punishes her children only because she loves them. The result is an original contribution to the literature on "affliction."

In Part II, "Female Witness and Inter-Confessional Dialogue," I explore the use of catechisms in inter-confessional devotional reading. Chapter 3 considers a woman who used the catechetical form to read and respond sympathetically to a prohibited Catholic devotional text. Katherine Thomas was a wealthy widow and mother from a small town in Herefordshire near the Welsh border – an area with a high percentage of Catholics and home to a Jesuit seminary at Cwm. Thomas' catechism is based upon her reading a copy of John Heigham's *Life of Christ* that had been smuggled into England at least fifty years earlier. Because Heigham's *Life* was composed for the community of nuns at Gravelines, it creates a narrative that emphasizes the centrality of women to Christ's life, death, and resurrection. Thomas' catechism condenses the final 200 pages of Heigham's *Life* to highlight his account of Christ's post-resurrection appearances, a sequence that relates how Christ first appeared to his mother and Mary Magdalene, thus emphasizing women's ability to serve as resurrection witnesses and contributing to ongoing debates concerning women's ability to teach religious truths. Thomas also imaginatively includes in her catechism narrative details not found in scripture, such as

Christ's final meal at the house of Mary Magdalene, thus depicting the importance of women as supporters of the early Christian community.

In Chapter 4, I consider how Barbara Slingsby Talbot, a Church of England loyalist, used the catechetical form to intervene in late seventeenth-century debates concerning the toleration of English Catholics. Talbot's manuscript, Huntington Library HM 43213, is a small text formatted to resemble a Protestant devotional manual and catechism. In a brief preface, Talbot describes HM 43213 as a redacted version of a book sent to her by her late father, Henry Slingsby, a Royalist executed by Oliver Cromwell in 1658. Although she treasures the book as "the last legacie" of her father, Talbot explains that she has redacted it before circulating because it contains material "contrary to the faith and Doctrien of the Church of Ingland." I have identified Henry Slingsby's book as *The Key of Paradise* (5th ed., 1622), a Catholic devotional manual published by the Jesuit John Wilson. Talbot's manuscript largely preserves the order and content of *The Key of Paradise*, only revising the Catholic elements. She reads her father's text sympathetically, remarking that it contains much in it that is "pious and useful" despite its Catholicism. I argue that Talbot revised her late father's devotional manual in 1686 precisely to intervene in contemporary debates occasioned by the accession of the Catholic James II.

Part III, "Print and Polemic," looks at two women who drew upon the genre's association with pious female domesticity to publish catechisms that intervened in Civil War politics. Chapter 5 examines *A Catechisme of the Severall Heads of the Christian Religion*, published by Dorothy Burch in 1646. Burch was a godly wife and mother who lived in Strood, a small town near Rochester. I demonstrate that her decision to compose and publish her catechism was intimately connected with religious conflicts that reflect the widespread controversy caused by Laudian reforms in Kent. Strood's parish church, St. Nicholas, was served ably by John Chamberlain, a godly minister, for over thirty years. But when Chamberlain died in 1639, he was replaced by John Mann, a High Church curate, as part of Archbishop's Laud's efforts to ensure conformity. Conflicts quickly ensued between Mann and his working-class parishioners. Characterizing herself as the spokeswoman for her godly, but minimally educated community of fishermen and oyster-dredgers, Burch explains that she composed her catechism to counter Mann's characterization of the parishioners of St. Nicholas as "a poor, ignorant and simple people, who knew nothing of God." Under the urging of "one of near relation," Burch agreed to publish her catechism.[28] It was printed by Mathew Simmons (the radical publisher of Milton's prose tracts), perhaps as a demonstration of the informed piety of humble Kentishmen. Burch's catechism thus exemplifies how one early modern woman exerted the authority accorded to her as a mother, as well as the accrued power of the printing press, to contest a most unchristian disdain for the lowly.

In Chapter 6, I address the use of catechetical form by separatist, antimonarchical women, exemplified by Mary Cary's *The Resurrection of the Witnesses* (1653). First published in 1648, this work is an extended exegesis of Revelation 11:1–14 that predicts the success of Cromwell's New Model Army. A founding member of the Fifth Monarchists, a millenarian organization, Cary denies speaking as a prophet – the strategy used by her contemporary Anna Trapnel to authorize her entrance into the public sphere. Instead, in her 1653 revision of *The Resurrection of the Witnesses*, Cary claims authority on the basis of her domestic scriptural study: "But only this do I assert, that I have from my child-hood, but especially since I was fifteen years of age, been (I doubt not but I may say) by the spirit of God set upon a serious and continual study of the scriptures in general, and more particularly, of the book of Revelation." She concludes: "This, I say, is all that I assert concerning this, and I have no other grounds but these for these things."[29] Cary includes several catechisms within her prose exegesis. By using the catechetical form, Cary assumes the authority ceded to women in domestic religious instruction to comment upon contemporary political events. Protestant ministers objected to Cary's text on these grounds: *The Account Audited* (1649) charges that Cary's exegesis is faulty because it is based on oral, not written, scriptural study – the former being implicitly associated with women. *The Resurrection of the Witnesses* thus provides insight into the catechism's role as a genre that straddled both writing and orality, and the way in which these modes of discourse were gendered in early modern England.

Notes

1. Samuel Hieron, *The Doctrine of the Beginning of Christ* (London, 1620), Sig. C4r.
2. Studies that emphasize the centrality of catechisms to early modern women's education include Kenneth Charlton, *Women, Religion, and Education in Early Modern England* (London: Routledge, 1999); Ian Green, *The Christian's ABC: Catechisms and Catechizing in England, 1530–1740* (Oxford: Oxford University Press, 1996); Margaret Spufford, "First Steps in Literacy: The Reading and Writing Experiences of the Humblest Seventeenth-Century Spiritual Autobiographers," *Social History* 4 (1979): 407–45. I discuss several sixteenth-

and seventeenth-century first-person narratives that mention maternal catechesis in Chapter 1.
3. This association persists despite the work of literary scholars Stanley Fish, *The Living Temple: George Herbert and Catechizing* (Berkeley: University of California Press, 1978) and Dennis Danielson, "Catechism, *The Pilgrim's Progress*, and the Pilgrim's Progress," *Journal of English and Germanic Philology* 94.1 (1995): 42–58.
4. Debora Shuger, *Habits of Thought: Religion, Politics, and the Dominant Culture* (Toronto: University of Toronto Press, 1997), 4.
5. Michelle Dowd similarly praises methodology that allows critics to shift their "focus away from the exceptional or oppositional aspects of women's textual lives (e.g. their resistance to male authority)" and consider "instead their embeddedness within a range of discursive contexts, including the orthodox as well as the more radical." "Genealogical Counter Narratives in the Writings of Mary Cary," *Modern Philology* 109.4 (2012): 440–62, footnote 4. Erica Longfellow makes a similar point regarding *Eliza's Babes* (1652) in *Women and Religious Writing in Early Modern England* (Cambridge: Cambridge University Press, 2004). "The book's obscurity seems due to a combination of its scarcity, a mistaken assumption that it is intended for children, and the preference of many feminist scholars for texts that are either religiously or politically radical or of high literary quality, of which *Eliza's Babes* is neither" (123).
6. Kate Narveson briefly discusses the catechetical compositions of Lady Fitzwilliam and Lady Montagu in *Bible Readers and Lay Writers in Early Modern England* (Aldershot: Ashgate Press, 2012), 138–9. Siobhan Keenan discusses the original elegies contained in Katherine Thomas' manuscript miscellany but does not remark upon the catechisms. "Embracing Submission? Motherhood, Marriage, and Mourning in Katherine Thomas's Seventeenth-Century Commonplace Book," *Women's Writing* 15.1 (2008): 69–85. Burch is mentioned briefly in Sylvia Brown's "The Eloquence of the Word and the Spirit," in *Women and Religion in Old and New Worlds*, ed. Susan Dinan and Debora Meyers (New York: Routledge, 2001), 194. Phyllis Mack devotes a paragraph to Burch's authorship in *Visionary Women: Ecstatic Prophecy in Seventeenth-Century England* (Berkeley: University of California Press, 1992), 121. Jeremy de Groot looks at Barbara Talbot's exercises in French translation in "'Everyone Teacheth After Thyr Owne Fantasie': French Language Instruction," in *Performing Pedagogy in Early Modern England*, ed. Katheryn Moncrief and Katheryn McPherson (Aldershot: Ashgate, 2011), 33–52. Mary Cary has received the most extensive discussion; see especially David Lowenstein, "Scriptural Exegesis, Female Prophecy, and Radical Politics in Mary Cary," *Studies in English Literature* 46.1 (2006): 133–53. I provide a fuller bibliography of Cary's writings in Chapter 6.
7. That Protestant women comment sympathetically on prohibited Catholic devotional manuals challenges commonly held beliefs concerning Protestant-Catholic relations in the period. Richard Strier aptly declares that we as critics

need to oppose "any sort of approach to texts that knows in advance what they will or must be doing or saying or, on the other hand, what they cannot possibly be doing or saying." *Resistant Structures: Particularity, Radicalism, and Renaissance Texts* (Berkeley: University of California Press, 1995), 2.
8. Kimberly Ann Coles, *Religion, Reform, and Women's Writing in Early Modern England* (Cambridge: Cambridge University Press, 2008), 2.
9. Unless otherwise noted, all scriptural references are to the Geneva Bible, *The Bible: That Is, The Holy Scriptures* (London, 1610), held by The Newberry Library. The Geneva Bible's extensive annotations and cross-references made it a logical choice for women readers who, as Femke Molekamp has remarked, were "an important group targeted by the Geneva Bible reading aids." *Women and The Bible in Early Modern England* (Oxford: Oxford University Press, 2013), 28. The 1610 version includes Lawrence Tomson's translation and notes to the New Testament, first published in 1576 and included in Roman quartos from 1587, and Franciscus Junius' 1599 virulently anti-papist notes on Revelation (Molekamp, *Women and the Bible*, 29). All of the female catechists I consider composed their texts after 1603, making it likely that they would have used an edition that included these new translations and notes. I have also, whenever possible, checked female catechists' scriptural verses against *The Geneva Bible: A Facsimile of the 1560 Edition* (Peabody, MA: Hendrickson Publishing, 2007) and *The Holy Bible, 1611 Edition; King James Version* (Peabody, MA: Hendrickson Publishing, 2011). I discuss the female catechists' use of various editions of the Bible more extensively in Chapters 2 and 6.
10. Longfellow, in *Women and Religious Writing*, describes how "an account book of an unnamed London congregation for 1652–4 records the debate caused by a woman's refusal to attend a meeting." The woman, Anne Harriman, explained her decision by stating that " … she could not walk where she had not liberitie to speak." "Anne Harriman's declaration," Longfellow writes, "thus highlights the faultline between the duties expected of all Christians – which must sometimes be carried out in public, open to view – and the restrictions placed upon women" by the Pauline command in 1 Corinthians 14:34 (159).
11. Janet Adelman, *Suffocating Mothers: Fantasies of Maternal Origin in Shakespeare* (London: Routledge, 1992); Coppelia Kahn, "The Absent Mother in King Lear," in *Rewriting the Renaissance: The Discourses of Sexual Difference in Early Modern Europe*, ed. Margaret Ferguson, Maureen Quilligan, and Nancy Vickers (Chicago: University of Chicago Press, 1985), 33–49. Frances Dolan, *Dangerous Familiars* (Ithaca, NY: Cornell University Press, 1994). Mary Beth Rose relates the absence of mothers on the English stage to the generic demands of tragedy in "Where are the Mothers in Shakespeare: Options for Gender Representation in the English Renaissance," *Shakespeare Quarterly* 42.3 (1991): 291–314.
12. Michelle Dowd, "Genealogical Counter-Narratives in the Writings of Mary Carey," *Modern Philology* 109.4 (2012): 440–62, 442. Much work has been devoted to the maternal legacy, examining the ways in which a balance is

negotiated between the occasion of writing – the prospect of maternal death – and the agency manifested by authorial composition. See Wendy Wall, "Dancing in a Net," in *The Imprint of Gender: Authorship and Publication in the English Renaissance* (Ithaca: Cornell University Press, 1993), 279–340, especially 283–95. Kristen Poole, "The Fittest Closet for All Goodness": Authorial Strategies of Jacobean Mothers' Manuals," *Studies in English Literature* 35.1 (1995): 69–88; Sylvia Brown, "Over Her Dead Body": Feminism, Post Structuralism, and the Mother's Legacy," in *Discontinuities: New Essays on Renaissance Literature and Criticism*, ed. Paul Stevens and Viviana Comensoli (Toronto: University of Toronto Press, 1998), 3–26. Jennifer Louise Heller provides an extensive discussion of the genre in *The Mother's Legacy in Early Modern England* (Aldershot: Ashgate, 2011). Kathryn McPherson and Kathryn Moncrief examine early modern motherhood as a performance in their respective collections, *Performing Maternity in Early Modern England* (Aldershot: Ashgate, 2008) and *Performing Pedagogy in Early Modern England: Gender, Instruction, and Performance* (Aldershot: Ashgate, 2011).

13. Catechizing is "milke for babes, whereas preaching is meate for men that are of age." Henry Leslie, *A Full Confutation of the Covenant* (London, 1639), Sig. A2r.
14. Eamon Duffy, "The Long Reformation: Catholicism, Protestantism, and the Multitude," in *England's Long Reformation, 1500–1800*, ed. Nicholas Tyacke (London: University College London Press, 1998), 33–70, 43.
15. Green, *The Christian's ABC*, 65–6. Much of the information in the preceding paragraph is derived from Green's magisterial work. My definition of catechism rests upon Green's: "Any form which was in question-and-answer and in which the basic intention of the author seemed to have been to provide instruction on a religious topic, broadly defined" (52).
16. In the mid-sixteenth century, English Catholics followed the lead of Protestant ministers and began producing catechisms for their faithful. These catechisms differ importantly from Protestant catechisms and regrettably lie outside the boundaries of this study.
17. I follow Patrick Collinson in defining the term "Puritan" as "a hotter sort of Protestant." I agree with him that differences between Puritans and their opponents in the Church of England "were differences of degree, of theological temperature so to speak, rather than fundamental principle." *The Elizabethan Puritan Movement* (Berkeley: University of California Press, 1967), 26–7. Drawing upon this definition, I use the terms "Puritan," "godly," "evangelically minded," and "evangelical Protestant" interchangeably. I also rely upon the work of John Spurr, who describes Puritanism as a belief system that "placed a high value on a reformed, parish based, national church and a strong parish ministry; at least some set forms of worship were judged necessary, as was an educated and trained clergy." "From Puritanism to Dissent, 1660–1700," in *The Culture of English Puritanism, 1560–1700*, ed. Christopher Durston and Jacqueline Eales (New York: St. Martin's Press,

1996), 234–65, 235. In contrast, I use the term "separatist" to designate those men and women whose theology differed "on fundamental principle" from Church of England theology.

Following Judith Maltby, I describe the men and women who "found authenticity, comfort, and renewal in conformity to the official and lawful forms of the Christian religion as offered by the Church of England" as "Prayer Book Protestants," "Protestant conformists," "Church of England loyalists," and (rarely) "Protestants." "Suffering and Surviving: the Civil Wars, the Commonwealth, and the Formation of 'Anglicanism,' 1642–1660," in *Religion in Revolutionary England*, ed. Christopher Durston and Judith Maltby (Manchester: Manchester University Press, 2006), 158–80, 159. I avoid "Anglican" since, as Maltby rightly notes, the term "begs enormous scholarly and historical questions, as it treats the emerging multi-denominational character of English Christianity after 1660 as a foregone conclusion" (159).

18. Janel Mueller, "A Tudor Queen Finds Voice: Katherine Parr's *Lamentation of a Sinner*," in *The Historical Renaissance: New Essays on Tudor and Stuart Literature and Culture*, ed. Heather Dubrow and Richard Strier (Chicago: University of Chicago Press, 1988), 15–47 and "Devotion as Difference: Intertextuality in Queen Katherine Parr's Prayers or Meditations," *Huntington Library Quarterly* 53.3 (1990): 171–97; *Silent But for the Word*, ed. Margaret Hannay (Kent, OH: Kent State University Press, 1985); Erica Longfellow, *Women and Religious Writing*; Katherine Narveson, *Bible Readers and Lay Writers*; Femke Molekamp, *Women and the Bible*.

19. Alistair Fowler, *Kinds of Literature: An Introduction to the Theory of Genres and Modes* (Cambridge: Harvard University Press, 1982), 44–5.

20. Julie Crawford, "Literary Circles and Communities," in *The History of British Women's Writing, 1500–1610*, ed. Caroline Bicks and Jennifer Summit (Basingstoke: Palgrave Macmillan, 2010), 34–59, 35.

21. Sarah Ross, "Early Modern Women and the Apparatus of Authorship," *Parergon* 29.2 (2012): 1–8, 5.

22. Fowler, *Kinds of Literature*, 42.

23. Joshua Scodel similarly emphasizes both the materiality of a genre and its relation to social and political circumstances in *The English Poetic Epitaph: From Jonson to Wordsworth* (Ithaca: Cornell University Press, 1991). On the materiality of early modern women's reading practices, see Heidi Brayman Hackel, *Reading Material in Early Modern England: Print, Gender, and Literacy* (Cambridge: Cambridge University Press, 2005); Helen Smith, *Grossly Material Things: Women and Book Production in Early Modern England* (Oxford: Oxford University Press, 2012).

24. Victoria Burke, "Ann Bowyer's Commonplace Book (Bodleian Library, Ashmole MS 51): Reading and Writing among the 'Middling Sort,'" *Early Modern Literary Studies* 6.3 (2001): 1–28. Also, Margaret Ezell, *Social Authorship and the Advent of Print* (Baltimore: John Hopkins

University Press, 1999); Harold Love, *Scribal Publication in Seventeenth-Century England* (Oxford: Oxford University Press, 1993); Arthur Marotti, *Manuscript, Print, and the English Renaissance Lyric* (Ithaca: Cornell University Press, 1995).

25. Ezell remarks in *Social Authorship*, "Current modes of analyzing authorship do not deal with this type of author who has no desire to publish or 'go public' except to form theories to explain the motivation behind what we see as authorial self-destruction" (43). D. F. McKenzie declares more bluntly, "Apart from brief accounts by Cameron and Love, and the invaluable index volumes edited by Peter Beal, the extent, implications, and normalcy of scribal publication have remained unreported and unstudied." "Speech—Manuscript—Print," in *Making Meaning: Printers of the Mind and Other Essays*, ed. Peter D. McDonald and Michael F. Suarez (Amherst: University of Massachusetts Press, 2002), 235–58, 247.
26. Personal communication, *Sixteenth Century Studies Conference*, Cincinnati, Ohio, 2012. See also Micheline White, "Power Couples and Women Writers in Elizabethan England: The Public Voices of Dorcas and Richard Martin and Ann and Hugh Dowriche," in *Framing the Family: Narrative and Representation in the Medieval and Early Modern Periods*, ed. Rosalynn Voaden and Diane Wolfhal (Tempe: Arizona Center for Medieval and Renaissance Studies, 2005), 120–38.
27. Micheline White, "Women Writers and Literary Religious Circles in the Elizabethan West Country: Anne Dowriche, Anne Lock Prowse, Anne Lock Moyle, Elizabeth Rous, and Ursula Fulford," *Modern Philology* 103.2 (2005): 187–214, 188.
28. Dorothy Burch, *A Catechisme of the Severall Heads of the Christian Religion* (London, 1646), in *Catechisms Written for Mothers, Schoolmistresses, and Children, 1575–1750*, ed. Paula McQuade (Aldershot: Ashgate, 2008), Sig. A3v.
29. Mary Cary, *The Resurrection of the Witnesses* (London, 1653), *Early English Books Online* (III:E.719 [2]), Sig. D1v.

PART I

Domestic Catechesis and Female Authorship

In Part I, I examine the practice of maternal catechesis within the early modern household. Chapter 1 investigates the manuscript compositions of two women: Katherine Thomas, a Herefordshire widow and mother, who composed a lively historical catechism tailored to the interests of her children, and Lady Ann Montagu, who transcribed a print catechism, along with an original poem dedicated to her stepchildren, in her loose papers. Thomas' catechism is a working text, designed for use in household religious instruction; Lady Montagu's composition, in contrast, draws upon the prestige accorded to women as domestic catechists to legitimate her authorship. In Chapter 2, we turn to another domestic catechist, Lady Katherine Fitzwilliam, who, like Thomas, includes in her manuscript miscellany a catechism designed especially for children. Fitzwilliam's catechism, predating Thomas' by at least fifty years, is situated in a manuscript matrix of three more advanced catechisms clearly intended for use in the household. Examining Fitzwilliam's work in the context of these other three will deepen our understanding of the relation between maternal catechesis and original composition by women in seventeenth-century England.

CHAPTER I

"Mother Bare Me"
Catechisms and Maternity in Early Modern England

Q. But what Mothers have you?
A. I have Mother Earth and I have Mother Eve, Mother bare me and
Sion the Mother of us all if we be the faithful Children of God.
W. B. *The Farmer's Catechize* (1657)[1]

Introduction

In *The Pilgrim's Progress*, Christian's wife is visited by Prudence, who wants to "see how Christiana had brought up her children." She accordingly asks "leave of her to catechise them." Although catechesis is ordinarily conceived of as the rote rehearsal of questions and answers, Prudence personalizes her instruction: she addresses each child by name, asks each if he is willing to be questioned, and tailors her questions according to the child's age and ability. The boys answer Prudence's questions admirably, and she praises them individually: "you are a very good boy ... one that has learned well." Prudence concludes her catechesis with two suggestions: the boys, she says, should "continue much in the meditation of that book that was the cause of your father's becoming a pilgrim," and they should "still harken to your mother, for she can learn you more."[2]

That *The Pilgrim's Progress* contains this representation of catechesis is not surprising: Bunyan's debt to popular religious literature (in which catechisms play a central role) has often been remarked.[3] I am interested in this exchange because of its two underlying assumptions: that the purpose of catechesis is to teach children to read the Bible on their own and that providing this training is the responsibility of the mother. The goal of catechesis in teaching children to read the Bible accords with the Protestant emphasis upon *sola scriptura*. But what of the second assumption – that in seventeenth-century England, mothers were responsible for the catechetical instruction of their children? Bunyan depicts

Christiana as the boys' primary teacher: "You are to be commended," Prudence remarks, "for thus bringing up your children."[4]

This chapter will demonstrate that maternal catechesis constitutes a vital but under-acknowledged area of female agency in early modern England. Studying it provides insight into what I term "everyday maternity": the ordinary interactions between mother and child that constitute the majority of one's experience of either mothering or being mothered. Like literary and dramatic treatments, these are of course representations. But scholars have tended to overlook representations of this sort, in part because they do not subvert cultural norms and in part because much of the evidence for everyday maternity survives only in manuscript. Maternal catechizing, with its emphasis upon a mother's intellectual ability, her love for her children, and the sustained engagement between herself and her child, provides a valuable site to start an inquiry into maternity in early modern England.

This chapter has three parts. In the first, I draw upon published catechisms, spiritual autobiographies, letters, and journal entries to trace the role played by mothers in catechesis. Although historians have acknowledged the importance of mothers as teachers in early modern England, there has been little inquiry into the impact of such instruction upon popular images of maternity. Maternally directed catechisms, written for mothers to use in educating their children, depict mothers as literate, intellectually eager, and engaged in their children's intellectual and moral development. They are motivated to instruct their children because they love them. By requiring a child to memorize his catechism, a mother fosters his lifelong spiritual growth. As adults, early modern men and women describe childhood catechesis as the time when they became aware of their mother's love. This love, moreover, is not one-sided: mothers emphasize that the love that they feel while instructing their children shapes their own spiritual and intellectual development.

In the second part of this chapter, I explore maternal catechesis in the manuscript miscellany of Katherine Thomas, a mother of five children who lived in a small village near the Welsh border. Katherine Thomas' manuscript miscellany, composed over thirty years, mixes passages from popular devotional manuals and original compositions. Thomas' original compositions include prayers, elegies, a maternal legacy, and two catechisms. Siobhan Keenan has explored Thomas' elegies, but Thomas' two catechisms have yet to be studied.[5] In Chapter 3, I focus on Thomas' second catechism; here, I discuss her first catechism, *Places of Scripture*, a historical text that Thomas likely used in the education of her children. It provides an image of a mother who is aware of her children's interests and designs her catechetical lesson around them. Because it includes questions that focus on sensational or dramatic incidences from the Old and New Testaments, it suggests that maternal catechesis could both instruct and give pleasure to children.

The third part of this chapter explores the role of maternal religious instruction in the loose papers of Lady Ann Montagu. These loose papers include both an original poem of 160 stanzas and a catechism by Joseph Hall. One might be tempted to distinguish between Lady Montagu's 'literary' poem and her 'non-literary' catechism, but I would suggest that these distinctions do not convey Montagu's understanding of these two works.[6] Although their genres are disparate, the poem and the catechism cohere in representing Lady Montagu as a loving, devout, and literate mother. Montagu's loose papers suggest that textual records of maternal catechesis, in various forms, could serve multiple functions. On the one hand, they provide evidence of a mother's love for her children and her concern for their spiritual well-being, as we see in the household devotionals of Katherine Thomas (and, as we shall see in Chapter 2, of Lady Katherine Fitzwilliam.) On the other hand, as textual representations of such devotion, they could legitimize female authorship and perhaps promote a familial reputation for godliness.

The Role of Mothers in Domestic Catechesis

Mothers were the primary teachers of very young children in early modern England.[7] The reasons for this are in part economic: very young children could not contribute to the family economy, so they were kept at home under the care of their mothers, who, among other activities, would work through the catechism with their children. This instruction served a dual purpose: it taught children how to read at the same time that it instructed them in the basics of religion. George Herbert urges as the primary duty of a minister's wife the "training up of her children and maids in the fear of God, with prayers, and catechizing, and all religious duties."[8] The Scottish divine John Willison reminds mothers that "children are mostly under your care in their tender years, and you have the best opportunity to teach them to know God, and pray to him; to love Christ, and hate sin: the impressions they receive from you, ordinarily abide with them afterwards."[9] This practice was prevalent in Puritan families and may account for their higher literacy rates. But non-godly families followed this model as well. We know, for example, that Shakespeare was familiar with the popular *ABC with the Catechism*; it is likely that he, like so many other contemporaries, learned to read by memorizing its alphabet and then sounding out the words of the catechism with his mother.[10]

How are we to conceptualize this dual use of catechisms? One aspect is their ubiquity; they were found in (nearly) every house. Another aspect is the simplicity of basic catechisms: because they eschewed complex vocabulary and syntax, these catechisms were ideally suited for reading instruction. Because of the ubiquity of catechisms and the simplicity of the catechetical form, readers recognized that they were books that could be used to teach others how to read; booksellers and printers recognized how readers were using these works and adapted their contents accordingly. We know, for example, that as early as the 1550s, catechisms were being printed together with ABC's. This confirms Roger Chartier's suggestion that changes in the physical form of the printed book simultaneously respond to and shape reading practices.[11]

Early modern spiritual autobiographies, letters, and journals further confirm the importance of mothers in the teaching of reading. Margaret Spufford quotes from the diary of James Fretwell, who described his mother's efforts as follows: "She took me under her pedagogy until I could read in my Bible and thus she did afterwards by all my brothers and sisters ... And as my capacity was able, she caused me to observe what I read, so I soon began to take some notice of several historical passages in the Old Testament." A member of Thomas Shepard's Cambridge Massachusetts Bay Colony congregation confirms the purpose of catechetical instruction: "My education was in a religious manner from a cradle in that I was trained up to read scripture." Widely read in theology, Lady Brilliana Harley was responsible for the early education of her children. Barbara Slingsby Talbot, a catechist I discuss in Chapter 4, was taught by her mother to read and say the catechism before she was five years old. The Massachusetts Bay Colony minister Increase Mather underscores the gender differential that underpinned much early modern instruction: "I learned to read of my mother. I learned to write of my father, who also instructed me in grammar learning."[12]

The ABC with the Catechism

Although early modern catechisms differ in length, style, and tone, most are variations on the catechism included in the *Book of Common Prayer*. The majority follow a standard format: first questions and answers concerning the creed, then the Ten Commandments, the Lord's Prayer, and the sacraments. Ian Green terms these items the catechetical staples.¹³ While we can discern some points of theological contention within the catechisms, the vast majority avoid religious polemic.¹⁴

Most early modern catechisms acknowledge that the acquisition of basic literacy is a gradual process. Many popular ones begin by introducing children to the numerals and the letters of the alphabet. A catechism published in 1626 advertises itself as a text that can be used both to teach religious doctrine and the alphabet: *An ABC or Holy Alphabet, Conteyning Some Plaine Lessons Gathered Out of the Word, to the Number of the Letters of the English Alphabet to Enter Young Beginners into the Schoole of Christ.* *The ABC with the Catechism* (perhaps the most popular of these collections) begins with a chart that contains all of the numerals from one to three hundred, in "letters and figures." A marginal note explains that it teaches "How to know the names of numbers, both by letters and figures from one to three hundred etc." The second page contains a table with the alphabet in three different fonts and is headed "The ABC." First listing all of the letters of the alphabet in both upper and lower cases, the vowels are then conjoined with select consonants: a, ab, ac, ad, af, ag, etc. After rehearsing all of the vowels, the text concludes with a simple sentence: "In the name of the Father, and the Son, and of the Holy Ghost. Amen." The pedagogy of this text is explicit – a fact which perhaps helps account for its popularity. A child begins by recognizing the letters of the alphabet. Once she learns to combine them, she is encouraged to practice reading with the catechism, the first sentence of which reads, "What is your name?"¹⁵ Writing in the eighteenth century, Isaac Watts sums up the process: "When a child learns to read, do we not first teach him to know the letters, and then to join syllables and words? After this, some short and easy lessons are appointed him; and then some that are longer and more difficult."¹⁶

Edmund Coote's *The English Schoolmaster* contains an influential early modern catechism; it also offers a model of gradual language acquisition. Although Coote designed his text for schoolmasters, its marginal notations offer insights into how catechisms were likely used by mothers to teach basic literacy within the home. After providing the letters of the alphabet in different fonts, it opens with a lesson on syllables: "ab eb ib ob ub / ad ed id od ud." The chapter heading makes clear its initial goal: "teaching to read syllables of two letters." Throughout the opening chapters, marginal glosses provide pedagogical advice, urging the instructor to adapt lessons to individual scholars. "When your scholar hath perfectly learned his letters, teach him to know his vowels and after two or three days when he is skillful in there, teach him to call all the other letters consonants." Chapters conclude with sentences designed to allow the child to practice the principles that she or he has just learned. The second chapter, for example, concludes with "Boy go thy way up to the top of the hill and get me home the bay nag." A marginal note explains that this "frivolous" sentence has been designed "only to teach distinct reading."[17]

Only after she has completed many such lessons does the child proceed to Coote's *A Short Catechism*. From the first, Coote warns against advancing too quickly, using an introductory dialogue to model appropriate and inappropriate responses. Robert, eager to please his teacher, wants to move ahead: "But now let us look into our catechisme, for our Master will examine us next in that." But John (clearly the better student) reminds Robert of the importance of assured mastery of basic elements: "Nay, by your leave, we shall first read over againe what we have learned, with the Preface, Titles of Chapters, and Notes in the margents of our Books, which we have omitted before, because they were too hard; for we shall go no further before we be perfect in this."[18] Not all early modern catechisms follow this step-by-step approach; some catechisms do not seem to have been intended to teach reading at all; instead, they provide (sometimes quite advanced) religious instruction. But many catechisms seem to have been designed as gateway texts to literacy in the early modern world.

Catechisms as an Introduction to Print Culture

Margaret Spufford and Tessa Watt have brought to scholarly attention a subset of inexpensive religious literature – cheap print – that was available to all but the lowest of early modern society.[19] When recounting his childhood in a remote village in Wales, the godly minister (and future Fifth Monarchist) Vavasor Powell remarks that, as a child, "either Hystorical or Poetical Books, Romances and the like were all my delight." Richard Baxter's youthful tastes ran to "Romances, Fables, and old Tales." Working-class women also actively participated in this emergent print culture, although their reading habits are less easy to ascertain because they were less likely to keep commonplace books. The serving girl Katherine Branch was familiar with the catechism and the primer, as well as some popular verses. John Bunyan states that when he married his wife, they had "not so much household stuff as a dish or a spoon between us," yet she possessed copies of Arthur Dent's *The Plainman's Pathway to Heaven* and Lewis Bayly's *The Practice of Pietie*, which had been given to her by her father. Hailing from a spectrum of social classes, the women narrators in Vavasor Powell's *Spirituall Experiences of Sundry Beleevers* reveal their familiarity with a variety of popular religious works, including books by Erasmus and William Perkins, suggesting that the circulation of printed material among working-class women may have been greater than has been previously thought.[20]

Many catechisms explicitly seek to cultivate familiarity with the world of print. Presumably, a reader who becomes accustomed to seeing letters represented in several fonts in *The ABC with the Catechism* would be better prepared to encounter printed material. Catechisms designed for slightly older readers, such as Alexander Nowell's *A Catechisme, or First Instruction*, adopt a page layout with marginal glosses pointing the reader to other places of scripture and providing authorial commentary on a given passage.[21] Some Puritan ministers explained to beginning readers what these scriptural glosses were and how they functioned within the text. "They are orderly set down," explains the Massachusetts Bay Colony minister John Fiske in his catechism *The Watering of the Olive Plant*, "as they relate to the several sentences or parts in the answers." The popular catechist John Ball is even more explicit: "First that the letters, a, and b, and c etc. set over the Answere doe direct what part of the Answere the Testimonies of Scripture alleged doe serve to confirme. And the figures 1.2.3, etc. doe intimate what words, or which parts of the Answere, are explained into the Exposition."[22]

The Role of Memory

Such methods depend upon a well-developed memory. Children were expected to memorize entire catechisms. Catharine Burton (1668–1714), a Discalced Carmelite, recalls in her memoirs how she came to memorize a Catholic catechism:

> My mother died when I was eight years of age. She left eight children behind her. I was the youngest but three. My father took care to have us brought up to virtue and kept to our prayers morning and evening, besides the time in which the family met at litanies, which were never omitted. To encourage us the more, he promised money to those who best learnt their catechism. I generally carried it and was more pleased with the credit I gained than any other prize.

The Northamptonshire gentlewoman Elizabeth Isham recounts weekly childhood catechetical sessions that caused her a great deal of anxiety: "I remember the paines I tooke saying it every night to my selfe for feare lest

I should forget it . . . .." The Protestant minister Josias Nichols urges parents not to underestimate the memory of even a very young child:

> it will not bee amisse to cause the learner to repeate without booke, the places where all the stories and sentences are written: and herein the teacher may use his discretion to teach them more or less of the like sort and easiness and he shall find that a little childe will beare very much more, then a man that hath not tried would beleeve.[23]

This reliance upon memorization led some contemporaries to criticize early childhood catechesis as mindless repetition or "parroting." Even George Herbert, an advocate of catechesis, admits that "many say the catechism by rote, as parrats, without ever piercing into the sense of it."[24] Ministers attempt to counteract this charge by insisting that children should understand what they are reciting. Isaac Watts, for example, argues that memorization and comprehension can – and should – go hand in hand. He writes that "whatsoever catechisms are impressed upon the Memories of Children in their most tender years they should be taught the Meaning of them, as far as possible, as fast as they learn them by heart." Watts is a theorist of catechizing, so his discussion is more theoretical than most. But even within working catechisms there is evidence that the authors want to make sure that the child understands what he reads. In *The Mother and Child*, the fictional mother asks a child who has answered a complex question concerning the resurrection of the body:

M. Do yee beleeve that your bodies shall rise again?
C. Yea, but of another qualitie.
M. What reason have ye for it?

Earlier, she requires the child to articulate what it means for Christians personally that Christ will come in judgment: "What is it to us, that Christ shall come to judge? Great comfort," the child replies.[25]

But there was no escaping the fact that catechesis demanded a great deal of rote rehearsal. In *Of Domesticall Duties*, a published account of lectures originally delivered to his Blackfriars congregation, William Gouge defends memorization on three grounds. First, it sets the child on a virtuous path while she is still young. "It is better," explains Gouge, "that they should be framed and squared to a good course, before they can discerne betwixt good and evil, then be suffered to runne on in evill, till they get an habit therein; which after it is got, will hardly be cast off." Second, it emulates upper-class educational practice by training very young children. "What may bee the reason" queries Gouge, "that children of Kings and great men are commonly of more understanding at twelve or fourteen years of age then poore and meane men's children at seventeen or eighteen but that they are sooner, and better instructed." Finally, memorization is an investment that will yield interest when the child matures: "As by age their understanding commeth to more and more ripenesse, they will more and more conceive that which at first they did not so well understand." A catechizing mother is like a farmer who sows "in the winter, to receive a crop the harvest following." "Children," Gouge concludes, "are to be instructed betimes even for the benefit that may be after reaped."[26]

What does Gouge mean when he refers to the yet-to-be reaped "benefit" of childhood memorization? To understand Gouge's metaphor fully, we need to consider the rhetorical structure of Puritan sermons and treatises, which relied upon Ramist logic in which axioms move "from the most general to the more particular." Protestant ministers represented this structure with diagrams "showing the division of the whole into parts according to categories called heads, topics, or commonplaces."[27] Arnold Hunt helpfully compares this rhetorical structure to a mental filing system, where the "heads" serve as large folders into which smaller folders, containing more particular demonstrations or applications, can be placed. Godly ministers urge readers or auditors to mark the doctrine's "head" or "application" as well as its "use." "Thus much of the doctrine and this question. The use follows," writes one minister. Another urges: "well we have heard of the parts, doctrines, and uses of this text. Nowe followeth the application...."[28]

Puritan ministers relied upon this rhetorical structure in part because they believed it was easily apprehended – unlike scholastic argumentation. But many godly women and men were nonetheless unable to remember (or even understand) religious material that they heard or read. This was especially true of those who lacked a formal education. Nehemiah Wallington, for example, was an enthusiastic sermon-goer, sometimes attending multiple sermons in one week. But he was unable to remember the sermon subsequently.[29] Isaac Watts provides the example of a woman, who, "falling under sensible convictions of her want of Religion and Piety towards God, and having been told that the Bible was the Book whence she was to learn her duty... betook herself to read several of the first Chapters of Genesis." But since she lacked knowledge of the basic heads of religion, she was unable to do so and "she labored and wearied herself in that Search with very small Advantage."[30]

Memorizing the catechism was intended to address such difficulties: by informing children of the key doctrines of the Protestant faith, it enabled them to refer to these doctrines when they subsequently encountered more advanced oral or written instruction. In Patrick Collinson's words, "those who listened to sermons and read the Bible did so with faculties trained by catechisms–trained, that is, to arrange what they heard in formal rhetorical structures."[31] The godly minister John Downame suggests that this training is the primary benefit of early catechesis: when children have been "grounded in the principles and maine parts of divinity" through catechesis, they can "referre all things [they] heare to their heads." Ministers describe catechetical memorization as a crucial building block that will enable men and women to understand more sophisticated instruction, as William Perkins urges users of his catechism: when "ye have them without book and the meaning of them withal, then learn the exposition also: which being well conceived, and in some measure felt in the hart, ye shall be able to profit by Sermons, whereas now yee cannot." John Hoffman, minister at Wotton, Oxfordshire, colloquially writes, "sermons without knowledge and understanding of the fundamental truths are as if you should set a brown loafe and cheese before infants that call for milke."[32] As Perkins and Hoffman suggest, the primary purpose of such instruction was improved understanding of basic doctrine. But ministers recognized that memorization potentially provided early modern men and women with a powerful analytical tool for organizing, storing, and understanding more advanced religious instruction independently. As the Bradford minister John Ball explains, catechesis enables the godly man to "refferre that which hee heareth in the publicke assembly, or readeth in Godly and learned Bookes, to some head, apply it to the right purpose, treasure it up in safe memorie for use in time of need and have in readiness to answere the gain-sayers."[33]

It would be a mistake, however, to conclude that mothers saw memorization primarily as a means of improving the intellect. A mother catechized her child because she believed it would benefit her child's soul. By encouraging her child to memorize her catechism, a mother demonstrated her loving concern for her child's lifelong spiritual development, a development that was facilitated by the child's ability to organize and to process religious doctrine. She also provided her child with a treasury of religious knowledge that the child could draw upon when confronting spiritual problems such as doubt or despair. Ideally, this maternal training enabled the child, when she matured, to recreate a sermon from memory for those who had not heard it, allowing her to experience both the pleasure of helping others and the satisfaction of being trusted as an authority. It also enabled her to instruct the less informed. Watts recounts how the woman who was initially unable to understand the Bible began to grasp it when she was "by the Information of other Christians ... led into the knowledge of the chief Principles of the Christian Religion...."[34] Far from mindless recital, catechetical repetition needs to be understood within the broader early modern understanding of memorization as enabling spiritual growth and fostering godly community.

Maternally Directed Catechisms

Mothers saw such catechetical instruction as part of their household duties. John Willison links catechetical instruction with more general forms of instruction in his *The Mother's Catechism For the Young Child*: he argues that just as parents teach children "how to speak and go," they should provide them with religious education. Catechetical instruction was integrated within the day's activities. The Warwickshire Record Office contains a memorandum written on the back of two unfinished letters concerning the upbringing of Penelope and Kate Mordant. The instructions show that catechizing was part of the morning routine: "As soon as they are up and dressed, they are to be heard to say their prayers, wash their hands, then say their catechism, eat their breakfast, then dress their hair." Elizabeth Isham recalled in her *Book of Rememberance* reciting the catechism as a child with "her brother and sister every Sabbath when our turns came, in the after Noone." Another woman from the North of England describes discussing religious questions with her child before he goes outside to play. In *The Mother's Catechism*, Richard Baxter depicts a mother who must confront a child who tells her he would "play and talk of somewhat else than learn my catechism. I do not love it."[35]

Printers designed catechisms specifically for busy mothers. These maternally directed catechisms seem to have been designed with multitasking in mind: many are quite small, so that a mother can hold the book in one hand while she attends to her children with the other. The title page of *The Mother and the Child* emphasizes the work's question-and-answer format, its "short" and "brief" meditations, and its usefulness "for the fitting of little children for the publicke ministry" or sermons and communion. It is compact (94 mm by 43 mm), printed in black letter, and easily memorized. It is described as an accessible version of John Craig's popular, *A Short Summe of the Whole Catechisme*.[36] As evidence of widespread popularity and use, John Willison's *The Mother's Catechism* went through more than twenty editions, was translated into Gaelic, and was used in England, Scotland, and the American colonies. This popularity in turn suggests the increasing importance of women as consumers in a growing print marketplace. By the late seventeenth century, Richard Baxter would utilize the title, *The Mother's Catechism*, in a work that was not, in fact, a traditional catechism.[37]

To Be Opened at First

Although written, in theory, for children, numerous catechisms published in England between 1550–1700 make few concessions to either a child's reading ability or attention span. The much-reprinted *Westminster Shorter Catechism* was notoriously difficult, as this typical exchange shows:

> Q. What especial act of providence did God exercise towards man, in the Estate wherein he was created?
> A. When God had created man, he entered into a Covenant of life with him, upon condition of perfect obedience, forbidding him to eat of the Tree of the Knowledge of Good and Evil, upon pain of death.

It is not impossible for a child to memorize such a passage; many children did. But it is difficult to imagine a child of seven or eight understanding either the question or its answer. This is perhaps why so many guides to the *Westminster Shorter Catechism* appeared in the seventeenth and eighteenth centuries. Some of these guides, however, were no more accessible than the original.[38]

By contrast, maternally directed catechisms tailor their presentation of religious doctrine to a child's limited attention span. Ian Green describes these texts as "on the whole more indulgent or realistic."[39] I suggest that this sensitivity to its child-audience is one of the defining characteristics of maternally directed catechisms. John Craig's *The Mother and The Child*, for example, opens as follows:

MOTHER. Who made you?
CHILD. God.
M. Why did God make you?
C. To serve him.
M. How will God be served?
C. According to his word.

The exchange is lively and engaging: the mother asks a brief question; the child responds.[40] The religious beliefs covered in this exchange are fundamental ones, including the origin of man, the purpose of man's existence, and the necessary reliance upon the Bible to determine how God wants to be worshipped. But the manner of presentation makes these beliefs easily apprehended by a small child. The content and vocabulary of another maternally directed catechism, *The First Book for Children*, are directed towards the somewhat older child: "Q. What is the Work of Creation? A. The work of Creation is God's making all things of Nothing, by the Word of his power, in the space of six days, and all very good."[41]

Many such catechisms were designed to prepare children to receive the sacrament of the Lord's Supper, which typically occurred at the age of seven or eight. These pithy, direct, and engaging texts enable the mother to furnish the child with a basic doctrinal understanding necessary to receive the sacrament. The Cranbrook minister Robert Abbot prefaced his longer catechism, *Milk for Babes* (1646), with two shorter catechisms. The first catechism expounds the doctrine of the trinity, the Ten Commandments, and the sacraments; the second very briefly digests fundamental tenets of faith for a young child. For example, it asks the child to "Give me the summe of Religion in one sentence? A. A sinner, being justified by faith, is bound to live a godly life." And, "Give me the summe of Religion in four words? A. My Generation, Degeneration, Regeneration, and Glorification."[42]

Catechisms for Various Ages and Abilities

Beginning in the seventeenth century, some catechetical authors began to gradate their presentation of religious content. George Herbert observes that the country parson "exacts of all the Doctrine of the Catechisme; of the younger sort, the very words; of the elder, the substance."[43] Isaac Watts advocates a four-stage program of catechesis, beginning with very young children: "Tis certain," writes Watts, "that at the Age of three or four Years old, a Child may be taught to know something more than mere Words and Terms; he may attain such Ideas both of the God that made him, and of his duty to his Maker, as is necessary for his share of Practice in that infant state." Watts acknowledges that the lesson could be extended to original sin and humankind's need for a Savior, "but in the very first Catechism tis hardly necessary for a young child of four years old." Underpinning Watts' advice is his awareness of how a child's intellectual abilities and emotional needs evolve as he develops: "At seven or eight Years of age, he can receive more of the Truths and Duties of Christianity than he can at four: and the same remark can be repeated concerning a child of ten or twelve years old, and concerning a youth of fourteen or fifteen."[44]

This gradated questioning comes alive in *The Pilgrim's Progress*. Prudence begins with the youngest: "Come, James, can thou tell who made thee?" This is the same question that Watts would place first. She asks James four additional questions, "Canst thou tell who Saves thee?" and "How doeth God the Father save thee?" "How doth God the Son save thee?" and "How doth God the Holy Spirit save thee?" Prudence questions the next oldest child, Joseph, concerning the nature of Man and "God's design in saving of poor men." When she questions Samuel, the second oldest child, Prudence's questions are otherworldly: they concern the nature of heaven, hell, and the beatific vision. But the eldest child, Matthew, is asked the most difficult questions, which include the status of the human body at the resurrection and theological arguments concerning the nature of God.

PRU: How believe you as touching the resurrection of the dead?
MAT: I believe they shall rise the same that was buried: the same in nature, though not in corruption.
PRU: Was ever anything that had a being, antecedent to, or before God?
MAT: No, for God is eternal, nor is there anything excepting himself that had a being until the beginning of the first day.[45]

Bunyan's representation of this age-appropriate catechesis arguably reflects actual practice. Josias Nichols urges parents similarly: For "the first order, from the time that children can speak," it "shall bee good to teach them (as the manner of all Christians is) to say without book distinctly: The Lord's prayer, the Creede, and the tenne Commandments." Nichols then continues, "after they have been thus trayned a while and can answere as children, readily to these: then let them learne that short Catechism without booke which beginneth after this sorte: Who made thee? God. What is God? He is Almightie, etc." Nichols reminds parents that this catechism "may be bought for the valew of a pennie in the booksellers shops." The parent should then teach the child "some short stories and sentences of holie Scripture." Only when the child can cite a scriptural support for each commandment as well as recite "the 1, 15, 112, 127 and 128 Psalms" from memory can the parent proceed to what Nichols terms the "second order of instruction, for the opening of the understanding."[46]

The Historical Catechism

Unlike traditional catechisms, which sought to teach fundamentals of the faith, historical catechisms were designed to acquaint children with scriptural personages and events. These works focused upon sensational Old and New Testament stories to attract young minds otherwise uninterested in religion. Their aim, remarks Eamon Duffy, "was clearly to get the youngster searching through his bible and references were provided."[47] With his characteristic attention to detail, Watts advises that historical catechisms should be designed for children between the ages of seven and fifteen, and he urges a focus on stories interesting to children. These are of two types. First are stories "particularly such as relate to Parents and to Children, in which their Stage of Life has a very peculiar Interest. Therefore, it may be proper to insert the Carriage of Cain to his brother" or even "of Timothy and of Christ himself in their younger Years." Second are Old Testament stories that "have any Thing marvelous or extraordinary in them; for this more sensibly attracts the Minds of Children and gives them most Delight in Learning."[48] Ian Green remarks that schoolmasters also recommended historical catechisms "for teaching and exercising boys in scriptural knowledge"; he observes that a version of the popular historical scripture catechism *The Way to True Happiness* was "bound in with many octavo copies of the Bible from the 1620's to the 1640's, despite official warning against this practice in 1628."[49]

Successful historical catechisms follow these principles. Watts includes the following exchange:

> Q. What fault was Noah guilty of?
> A. At one particular time, he was intoxicated with drinking wine.
> Q. What crime was Ham guilty of?
> A. He made sport with his father and was cursed.

Again, when the mother in Baxter's *The Mother's Catechism* tells how Cain envied Abel and so killed him, one can almost hear the excitement (and implicit acknowledgement of sibling rivalry) in the child's response: "Did the first man that was born kill his own brother? What made him kill him?" Another popular historical catechism, *The First Book for Children*, covers the same material and includes vivid woodcuts illustrating the stories. When it discusses Cain and Abel, for example, the woodcut depicts a club-wielding Cain smiting a smaller, prostrate Abel. The catechism's questions also appeal to a child's love of superlatives: "Q. Who was the strongest Man? A. Samson, who slew a thousand Philistines with the Jaw-bone of an ass and at his Death slew many more, by pulling down the Pillars of the House."[50] It was possible, of course, for a child to get lost in these stories and miss the larger instructional goal. But in most cases, what we have is an extension of the principle of tailoring catechesis to a child's capacity and thus providing for a child's continuing spiritual growth.

Images of Maternity

Maternally directed catechisms offer depictions that belie both early modern and contemporary scholarly stereotypes of maternity.[51] These mothers are intellectually capable, with a deep knowledge of their faith, regardless of their social status or economic standing. Chapter 5 examines Dorothy Burch, author of *A Catechisme of the Severall Heads of Christian Religion*, and a mother of five children. Burch had no formal education and was in all likelihood a tradesman's wife. Yet Burch ably distinguishes justification, sanctification, and conversion before giving eight reasons why "the people of God," ought "to do good works, seeing they justify us not," all of which are supported with appropriate scriptural citations. Mrs. J.C., author of *The Mother's Catechism*, articulates the distinction between "a covenant of works" and "a covenant of grace": "The covenant of works requires perfect personal and perpetual obedience, leaving no room for Repentance or a Mediator: but the Covenant of Grace accepts of sincere Obedience on Account of the Obedience of another, and there is room for Repentance and a Mediator." The mother in Willison's *The Mother's Catechism* requires her child to confirm that "Christ's righteousness [is] the only meritorious cause of our justification." The intellectual complexity of these positions suggests that whatever the official belief in women's inferiority, it was not confirmed by women's participation in religious discussions. Bunyan dates his conversion to overhearing "three or four poor Women, sitting at a door, in the sun talking about the things of God." This passage is justly famous for the simplicity and directness of its language. But what is perhaps most pertinent is what the women discuss: "a new birth, the work of God on their hearts, also how they were convinced of their miserable state by nature." "They were far out of my reach," concludes Bunyan.[52]

Marginal notes prompt mothers looking for a more sophisticated exposition of religious doctrine to consult outside texts. A gloss in *The Mother and the Child* exhorts "those that will see further of this, look at his Majesties Catechisme made by Mr. Craig." For his part, Willison urges mothers (and fathers) to give their children additional reading material: "provide Bibles for them, together with *Confessions of Faith*, Vincent's *Catechism*, Guthrie's *Trial of a Saving Interest*, and such little books."

This suggests that mothers could have discretionary time and income that they could use to purchase books.[53] The mothers in these catechisms are vivid, realistically depicted characters. No mere stock figures used to advance an argument, they display good critical-thinking skills. Like the schoolmasters in other catechisms, these mothers ask children questions designed to ensure that a child grasps what is being discussed. During a discussion of the creed, the Mother in *The Mother and The Child* asks: "What is meant by sitting at the right hand of God?" After the child gives an appropriate answer, Mother questions further: "Hath God a right hand?" No, replies the child, "but it is spoken for our capacitie." The mother recognizes that her child may not understand metaphor as such, so she checks to see if he understands not only what it signifies but why it is used. In Mrs. J.C.'s *The Mother's Catechism*, Mother is an engaged teacher. While relating the consequences of the Fall, she recognizes that the child might not grasp the significance of Eve's transgression, so she asks: "Was it not a little Sin to eat a little Fruit?" The child's response "No; for being forbidden, it became Disobedience and Rebellion against God" shows her good understanding.[54] In *The Mother and The Child*, the mother models intellectual persistence. After rehearsing the various titles of God, she asks her child, "What gather yee of this?" Later she questions him, "Why doe you say I beleeve and not wee beleeve?" Similarly in Dorcas Martin's *The Manner How to Examine*, the mother asks the child to "shew the reason" and tests his understanding of metaphor by asking "is Baptisme a washing of bodilie filthinesse?" In his *The Mother's Catechism*, Baxter inverts the usual roles so that the child asks the mother difficult questions, such as "What is a soul, Mother?" "How do you know we have Souls?" And, "Dogs and beasts do See and Feel, Have they souls?" The mother's answers – "Yes, they have souls . . . but their souls and ours greatly differ" – reveal her own knowledge.[55]

The mothers in maternally directed catechisms do not have a sentimental view of childhood. They know that children do bad things all the time and will continue to do so. In *The Manner How to Examine*, Mother asks, "Have we power of our selves to doo good and to keep us from evil? The child replies, " No, not so much as to think anie good thing." In Robert Abbot's catechism, the mother asks, "Art thou able to keep these commandments?" The child replies, "No: let me do what I can, yet I break them every day, more than I can expresse." Such remarks reflect the theological belief in innate depravity. Nor are the mothers in these works reluctant to teach their children the basic truths of the Christian faith – even if there is some chance that the children might be frightened.⁵⁶ For example, the Scottish minister John Willison reminds young readers of his catechism that "you may see Graves of your length, and sculls your size in the church-yard" and that "hellfire will burn green Trees, as well as old Stocks."⁵⁷ Katherine Fitzwilliam, discussed in Chapter 2, offers her children a detailed description of hell and then asks: "Q. How like you that cheere?" Such tactics defy modern ideas of childhood. But these mothers are motivated by concern for their children's salvation. They believe in heaven, hell, and predestination and insist that children understand and believe too. Such remarks demonstrate their resolve to have their children acknowledge religious truths fundamental to the Protestant faith.

The mothers represented in these works enjoy interacting with their children. "My child" and "My dear child" are the most common forms of address. They advise children how to comport themselves: in Dorcas Martin's catechism, the mother urges the child to "saie it with a high voice, and pronounce it well," confirming the orality of much catechetical instruction. But the most obvious way in which care is manifested is in the mother's willing engagement with her child for an extended period of time. In Baxter's *The Mother's Catechism*, Mother calls the child in from play: "Come, child, are you willing to be taught your catechism?" The child responds, "What is the catechism, mother?" After the mother explains, the child replies that he would still rather stay outside. But the mother proceeds to engage the child in learning the basic Christian truths – the nature of God, his relation to creation, and mankind's role in creation. She does so with patience and even gentle amusement. She encourages her child's interest with a brief astronomy lesson: "Many of the stars seem little to you, because they are many thousand miles from us and yet are many hundred times bigger than all this earth: and no man can tell how many thousand thousand miles there may be beyond all the stars which we can see. Do you not look up and wonder at this?"⁵⁸

This gentle banter between mother and child is mirrored in many of the plays of the period, from Lady Macduff in *Macbeth* to Ann Sanders in *A Warning for Fair Women*, who teases her froward child, calling him "Sir Sauce" but promising him a new suit if he works hard in school.⁵⁹ Maternally directed catechisms, then, offer an alternative model for early modern motherhood, one in which mothers are portrayed as capable of understanding – and even expounding – difficult theological concepts. At the same time, these mothers display a gentle, even amused tolerance of their children's resistance to religious instruction.

Maternal Love

Domestic catechesis depended on a mother's desire for her children's betterment, and it proceeded through conversational exchange, so it is unsurprising that Protestant ministers considered catechesis a vital manifestation of maternal love. Citing scriptural prototypes, the popular Puritan minister William Gouge links maternal nurture with teaching: "Let mothers especially note this point of timely nurture ... The grandmother Lois, and mother Eunice, first taught Timothy. Bathsheba taught Solomon when he was young. Oft doth Solomon warne children not to forsake their mother's teaching." As we have seen earlier, the Protestant minister Samuel Hieron makes maternal catechesis definitional to early modern motherhood: "Q: What is the mother's duty? A. To nourish her children and to instruct them. 1 Timothy 5.10." Josias Nichols similarly suggests that domestic religious instruction is the "natural" way for a woman to demonstrate maternal love:

> A woman, being the fruitfull vine on the house sides, in whose sight the children are tender and deare: can by no meanes shew their naturall love better then being alwaies at hand with their children and maides, to give them everyday in milde and pleasant manner some golden apples: wherewith the young babes will take such delight, that by the nourishment and exercise thereof, they will be made strong to confound the enemies of God and their countrie.[60]

Ministers describe a mother's willingness to adapt her instruction to her child's capacity as an act of love. "It is no disgrace to catechize plainly," writes the clergyman Richard Bernard, "learned fathers have done it, it argueth love and a desire to have the people understand us." Bernard is speaking of ministerial catechesis, but I would argue that his description of accommodation as demonstrating a speaker's love applies equally to maternal catechesis. Bernard supports his argument by referencing maternal communication: "a mother, speaking to her little babes, speaketh not, as to the older in yeeres but even as a childe to children, unto other, as becometh her to speak and fit for them to heare." Gouge describes appropriate instruction as "an evident sign of a parent's true love of his child" and subsequently reminds parents that "if a vessel have a little mouth ... we let the liquor fall by little and little according to the capacitie."[61] George Herbert describes such accommodation as the washing and cleansing "of things of ordinary use" to "serve for lights of Heavenly Truth."[62]

Early modern men and women consistently recall childhood catechesis as an experience in which they felt their mother's love. A female spiritual autobiographer recollects the pleasure she felt as a child when her mother taught her how to read:

> I was indeed the daughter of very godly and honest parents, who diligently brought up their children in the feare of God. My mother, who in her days was notified for a godly vertuous and religious Gentlewoman, shee, I say, from among twelve children chose me to set her love and affection upon, she told me it was because she saw something [of] a more tractablenesse and diligence to please her then in the rest, which when I perceived as then not being seven yeare old, I laid my self forth the more to give her content, who tooke great delight to instruct me, to hear me read, and ask her questions. She allotted me a portion of Scripture every day, as likewise a part of Erasmus Rotterdamus upon the four Evangelists, wherein we both took great delight.[63]

This account accords with what we have seen was the typical process of maternal catechesis. The author emphasizes that it is love that motivates her mother to teach her. But it is evidently love that also impelled her as a child to learn, "I laid my self forth the more to give her content." She emphasizes their mutual "great delight." Maternal instruction both arises out of and substantiates the love between mother and child.

Just as adults remember childhood catechesis as an experience of maternal love, mothers remark upon the love they feel while instructing their children. They suggest that this love has, in turn, contributed to their own spiritual growth. One woman movingly describes witnessing "before my face" the death of her husband and young child during a siege at Liverpool, only to take refuge with her "wounded childe, and a little daughter in a barn," where she found solace reading to them, "having gotten a peece of an old Bible."[64] Another woman provides the following account:

> About seventeen years since, a child of mine about six yeares of age, when I have bid him goe forth to play, he hath come in againe very solitary because other Children would swear... I would ask him, 'Robert, what ayleth you, why doe you not goe to play?' he would answer, That he had no fellowes to play withal, but such as would swear and the like, and they could not be (said he) Gods children. I would say, 'Why not Childe?' He then would say, 'No mother, though I am but a little way in my Booke, yet I have learnt, that God will not pardon such sinnes, as swearing'; I have sometimes said, 'Yes Child, I hope God will pardon them, else God help thy Father and God help us all.'

The mother's gentle humor is revealed in her reference to her husband's foul language. But this story is set within a larger narrative in which the child's reluctance impels the mother to deepen her relationship with

Christ: "considering my Childe, so young, should give me such instructions," the mother remarks, "hath proved a blessing to me, to bring me home to him."[65] At no point does this account suggest that mother and child are equals, but hierarchy does not prevent instruction. Put in slightly different terms, the learning that occurs during catechesis is not one-sided. Mothers are responsible for teaching, but this does not preclude the possibility that mothers can also learn from children.

Places of Scripture

We turn now to a child's catechism found in the household devotional of Katherine Thomas. I discuss Thomas' biography and characterize her household devotional in Chapter 3. Here, I focus upon Thomas' historical catechism, which I call *Places of Scripture*, to see what it can tell us about late seventeenth-century maternal catechesis.[66] *Places of Scripture* probably entered Thomas' manuscript miscellany sometime in the early to mid 1670s. This supposition is derived from its place in the miscellany. It is surrounded by other materials dating from the 1660s and 1670s, including, for example, Thomas' elegy for her daughter Dorothy, who died in 1665. This date also gains plausibility if Thomas included it for the use of her surviving children, who would have been between seven and ten years old at this time – approximating the age that Watts suggests is appropriate for historical catechesis.

Whether this catechism is an original composition or an adaptation of a published catechism is uncertain at present.[67] Departing from her usual practice, Thomas neither states that she took this catechism from another work nor claims to have composed it herself. Although the catechism begins with the Old Testament, it proceeds to questions from the New Testament. This following of the order of Scripture may suggest Thomas' authorship; it is easy to imagine that Thomas composed this catechism for her children while reading through the Bible from beginning to end. The Protestant minister Eusebius Pagit describes a similar process in his *Historie of the Bible*:

> When my children first began to speak for the furtherance of them and my servants in the knowledge of the Historie of the Bible after a Chapter read at our meals at dinner out of the Old Testament, at supper out of the new, I gave them by word of mouth only such observations as I thought fit for their capacity and understanding, and by their answers to my questions I daily took an account of how they understood and retained the same in memory.[68]

Pagit's explanation accords with common household practice among evangelical Protestants. The catechetical notebooks of the Henry family suggest similar familial instruction.[69] Some of Thomas' questions – such as the one about the three children put into the fiery furnace – resemble questions in Willison's *The Mother's Catechism*, although this resemblance may stem from their addressing the same passages of scripture. In what follows, I assume that Thomas composed *Places of Scripture* based upon her reading of similar historical catechisms. At the same time, however, my argument does not depend upon the catechism's originality; her selection and formatting of materials can still tell us a great deal about maternal practice.

Thomas opens with Genesis, but includes questions from Judges, Numbers, 2 Kings, and even the Psalms. After four pages of Old Testament questions, Thomas turns to the New Testament, drawing questions from all four evangelists (mostly Matthew, John, and Luke) as well as Acts. Most of the questions identify biblical personages and ask the child to name them. Some of these questions are easy for a child with a basic knowledge of the Christian faith: "Whoe was the first man and woman_____Adam and Eve." Others, however, require a minute knowledge of biblical history: "to whom did the Lord shew mercy to in Jericho, for Concealing ^his Spise, Joshua sent to Spie out the Land_____ Rehab the harlot and her fathers house." Some questions ask the child for a specific number to demonstrate familiarity with the details of a story: "Howe many days did Joshua and the people compass Jericho before the walls fell downe, by the Lord's command_____ 7 days."

Thomas places the questions on the left-hand side of the page. On the far left, in front of the question, she places a scriptural citation to which the question refers. On the first two pages of her catechism, these citations are general. The first reads simply "Genesis" and covers the fourteen questions that follow. The next citation, "Genesis X," relates to just one question, however: "Whoe was the Mighty hunter before the Lord_____ Nimrod." As Thomas continues through the books of the Old Testament, her citations are occasionally more precise. The question, "Whoe hid the wedg of Gould and the babylonish garment Contrary to the Lords Commandment" is preceded by a citation to "Joshua vii." But two questions about the exploits of Samson follow the citation of "Judges iii." This uneven pattern of scriptural citation suggests the unscholarly nature of Thomas' piety. By contrast, the formally educated godly minister William Perkins supports every answer in his catechism, *The Foundation of the Christian Religion* (1597), with multiple scriptural references.

Most printed catechisms are organized sequentially: a question on one line is directly followed by its answer on the next line. This arrangement insures a minimum of wasted space, as shown in John Willison's popular *The Mother's Catechism*. But Thomas correlates her question and answer on the same line, connecting them with a long horizontal pen stroke. The column of answers is labeled "Answere Child." Thomas does not adopt the page layout of printed catechisms; instead, her catechism adopts the layout of domestic account books. The account book of Joyce Jeffries (1638–48) is formatted identically.[70] Thomas' layout reflects the origin of *Places of Scripture* within the household and additionally suggests that she identified her domestic religious instruction with her other household responsibilities. At the same time, this format is preferable for a mother who wants to read through the catechism with her child: she could cover the answers on the right side of the page while helping the child practice reading the questions on the left.

Occasionally in Thomas, the answer directly follows the question as in "Which killed his brother Abill: wicked∧^Cain killd him." Here, Thomas corrects herself by crossing out the answer and rewriting it in the right margin: "~~wicked∧ Cain killd him~~ Cain killed him." Thomas will also revise a question that becomes too complex. In "Whoe Searved 2 seven years for his wife, rachel," Thomas continues "and wresled." But then she crosses the added phrase out, drawing a line connecting the first question with the answer: "~~and wresled~~——Jacob." Thomas then places the phrase "with God" above "Jacob": "~~and wresled~~——Jacob ∧^{with God}." This answers the implicit question in the crossed out phrase. These revisions suggest that Thomas may have been fearful of overextending her young children's capacities.

Thomas displays both her familiarity with the genre of the historical catechism and her awareness of a child's interests in her formulating questions containing superlatives.

Whoe was the proudest king_____	King Nabucodnezer:
Whoe was the Strongest man_____	Samson:
Whoe deceived him with fayer words_____	dalilah:
Who was the fairest man_____	Absolon:

Such questions are a characteristic feature of historical catechisms and are designed to appeal to a child's interest in knowing who or what was the best in any particular category. Some of Thomas' questions require the child to pass moral judgment on a character's actions. For example, the question, "Whoe Commanded naboth to be Stoned to death?" must be answered, "wicked Jezebell." Such moralizing inculcates orthodox moral judgments.

As we have seen, Isaac Watts advised would-be authors of historical catechisms to focus on stories concerning parents and children and stories about miraculous events. *Places of Scripture* proceeds similarly. Besides the story of Cain and Abel, it includes such questions from 2 Samuel as "Whoe killd amasa (his mother's Sister's Sonn) Cruell_____Joab" and Genesis 11:28: "Whoe was the first sonn which died before his father in the Land of his nativity_____hamm the Sonn of terah." The catechism also includes the following questions on sensational episodes:

1 Samuel 24	Whoe cut off the Skirt of Saul's robe in the Cave_____david
1 Samuel 28	Whoe went by night to the witch of Endor for Counsell_____ K. Saule
2 Kings 2	How many Littell Children did 2 Bares kill for Calling of Elisha "bald head"_____42 Children

Bears devouring sassy children, an Old Testament patriarch slinking off in the middle of the night to visit a witch – this was exciting stuff for early modern children, like modern ones. Thomas Boston, later Minister at Simprin, confessed that as a child he read the Bible mostly out of "curiosity" about "the history of Balaam's ass" (Numbers 22:21–34).[71]

Thomas' questions from the New Testament show a similar awareness of what her children might find interesting, although the material was less sensational:

St. Luke XIX	Whoe climed up in a Sycomore tree to See our Saviour Jesus Christ as he passed by Jericho_____ Littell Zaccheus the publican.
Matthew 24:23	Whom did they Compell to bare the Cross after our Saviour Jesus Christ to Mount Calvery_____Simon of Cyrene.

Thomas misidentifies the scriptural reference for her second question, which in actuality derives from Mathew 27:32, but by including questions of this kind within her catechism, Thomas reveals not only her awareness of a child's interests but also her commitment to tailoring her religious instruction to meet these interests. Doing so requires the ability to stand outside of one's self and one's own interests and imagine what another being might find interesting. This reflects Thomas' sense of audience, just as her formatting suggests her sense of how to use her text to teach a child to read. Both were generated through daily, loving interaction. A handwritten catechism, designed for household use, *Places of Scripture* provides a fascinating look into the dynamics of maternal catechesis in seventeenth-century England – and the love that it enacted.

"Children Deare": The Audience of Lady Montagu's Loose Papers

Carefully transcribed and prepared, Lady Ann Montagu's collection of texts challenges our contemporary understandings of originality and genre. Born in 1573, she was the daughter of John Crouch of Buntingford in the county of Northampton. She married Edward, Lord Montagu in 1625, when she was fifty-one years old. He was her fourth husband.[72] Lord Montagu had married twice previously and had four young children, Frances (b. 1613), Edward (1616–84), William (1619–1706), and Christopher (1620–41). The childless Lady Montagu dedicates her writings to her stepchildren, to whom she "has been . . . mother these eleven years." The collection therefore dates to 1636/7.[73] Held by the Northamptonshire Record Office, this collection consists of loose papers, the penultimate step before manuscript collection.[74] These loose papers contain original and copied works in various genres, including a mother's legacy, an original poem, a transcribed catechism, Eucharistic instructions, and a prayer.

Edward Lord Montagu was an evangelically minded Protestant, whom King James I claimed "smelt a little of Puritanism."[75] After the death of his father, Lord Montagu resided primarily at Boughton House in Northamptonshire where he used his authority within the region to promote godly ministers to local livings. He also established a Puritan lectureship at Kettering.[76] We know that Lord and Lady Ann Montagu structured their household according to the precepts urged by godly ministers. The Montagu family met for daily prayer and attended weekly services at Kettering. The boys were taught to read by memorizing scriptural verses. Visitors to Boughton House were impressed by the children's ability to recite verses from Proverbs from memory.[77] The godly minister Joseph Bentham memorialized the piety of the Montagu household in print when he published fourteen of his Kettering lectures as *The Society of Saints: or a Treatise of Good Fellowes and their Good-Fellowship*. Bentham dedicated the work to Lord and Lady Montagu's three sons and son-in-law and explained that its purpose was to demonstrate to the young men that "by walking in those ways trac'd out by your religious parents and describ'd in this Discourse, ye shalbe sure to please God, glad the good, put to silence the contrary-minded [and] declare your reverent esteem of your Godly Parents."[78]

In its emphasis upon the godly training of children, Lady Montagu's manuscript collection similarly attests to the religiosity of Lord Montagu's and her household. We don't know whether Lady Montagu intended her compilation for circulation outside of her family; it does not contain a preface or other indicators of non-familial readership. It is possible, however, that these textual representations were intended to circulate and buttress Lord Montagu's reputation within the region. Richard Cust has remarked that "much of Montagu's status in Northamptonshire rested on his reputation as a patron of godly ministers." Lord Montagu played a leading role in local politics. He was long valued by his neighbors as a godly gentleman and consistent spokesperson "for the country."[79] Like Bentham's published text, Lady Montagu's manuscript collection provided a powerful attestation of her family's domestic devotion (and thus, by extension, her husband's piety).

In the letter that prefaces the collection, Montagu writes that she has been inspired by motherly concern: "My deare children, I have often tymes had a desier in my harte and thougts to write som what to you which might bee som guide or rule to walke in a holy and christian lyfe as may bee pleasing to god and everlasting comfort to your owne soules." An original poem of 160 stanzas, written in ballad meter, follows this letter. Montagu opens by addressing her children directly:

> These verces for my children bee
> hope ing theyle reede the same
> and practise them theyle set them free
> from sinne and eke from shame (Stanza 1)
>
> O heare my children what I say
> and marke well what I write
> to practise it doe not delay
> it will your soules delight (Stanza 3)

The poem simulates an oral utterance or conversation even as it acknowledges that it is written: the children must "heare" what she "say[s]" as well as "marke" what she writes. Montagu develops the fiction of a conversation as she proceeds: "Com now my deare and let us talke / how to avoyde all strife / to have a care whilst wee live heare / to leade a holy lyfe" (Stanza 6). Subsequent stanzas offer practical advice: the children should integrate prayer into their daily activities by thinking of God as soon as they wake up in the morning: "The first thoughts of thy hart give god / in morne When thou dost wake / least Satan fills your harts with badd / and maks thee god forsake" (Stanza 10). They should pray once again when they get dressed: "When thou dost rise up in thy bed / thy cloathes for to put on / o cloath thy self with Christ's white robes / and Satan willbee gone" (Stanza 11). They should do so again at lunch: "When soe farr of the day is spent / and noone is com for meate / first pray to god thy foode to blesse /then maist thou saflye eate" (Stanza 26). Montagu also reminds her children to "looke what company you doe keepe" (Stanza 45), to avoid gluttony since "Satain loves such belly gods" (Stanza 64), and to keep the Sabbath day holy by singing "sweet psalmes aright / to heare, to medditate, and pray / all day untill the night" (Stanza 50). She even specifies their amount of scripture reading, urging them that if they read two chapters everyday "twill much rejoyce thy minde" (Stanza 16).

Although Lady Montagu alludes to various scriptural personages and phrases, she is uninterested in the nuances. This makes her unlike such godly catechists as Katherine Fitzwilliam, who, as we will see in the next chapter, everywhere reveals her love of the specifics of scripture. Lady Montagu urges her children to "But walke with god as enoch did / all the daies of your lyfe / it will you bringe to blessedenes / to live without all strife" (Stanza 40). She alludes to Genesis 5:22 and 5:24 without providing an accompanying citation or glossing Enoch as an example of Christian righteousness. Likewise, when Lady Montagu urges her readers to "Have the brest plate of righteousness" (Stanza 23), she alludes to Paul's letter to the Ephesians 6:14.[80] The image of the breastplate of righteousness became prominent in Protestant theology and was glossed by both Luther and William Tyndale. Montagu is either uninterested in or unaware of these resonances; for her, the breastplate is simply a sacred object that will bring "joy."

Lady Montagu's presentation of her materials shows care throughout. Her poem is consistently formatted to bring out its ballad meter and its abab rhyme scheme as well as its stanza divisions. She catches an instance of eyeskip and corrects it immediately (Stanzas 22–23).

> If you god's armor will put on
> ~~Which is a holy thinge~~
> ~~Your feete being shod with gospells peace~~
> against the evell day
> and gird your loyns with veryty
> it will you strength and stay

> Have the brest plate of righteousnes
> Which is a holy thinge
> Your feete being shod with gospells peace
> Much joy twill to you bringe

Further evidence of Montagu's concern for the layout of her composition can be found in her brief marginal headings placed to the left of her text: for example, "spirituall armor," "the word," "meate," "meditate," "saboth," "sacraments," "table," "doe good," "charity," and "peace." Emulating a printed text, these topical guides help the reader to locate specific subjects.

Following this original poem, Lady Montagu places her transcription of Joseph Hall's catechism, *A Briefe Summe of the Principles of Religion, Fit to be Knowne of Such as Would Addresse Themselves to Gods Table.* Hall's sermons and treatises were very popular; Lord Montagu quotes from Hall in a letter to his brother Henry.[81] Emulating the printed version, Lady Montagu centers her title at the top of a new sheet of paper but changes it slightly: "A breefe sum of the prinsipalls of religion by way of cattychisme." Where Hall emphasizes the work's utility to a general audience, Montagu emphasizes the work's genre and thus the importance of catechesis in domestic religious instruction. Lady Montagu's transcription is nearly exact: it varies from Hall's original primarily in its spelling. She also emulates the physical layout of Hall's text in her transcription. Like Hall, she aligns her text with the Q and A's as separate units of text. Lady Montagu's Q's and A's are elaborate, almost calligraphic forms, slightly larger than the other letters and more decorative. Overall, we see in Montagu's loose papers an attempt to emulate some print conventions in order to make her selections visually appealing and thus reinforce her importance as compiler of her book upon its readers.

When compared to other seventeenth-century catechisms, *A Brief Summe* is notable for its elegance and brevity: it consists of only twenty-five pairs of questions and answers. Ostensibly designed for a child preparing for first communion, *A Brief Summe* addresses a range of topics from the simple – "what is God?" to the more complex.

> Q. What shall wee bee
> A. At the generall resurection of all flesh those which are in part renewed heare shalbee fully perfected and glorifyfied in body and soule and all those which lived and died in their sinnes shalbee judged to perpetuall torments

In keeping with accepted practice, the catechism sidesteps doctrinal controversies over Catholic transubstantiation and Lutheran consubstantiation. Its conception of the Lord's Supper is that of mainstream Calvinist theology:

> Q. What is the use of the Lords Supper
> A. To bee a signe, a seale, a pledge, unto us of Christ Jesus given to us and for us

The catechism's intellectual and religious directness results from its pithy, memorable phrasing typified by its use of verbs in a range of tenses: "Q. what must wee know concerning our selves? A. What wee ware, what wee are and what we shalbe." And, "Q. what must wee know of god? A. what a one hee is, and what hee hath done." While brief, the catechism covers two of the four staple subjects of English catechizing: the Lord's Prayer and the sacraments of the Lord's Supper and baptism. It is, as Ian Green notes, "short but quite full."[82] By including a copy of this catechism in her manuscript, Lady Montagu demonstrates both her doctrinal knowledge and her sound literary judgment.[83]

Montagu concludes with brief instructions concerning the reception of the sacrament of the Lord's Supper and an extended prayer to be used at "morning or evening or any other time." Although I have not been able to locate a precise source, the set of instructions closely resembles similar ones found in catechetical manuals. It exhorts the communicant to reflect on her own sinfulness and reminds her of the distinction between the sacrament's "outward" and "inward" parts. The extended prayer may be Montagu's original composition, but its contents are wholly traditional. It begins with a meditation on Montagu's own sinfulness, "confesing" to Christ "from the bottom of my hart that I am less than the least of thy merits and most worthy of thy greatest punishments." It also reveals a characteristically Protestant insistence upon the inability of human beings even "think one good thought." It concludes by asking God to bless the King (Charles I) and the Queen (Henrietta Maria), to which Montagu adds, "enlighten her hart with the true understanding of thy holy word that shee may see the truth of religion" – an allusion to the Queen's Catholicism. The prayer continues with petitions for magistrates, ministers of the holy word, and "all our children."

My Loving Friend

Montagu concludes with two original short poems, also written in ballad meter. Montagu concludes the first poem by characterizing herself as "your love ing mother still / and ever your deare friend." A horizontal rule follows this final line. The second poem opens with a deliberately truncated line:

> This booke I give
> to you o reade the same
> and practice it grant you may live
> to glorifie gods name
>
> If you will gloryfie god heare
> your soule shall live for ever
> in heavenly bliss where is all chere
> all joy and in all pleasure
>
> Which that you may my prayer it
> shalbe for you to god
> that you may ever doe his will
> and so escape his rodd
>
> And so my leave I take of thee
> not knowing what may fale
> death may aproach before I see
> you any more at all
>
> And if wee meete not heare one earth
> in heaven I hope wee shall
> and there to live with christ from death
> with him in eternall
>
> Accept of this poore work of mine
> though scoole like phrase it makes no show
> but practice this your soule shall finde
> true joyes at last gods word saies so
>
> And so farwell and say no more
> but bid you now adue
> Gods grace inrich your soules with store
> your freind Ann Mountagu

Montagu appears to have subsequently completed the first line, inserting the metrically appropriate phrase "my loving friend" in darker ink (and a slightly cramped script). This insertion may reflect Montagu's presentation of her manuscript to her stepchildren. It was not uncommon for early modern women (and men) to use the language of friendship when addressing close kin.[84] Montagu's use of friendship rhetoric affirms her close kinship relation with her stepchildren and underscores the loving affection she feels towards them.

Activating the humility topos in the phrase "of school-like phrase it makes no show," she defends her authority by asserting that her work is virtuous and sincere. Twice, she affirms that she compiled her manuscript to encourage godly "practice" or behavior, an emphasis that helps explain the manuscript's juxtaposition of original and transcribed texts and echoes Joseph Hall's insistence in *A Brief Summe* that two "things" are "required of a Christian," "Knowledge and Practice."[85] Montagu's compositional practices seem to have been guided primarily by her desire to provide her children with worthwhile moral and religious instruction. Although in disparate genres, the four works included in Montagu's loose papers cohere in their representation of Montagu as a literate and devout mother who cares about the salvation of her children.

Conclusion

The study of catechisms opens up a revealing view of relations between mothers and children in early modern England. As primary teachers, mothers were responsible for teaching very young children how to read at the same time as they taught them the basics of their faith. Catechetical instruction offered women an opportunity to engage with complex religious doctrine in outside sources. Maternally directed catechisms depict mothers as intellectually engaged and aware of their children's interests. Adults remember childhood catechesis as an expression of maternal love, but this love did not affect only the children. The instruction they gave their children provided mothers with evidence of their children's love for them, which mothers describe as an impetus to their own spiritual growth.

The household devotional of Katherine Thomas typifies maternal catechesis in seventeenth-century England. Whether Thomas wrote the questions herself or copied them from a published source is unclear, but her choice of questions reveals her attunement to her children's developmental capacities. Moreover, the format of *Places of Scripture* resembles a household account book and thus indicates its origin in the household. The careful formatting suggests that the book had practical usefulness for Thomas and her children. The questions, with their emphasis on the amusing and the sensational, indicate that catechesis aimed at being enjoyable for both mother and child. For her part, Lady Ann Montagu draws upon the cultural authority accorded to domestic catechesis to represent herself as a devoted, literate mother who cares about her children's spiritual well-being. This representation may have supported her husband's reputation as well. She incorporates the text of Joseph Hall's catechism together with her original poetic compositions. Her collection of loose papers presents different facets of domestic religious instruction bearing witness to her command of her material.

Notes

1. W. B. *The Farmer's Catechize: Or a Religious Parly between Father and Son* (London, 1657), 56–7.
2. John Bunyan, *The Pilgrim's Progress*, ed. Roger Lundin (New York: Penguin, 2002), 214, 216–17. I thank my colleague John Shanahan for alerting me to this reference.
3. On Bunyan and popular religious culture, see William York Tindall, *Mechanick Preacher* (New York: Columbia University Press, 1934). On Bunyan and catechisms, see Dennis Danielson, "Catechism, The Pilgrim's Progress, and Pilgrim's Progress," *Journal of English and Germanic Philology* 94.1 (January 1995): 42–58. Bunyan published a catechism, *Instruction for the Ignorant* in 1675. In *The Collected Works of John Bunyan*, ed. John Gulliver (Philadelphia, 1874).
4. Bunyan, *The Pilgrim's Progress*, 215.
5. "Embracing Submission? Motherhood, Marriage, and Mourning in Katherine Thomas' Seventeenth-Century Commonplace Book," *Women's Writing* 15.1 (2008): 69–85.
6. On the development of the idea of "literature" and the consequent separation of "literary" and "non-literary" genres, see Trevor Ross, "The Emergence of 'Literature': Making and Reading the English Canon in the Eighteenth Century," *ELH* 63.2 (1996): 397–422.
7. See Margaret Spufford, "First Steps in Literacy," *Social History* 4 (1979): 407–35, who remarks that seventeenth-century spiritual autobiographies contain "quite a number of examples of mothers teaching reading" (435). Also see David Hall, *World of Wonders, Days of Judgment* (New York: Knopf, 1989), 21–71. Kenneth Charlton surveys multiple ways in which mothers taught their children in *Women, Religion, and Education* (London: Routledge, 1999). Certainly some fathers instructed their children. The celebrated divine Richard Baxter, for example, relates that his father taught him to read by working through the historical parts of Scripture. *Reliquiae Baxterianae: or Mr. Richard Baxter's Narrative of the Most Memorable Passages of His Life and Times* (London, 1696), 2. But mothers appear to have been the primary teachers.
8. George Herbert, *A Priest to the Temple or the Country Parson, His Character and Rule of Life* (London, 1671), 32.
9. John Willison, *The Mother's Catechism for the Young Child* (London, 1735), in *Catechisms Written for Mothers, Schoolmistresses, and Children*, ed. Paula McQuade (Aldershot: Ashgate Publishing, 2008), 4.

10. Ian Green, *The Christian's ABC: Catechisms and Catechizing in England* (Oxford: Oxford University Press, 1996), 170.
11. "The transformation of forms and devices by which a text is presented authorizes new appropriations and consequently creates new publics for and uses for it." "Laborers and Voyagers: From the Text to the Reader," *Diacritics* 22.2 (1992): 49–61, 56.
12. Margaret Spufford, *Small Books and Pleasant Histories* (Athens: University of Georgia Press, 1981), 24; Michael McGiffert, *God's Plot: Puritan Spirituality in Thomas Shepard's Cambridge* (Amherst: University of Massachusetts Press, 1994), 161; Jacqueline Eales, *Puritans and Roundheads: The Harleys of Brampton Bryan* (Cambridge: Cambridge University Press, 1991), 25; On Talbot, see *The Diary of Sir Henry Slingsby, of Scriven, Bart*, ed. Daniel Parsons (London, 1836), 3. On Mather, see Hall, *Days of Wonder*, 35. Charlton, in *Women, Religion, and Education*, concludes, "There was little debate, then, as to whether a mother should be a prime agent in the education of her children nor as to her purpose in so doing" (202).
13. Green, *The Christian's ABC*, 578.
14. Eamon Duffy describes the "conventional character" of "penny godly" catechisms: they "offer brief summaries of the essentials of the faith, commandments, Lord's Prayer, graces, and morning and night prayers, and rhymed psalm verses for devotional use." He concludes that they, along with the rest of the penny godlies, represent "the centre and the best of English Puritanism." "The Godly and the Multitude in Stuart England," *Seventeenth Century* 1.1 (1986): 31–55, 43, 49.
15. Only a few of these catechisms remain because they were cheaply printed and much used. I quote from the following: *The ABC: with the Catechism* (London, 1687), Early English Books Online (2281:02), Sig. A2. This edition, which is held by Cambridge University Library, is extensively annotated. I have also consulted the following editions: *The ABC with the Catechism* (Philadelphia, 1788), and *The ABC with the Catechism* (London, 1687), held by the University of Illinois, Champaign-Urbana.
16. Isaac Watts, *A Discourse on the Way of Instruction by Catechisms* (London, 1786), 17.
17. Edmund Coote, *The English Schoolmaster* (London, 1670), 1–3.
18. Coote, *The English Schoolmaster*, 32.
19. Spufford, *Small Books*; Tessa Watt, *Cheap Print and Popular Piety, 1550–1640* (Cambridge: Cambridge University Press, 1991).
20. Edward Bagshaw, *The Life and Death of Vavasor Powell* (London, 1671), 2. Baxter, *Reliquiae*, 2. On Branch, see Hall, *World of Wonders*, 42. Bunyan, *Grace Abounding*, 15. Vavasor Powell, *Spirituall Experiences of Sundry Beleevers* (London, 1653), Early English Books Online (180:E1389[1]). Powell's narrators mention books by William Perkins (117) and Erasmus (161), as well as a book called *The New Birth* (90).
21. Alexander Nowell, *A Catechisme, or First Instruction* (London, 1571).

22. John Fiske, *The Watering of the Olive Plant in Christ's Garden, or, a Short Catechism* (Cambridge, Massachusetts Bay Colony, 1657), 3. John Ball, *A Short Treatise Contayning All the Principall Grounds of Christian Religion* (London, 1617), Sig. A4v.
23. Father Thomas Hunter, ed., *An English Carmelite, The Life of Catharine Burton, Mother Mary Xavier of the Angels … Collected from Her Own Writings and Other Sources* (London, 1883), 25. Elizabeth Isham, *Book of Rememberance*, ed. Elizabeth Clarke and Erica Longfellow, Folio 10v. (web .warwick.ac.uk/English/perdita/Isham). On Isham, see also Margaret Ezell, "Elizabeth Isham's Book of Rememberance and Forgetting," *Modern Philology* (2009): 71–84. Josias Nichols, *An Order of Houshold Instruction* (London, 1596), Sig. C2v-C2r.
24. Herbert, *A Priest*, 69. On the charge that such learning was "but as to teach a parrot or such like unreasonable creatures," see William Gouge, *Of Domesticall Duties* (London, 1622), 545; also Watts, *Discourse*, 19–20.
25. Watts, *Discourse*, 34–5. John Craig, *The Mother and the Child* (1611), in *Catechisms Written for Mothers, Schoolmistresses, and Children*, ed. Paula McQuade (Aldershot: Ashgate, 2008), Sig. A10v; A7v.
26. Gouge, *Of Domesticall Duties*, 545.
27. Stephanie Sleeper, "Ramist Logic," in *Puritans and Puritanism in Europe and America: A Comprehensive Encyclopedia*, ed. Francis Bremer and Tom Webster (Santa Barbara: ABC-CLIO, 2006), 517–18. See also John Morgan, *Godly Learning: Puritan Attitudes towards Reason, Learning, and Education, 1560–1640* (Cambridge: Cambridge University Press, 1986), 106–12.
28. Arnold Hunt, *The Art of Hearing: English Preachers and Their Audiences, 1590–1640* (Cambridge: Cambridge University Press, 2010), 99–100. The ministerial quotes are from Thomas Taylor and Mr. Hutton and are quoted in Hunt, 100.
29. On Wallington, see Hunt, *The Art of Hearing*, 102.
30. Watts, *Discourse*, 9.
31. Patrick Collinson, "The English Coventicle," in *From Cranmer to Sancroft* (London: Hambledon Continuum, 2006), 159.
32. John Downame, *A Guide to Godlynesse* (London, 1622), 338; William Perkins, *The Foundation of Christian Religion* (London, 1597), Sig. Aa3v; John Hoffman, *The Principles of Christian Religion* (Oxford, 1653), Early English Books Online (1880:08), Sig. A3r. See also the minister Richard Bernard, who writes in *The Two Twinnes: Or Two Parts of One Portion of Scripture* (London, 1613) that "no art can be learned without principles; we are first babes in Christ and therefore need Milke before Strong meat: can a house be well built without a foundation?" (8).
33. Ball, *A Short Treatise*, Sig. A5r-A6v.
34. Watts, *Discourse*, 9. On sermon repetition, see Hunt, *The Art of Hearing*, 94–114. For examples of the less-instructed asking questions of better-informed community members, see Powell, *Spirituall Experiences*, 166–7; see also Michael McGiffert, *God's Plot*, 209, 217.

35. Willison, *The Mother's Catechism*, 3; Warwickshire Record Office, Cr1368 Vol 1/99, The Upbringing of Penelope and Kate Mordaunt; Isham, *Book of Rememberance*, Folio 10v; Powell, *Spirituall Experiences*, 52; Richard Baxter, *The Mother's Catechism or a Familiar Way of Catechizing Children*, in *The Practical Works of the Late Reverend and Pious Mr. Richard Baxter* (London, 1707), 29.
36. John Craig, *A Short Summe of the Whole Catechism* (London, 1632).
37. Further discussion of the information contained in this paragraph can be found in Paula McQuade, "Introductory Note," in *Catechisms Written for Mothers, Schoolmistresses, and Children*, ix–xliii.
38. *The Grounds and Principles of Religion Contained in a Shorter Catechism* (London, 1708), 5. Initially, the long and shorter catechisms were published together: *The Confession of Faith* and the *Long and Shorter Catechism* (Glasgow, 1675). On guides to the *Westminster Shorter Catechism*, see Green, *Christian's ABC*, 82–3.
39. Green, *Christian's ABC*, 214.
40. Craig, *The Mother and the Child*, Sig. A3.
41. The *First Book for Children (1705)*, in *Catechisms Written for Mothers, Schoolmistresses, and Children*, ed. Paula McQuade (Aldershot: Ashgate, 2008), Sig. B1r.
42. Robert Abbot, *Milk for Babes*, in *Catechisms Written for Mothers, Schoolmistresses, and Children*, ed. Paula McQuade (Aldershot: Ashgate, 2008), Sig. A8v, A8r.
43. Herbert, *A Priest*, 68.
44. Watts, *Discourse*, 18, 51, 18.
45. Bunyan, *The Pilgrim's Progress*, 213–16.
46. Nichols, *An Order of Houshold Instruction*, Sig. B8r–C1v, C1v–C1r, C2r.
47. Duffy, "The Godly and the Multitude," 44.
48. Watts, *Discourse*, 65–6.
49. Ian Green, *Print and Protestantism in Early Modern England* (Oxford: Oxford University Press, 2000), 152–3.
50. *Dr. Watts' Historical Catechisms*, ed. Joseph Priestly (Dublin, 1793), 11. Baxter, *The Mother's Catechism*, 32. *The First Book for Children*, questions 2 and 15.
51. The following paragraphs draw upon and greatly expand material in Paula McQuade, "Introductory Note," in *Catechisms Written for Mothers, Schoolmistresses, and Children*, xiii–xvi.
52. Burch, *A Catechisme of the Severall Heads of the Christian Religion*, Sig. A6r–A7v; Mrs. J.C., *The Mother's Catechism* in *Catechisms Written for Mothers, Schoolmistresses, and Children*, ed. Paula McQuade (Aldershot: Ashgate, 2008), 21; Willison, *The Mother's Catechism*, 18. Bunyan, *Grace Abounding*, in *Grace Abounding With Other Spiritual Autobiographies*, ed. John Stachniewski and Anita Pacheo (Oxford: Oxford University Press, 1998), 22.
53. Craig, *The Mother and the Child*, Sig. A12r; Willison, *The Mother's Catechism*, 4.

54. Craig, *The Mother and the Child*, Sig. A6v; Mrs. J.C., *The Mother's Catechism*, 13.
55. Craig, Sig. A5r, A4r; Martin, *The Manner How to Examine* in *Catechisms Written for Mothers, Schoolmistresses, and Children*, ed. Paula McQuade (Aldershot: Ashgate, 2008), 240. Baxter, *The Mother's Catechism*, 29.
56. Martin, *The Manner How to Examine*, 238; Abbot, *Milk for Babes*, Sig. A6v. Alec Ryrie has remarked that "while parents might have a rosy view of their cherubs, children themselves were consistently told that they were the firebrands of Hell." *Being Protestant in Reformation Britain* (Oxford: Oxford University Press, 2013), 429.
57. Willison, *The Mother's Catechism*, 6.
58. Martin, *The Manner*, 235; Baxter, *The Mother's Catechism*, 34–5.
59. *A Warning for Fair Women*, ed. Charles Dale Cannon (The Hague: Mouton, 1975), 106.
60. Gouge, *Of Domesticall Duties*, 546; Samuel Hieron, *The Doctrine of the Beginning of Christ* (London, 1620), Sig. C4r; Nichols, *An Order of Household Instruction*, Sig. B7v.
61. Bernard, *Two Twinnes*, 20; Gouge, *Of Domesticall Duties*, 537, 540.
62. Herbert, *A Priest*, 72.
63. Powell, *Spirituall Experiences*, 161.
64. Powell, *Spirituall Experiences*, 11–13.
65. Powell, *Spirituall Experiences*, 51–3.
66. National Library of Wales, MS 4340A. Katherine Thomas' Commonplace Book.
    Perdita Manuscripts: Women Writers, 1500–1700 describes it as "144 folio duodecimo" and notes that the "manuscript is divided into two sequences." *Perdita Manuscripts* observes that the first is copied from the front up to Folio 117r; the second sequence begins from the back; the first section is written horizontally and contains page numbers; the second section is transcribed vertically and does not. Because the two catechisms derive from this second section of the manuscript, I am unable to provide page numbers.
67. I have compared the following historical catechisms: *The Way to True Happiness* (London, 1642); John Hoffman, *The Principles of Christian Religion* (Oxford, 1653), Early English Books Online (1888:08); Ambrose Rigge, *Scripture Catechism for Children* (London, 1672).
68. Eusebius Pagit, *The Historie of the Bible* (London, 1628), Sig. A3r–A4v.
69. See two manuscripts held in Chetham's Library, Manchester, UK: Bailey Collection A.2. 125. Commonplace Book and Catechetical Instructions on Sabbath Evenings; Bailey Collection A.2.126. Commonplace Book; Scriptural Questions.
70. *The Business and Household Accounts of Joyce Jeffreys, Spinster of Hereford, 1638–48*, ed. Judith Spicksley (Oxford: Oxford University Press, 2012).
71. Spufford, *Small Books*, 25.

72. Esther Cope, *The Life of a Public Man. Edward, First Baron Montagu of Boughton, 1562–1644* (Philadelphia: The American Philosophical Society, 1981), 104.
73. Richard Cust, "Montagu, Edward, 1562/3–1644," in *The Oxford Dictionary of National Biography* (Oxford: Oxford University Press, 2004). (www.oxforddnb.com.ezproxy.depaul.edu/view/article/19007)
74. Northamptonshire Record Office, Montagu Vol.3, Folio 241. The Loose Papers of Lady Ann Montagu. The manuscript is unpaginated; I reference stanza numbers when possible.
75. Cope, *The Life of a Public Man*, 82.
76. Cust, "Montagu, Edward, 1562/3–1644."
77. Cope, *The Life of a Public Man*, 145, 141, 162–3.
78. Joseph Bentham, *The Society of the Saints: Or, a Treatise of Good Fellowship* (London, n. d.). Cope, *The Life of a Public Man*, 142, remarks that the book must have appeared "sometime between the marriage of Frances Montagu and John Manners in 1628 and Bentham's departure from Weekly in 1631."
79. Cust, "Montagu, Edward, 1562/3–1644."
80. Ephesians 6:14. "Stand therefore, and your loynes girded about with veritie and having on the brestplate of righteousnesse." Paul is referencing Isaiah 59:17. "For he put on righteousness, as an habergeon, and a helmet of salvation upon his head . . . ."
81. *A Brief Summe of the Principles of Religion*, in *The Works of Joseph Hall* (London, 1625), 799–800. Cope, *The Life of a Public Man*, 161.
82. Green, *The Christian's ABC*, 661.
83. Hall's *A Brief Summe* is included in other manuscript collections. See, for example, William Andrews Clark Library, MS 20009.13. Manuscript Notebook Containing Transcriptions of Several Different Works by Joseph Hall. Transcribed sometime in the mid-seventeenth century, the collection is clearly intended to be a treasured personal legacy, more valuable than a printed copy because of the care and effort that went into its transcription.
84. Shakespeare, for example, writes in *Two Gentleman of Verona* that "she is promised by her friends / Unto a youthfull Gentleman of worth" (3.1.106). James Kelly makes this meaning explicit in his *A Complete Collection of Scottish Proverbs*: "Friends agree best at a distance. By Friends here is meant relations." "Friend," *The Oxford English Dictionary Online*, March 2015. Oxford University Press. (www.oed.com.ezproxy.depaul.edu/view/Entry/74646).
85. Hall, "A Brief Summe," 799–800.

CHAPTER 2

"A Tender Mother"
Domestic Catechesis in the Household Devotional of Katherine Fitzwilliam (b. 1579)

Introduction

The small notebook of Lady Katherine Fitzwilliam (1579–1643), known as FH 246, is unknown to most scholars interested in early modern women's writing.[1] This is in part because Fitzwilliam chose to preserve her writings in manuscript rather than publish them, so her notebook in the Northampton Record Office has been less accessible than a printed book. But there is also a problem of genre. Fitzwilliam did not compose in such recognizably literary genres as spiritual autobiography or poetry. Her textual output consists largely of four catechisms of varied lengths written in her own neat italic hand. Nor is her writing politically or religiously heterodox, the kind of non-literary writing that is more focused upon by scholars.

But even a cursory glance at the notebook and its author suggests the manuscript's relevance to current scholarly interests. She, a daughter of Sir William Hyde, was born Katherine Hyde of Berkshire in 1579. In 1603, she married William Fitzwilliam V (later Baron Fitzwilliam) and went to live at his family estate in Milton, Northampton. They had five children: William (married Jane, daughter of Hugh Perry, Alderman of London 1638; d. 1659), Winifred (1608–35), Anna (b. 1610; died unmarried), Katherine (married Sir John Lee 1633), and John (1614–37).[2] The Fitzwilliams were godly Protestants of long standing; Katherine Hyde shared her in-laws' religious beliefs and their scripturalism. Fitzwilliam's authorship would also have been encouraged by familial links with other women writers: her mother-in-law, Winifred Mildmay, was the sister of Anthony Mildmay, husband of Lady Grace Mildmay (1552–1620), a prolific author of manuscript works. Apethorpe, the ancestral manor of the Mildmay family, was approximately fourteen miles from Milton. Fitzwilliam named one of her daughters Winifred arguably to signal her connection to the Mildmay family. She was also related (more distantly) to the well-educated and literate Cooke sisters.³ What we see, then, is a confluence of factors that scholars have identified as enabling early modern women's authorship: scripturalism and contact with other women writers, whether as part of a formal literary circle or through familial and regional association.

Like her learned female relatives and neighbors, Fitzwilliam merits the attention of scholars interested in the intersection of gender, religion, and authorship. Fitzwilliam likely used FH 246 as a household devotional, a compilation of religious texts designed for the education of a godly household. The manuscript is a small volume, approximately 4 by 6 inches. The title page bears an elaborate nameplate that indicates Fitzwilliam's ownership. Besides the four catechisms that account for nearly two-thirds of its contents, the manuscript contains prayers for women in childbirth and book and sermon notes. Fitzwilliam does not title her catechisms, so I refer to them by their first words: the first catechism, *Can It Be Otherwise*, addresses the nature of faith, individual assurance, how a Christian should deal with affliction, and the duties of a Christian – all topics characteristic of what Ian Green has termed "High Calvinist devotional works" reflecting the theology of Theodore Beza, Ursinius, and William Perkins.⁴ The second catechism, *The First Treatise Teacheth*, redacts into catechetical form a popular Calvinist devotional treatise. The third catechism, *A Larger Unfoulding*, amplifies a topic addressed by Fitzwilliam in her first catechism: the problems posed by affliction. And the fourth catechism, *A Child's First Lesson*, tailors Calvinist doctrine for a child of about seven or eight years old.⁵

Probably composed between 1603 and 1623, Fitzwilliam's four catechisms illustrate how motherhood could catalyze female authorship in early modern England.⁶ Fitzwilliam worked sequentially on these catechisms; she conceived the third catechism as an addendum to the first, shaping the volume's content according to the evolving needs of her children and household. These diverse catechisms suggest that Fitzwilliam, through domestic religious instruction, gained generic awareness and experience in argumentation and linguistic analysis. She also honed her sense of audience: the question-and-answer series of her final catechism, *A Child's First Lesson*, are carefully tailored to the interests and abilities of a very young child, unlike those in her first catechism, which are designed for a more religiously advanced audience. Fitzwilliam evidently drew upon what she learned from domestic catechesis when composing her second catechism, her original redaction into catechetical form of Richard Rogers' *Seven Treatises* (1603). As we shall see, a Protestant minister published a similar catechetical redaction, so maternal catechesis equipped

Fitzwilliam with textual and linguistic skills that in some sense competed with ministerial authority.[7] We see further evidence of such competition in the third catechism, *A Larger Unfolding*, where Fitzwilliam contributes to the late sixteenth-century Calvinist literature concerning affliction by conceptualizing God as a "tender mother" who punishes her children with afflictions in order to make them stronger.

The four catechisms contained in FH 246 emphasize a mother's concern for her children's spiritual well-being. To be sure, the intimacy between mother and child that is reflected in Fitzwilliam's catechisms differs from our modern Freudian-influenced understanding of motherhood. When we read these exchanges carefully, we discover evidence that early modern mothers cared for their children's spiritual health: Fitzwilliam describes in lurid detail the pains of hellfire in order to discourage children from sin. But we also find intimations of the pleasure that can result from a shared textual analysis and even, arguably, a wry sense of humor. Although the image of motherhood that emerges from Fitzwilliam's catechisms does not conform to our contemporary understandings, it is not joyless.

Originality

We know that Lady Katherine Fitzwilliam composed her second catechism based upon her reading of Richard Rogers' *Seven Treatises* (1603). Fitzwilliam begins her engagement with this text by recasting it in outline form. In the far left margin of this outline is a page number keyed to Rogers' text, along with a letter designating the paragraph in *Seven Treatises* from which she derives the point in question. So, for example, Fitzwilliam has placed the designation "Pag. 2" next to the numerical designation "1" and directly below she places the letters H.I. – letters keyed to paragraphs in *Seven Treatises*. Such notations would allow Fitzwilliam (or her reader) to return to the original as needed. Only later in her notebook does she recast the outline as a catechism. Several early modern women performed similar redactions of complex and difficult material into catechetical form. Ian Green remarks that "authors who had been exposed ... to catechisms as part of their Christian education had no qualms using questions and answers to teach this essential information."[8]

Did Fitzwilliam herself write rather than redact or copy the other three catechisms? There are good reasons to think that they are original compositions. I have not found a source text for these catechisms among 180 catechisms published between 1580 and 1630. This contrasts with the ease with which I found the original catechism that provides the basis for the catechism of Lady Ann Montagu as well as the source text for Fitzwilliam's second catechism. Fitzwilliam's catechisms also differ from most published catechisms in the topics they address. As we have seen, Ian Green identifies "four staples" discussed in most sixteenth- and seventeenth-century catechisms, all of which are found in the catechism contained in the *Book of Common Prayer*. Calvin addresses the Apostles Creed, the Ten Commandments, and the Lord's Prayer in his *Catechism or The Manner How to Examine Children* (London, 1556 English translation). To give but two additional examples: Robert Fenton's very popular *So Short a Catechism* (at least twelve editions between 1582 and 1662), written to help children prepare for the Lord's Supper, covers the creed and the sacraments of baptism and communion and includes select prayers in just five pages; Martin Fist's *A Brief Catechisme of the Christian Religion* (1624) devotes twenty-five pages to discussing just the sacraments. The majority of catechisms published between 1580 and 1630 cover at least one of these staple subjects; by contrast, Fitzwilliam covers none. In a random sample that I made of twenty-five catechisms written between 1580 and 1630, only four (16 percent) did not discuss at least one of these staple subjects. Furthermore, the answers to Fitzwilliam's catechisms consist largely of scriptural texts; this too marks her catechisms as unusual (though admittedly not unique).[9]

It is possible that the three catechisms are the result of collaboration between Fitzwilliam and a godly minister associated with her family. Green and Cliffe have noted the close connections between Puritan ministers and members of the aristocracy and gentry.[10] In the prefaces to their published ministerial catechisms, Protestant ministers sometimes indicate that their text is a record of an originally oral performance within a noble household and imply that they performed such duties together with the noblewoman and her children. Robert Abbot, "preacher of God's word at Southwick in Hampshire," for example, includes two dedicatory epistles in his published catechism, *Milk for Babes*. The first is dedicated to Lady Honoria Norton; in it, Abbot claims that she has "had experience of the power and profit of it in your family and in the congregation over which you have care" and that she has now, "by entreating commands and commanding favors" urged him to publish it. In the second, which is dedicated to Lady Mary Bakere and Lady Unton Dering, Abbot insists that "there is none of you both, but have in your families, heard me open these grounds either to your children or servants."[11] It is possible that Fitzwilliam's three catechisms apparently lacking published sources reflect such ministerial catechesis, although there is no evidence of this in Fitzwilliam's manuscript.

Another possibility is that Fitzwilliam copied three of the four catechisms from several as-yet-unidentified sources, weaving selected passages together to form new works. Her catechisms would thus resemble prayer collages and other devotional material composed by early modern women, such as Lady Anne Clifford, Lady Grace Mildmay, and Lady Anne Halkett, which similarly combine "some fixed and some improvised elements."[12] Susan Felch suggests that critics adopt "a robust, multi-dimensional and non-individualistic account of linguistic activity that ... fits both the production and the function of women's written prayers."[13] But while this approach illuminates prayers and psalm collages, it sheds less light on women's catechetical compositions. Fitzwilliam's first, third, and fourth catechisms do contain echoes of other texts, but these echoes are never verbally exact and are largely topical.[14] They more likely attest to Fitzwilliam's extensive religious reading – and her participation in certain strains of godly piety – than to her compositional strategies.

A final possibility is that Fitzwilliam composed all of the catechisms, not just the second, based upon her reading of devotional prose. Her third catechism, for example, begins with a summative sentence that appears to display the Ramist reasoning characteristic of university-trained clergy: "Out of the scriptures before alleged touching afflictions, two things maie be learned. First what a Christian's duty is concerning afflictions. 2. What he must do to enable himself to better bear them." But two factors prompt caution in this matter. First, I have not been able to find a prose source for these catechisms, although subsequent research may discover one. Second, when Fitzwilliam redacts prose works, she usually provides page numbers in the left margin that are keyed to the source text. This is characteristic procedure not only in her second catechism, but also in a prose summary of a devotional work to which she give the title, *Directions to Those That Have Attained Faith*. The other catechisms lack similar marginal notations, an omission that may indicate that they are original compositions.

I think it is most likely that Fitzwilliam composed the three remaining catechisms herself, perhaps based upon her wide-ranging devotional reading. A notebook used by the non-conformist minister Phillip Henry to educate his daughter Sarah and son Mathew provides an analogue to Fitzwilliam's manuscript, revealing that home catechesis could be intellectually challenging as well as spiritually demanding. Among the topics that fourteen-year old Sarah Henry is asked to address is "What do the Scriptures say concerning the omniscience of God?"[15] As we will see in Chapter 5, Dorothy Burch composed and published her own catechism in 1646; her preface describes her writing process: "it came into my minde to see what God had taught me," so "I put pen to paper ... asking myself questions, and answering of them."[16] If Burch, a working-class wife and mother, could compose a catechism, surely Lady Fitzwilliam could as well. As the female head of a household, she would have rehearsed the catechism's exposition of scripture with her children (and perhaps her servants), learned to recognize catechetical argumentation and discerned how the catechisms tailor their presentation of religious doctrine to various audiences, even if hers were not original compositions.

Household Publication

When Katherine Hyde married William Fitzwilliam in 1603, she entered into a godly family with a tradition of religious reading and writing. Fitzwilliam's father-in law, William Fitzwilliam IV, was well known at the Elizabethan court as a committed Puritan. As early as 1569, he was in London with his neighbor Walter Mildmay, who was Chancellor of the Exchequer and also a godly Protestant. As we have seen, Fitzwilliam married Mildmay's daughter Winifred, who was the sister-in-law of Grace Sharrington Mildmay. Grace Mildmay was preparing her voluminous manuscript meditations to pass down to her daughter between 1610 and 1620, when Katherine Fitzwilliam would have been mistress at Milton.[17] During his time at court, Fitzwilliam IV benefited financially from his prominence within evangelical Protestant circles; at his death in 1618, he had increased his family's fortune in large part due to his effective manipulation of godly patronage.[18] We know less concerning the religious commitments of Katherine's birth family, the Hydes of Kingston Lisle, Berkshire, who were of slightly lower social status than the Fitzwilliams, but considering William Fitzwilliam IV's predilection for associating with other evangelical Protestants, it is likely the Hydes were also committed Protestants.

Lady Fitzwilliam wrote FH 246 with the intention that it would be read and used by others. This is confirmed by its table of contents (TOC), which is keyed to the first catechism only, thus suggesting that Fitzwilliam composed the texts in her manual sequentially. The TOC foregrounds the exposition of the Calvinist doctrine of assurance in the first catechism. It begins by asserting that without divine grace, all people, including children, are in "danger of destruction"; it then argues that this awareness of our danger should impel us to seek safety in the righteousness of Christ and that the believer can rest in that righteousness only through faith.

The subjects are sequentially numbered and logically ordered: knowledge of the danger of damnation, for example, leads one to seek Christ. And each numbered topic is followed by a page number, which is keyed to the page in Fitzwilliam's manuscript where the topic is discussed; for example, the fifth topic, "How Christ is made our Righteousnes" is followed by the identification "pag. 4," indicating its location in Fitzwilliam's manuscript. As I have suggested, Fitzwilliam's third catechism, *A Larger Unfolding* also contains numerical references to the first catechism. Because FH 246 contains both a table of contents and these numerical references, it was likely to have been designed for communal reading, perhaps by multiple readers.[19]

Nonetheless, FH 246 differs from many other devotional notebooks by seventeenth-century gentlewomen in paying little attention to visual aesthetics. Kate Narveson recounts the attention to detail that Fitzwilliam's neighbor, Lady Grace Mildmay, lavished upon her writings.[20] Lady Fitzwilliam's book is less carefully crafted; its table of contents is simple and even utilitarian in design. This suggests that Fitzwilliam did not compose her book as a presentation copy, designed to circulate among friends and neighbors, unlike the manuscript catechism transcribed by Barbara Slingsby (discussed in Chapter 4).

So why did she write it? I think that the likeliest explanation is that Fitzwilliam designed FH 246 for the religious education of her household.[21] In early modern England, domestic religious instruction included bible reading, psalm singing, and sermon repetition. *A Garden of Spirituall Flowers*, for example, advises the godly householder that before the afternoon service, he should "assemble thy Family together, confer with them what they have learned at the Sermon; instruct and Catechize them; read, or cause them to be read somewhat of the Bible, or some other godly Booke unto them."[22] The notebooks used by the Henry family reflect their weekly practice of catechesis, sermon repetition, and scripture reading. One of the notebooks bears a carefully formatted title page that reads "Questions of Conference in the Family." The first question reads, "What are the scriptural attributes of God the Father?" and is followed by an answer that cites John 3:17 and concludes, "this is life eternal." Another notebook contains sermon notes.[23] Lady Fitzwilliam's manuscript miscellany similarly contains sermon notes and prayers in addition to her four catechisms. This mixture reflects the idealized household practice urged by devotional manuals (and enacted by the Henry family) and arguably supports my claim that she composed FH 246 to assist with her domestic religious instruction. FH 246 thus belongs to a subgroup of women's writing in early modern England, which Kate Narveson terms "household publications," works "conceived both as products, material books to be left as legacies, and as texts subject to revision."[24]

Multiple godly women seem to have composed similar works containing catechisms, sermon notes, and scriptural passages. In a quote that aptly illustrates the linkage between sermon repetition and catechesis, the Puritan minister Nathaniel Parkhurst describes how it was the common practice of Lady Elizabeth Brooke after hearing sermons to "write the substance of them into Question and Answers or under Heads of Common Places, and then they became to her Matter for repeated meditation."[25] Mothers instructed children and stepchildren how they might recreate sermons that they had heard, just as they provided them with catechetical instruction. Lady Elizabeth Langham, for example, taught her eleven-year-old stepdaughter to repeat sermons that she had heard, "and by her instructions so methodised the memory of this young Child, that she was able to Analise a Sermon containing thirty or forty particular Heads, with the most remarkable inlargements upon them."[26] Mrs. Katherine Clark (wife of the godly divine Samuel Clark) left "many volumes" of sermon notes, which she "made good use of by frequent reading and meditation"; she also transcribed passages from books written by godly divines and "instilled" into her children a knowledge of "the first grounds and Principles of Religion," presumably through catechesis.[27]

These examples suggest that FH 246 reflects common practice among seventeenth-century godly women. But most female-authored household devotionals have yet to be recovered, and so, as Femke Molekamp observes, "it is left to us to imagine what precise form they took."[28] I would suggest that FH 246 is unusual only because it survived. It offers a glimpse into a common form of textual production among seventeenth-century women, a glimpse that is otherwise blocked by textual impermanence.

Catechisms and Sermon Notes

Before we turn to Lady Fitzwilliam's catechisms, I'd like to pause briefly to consider in more detail the relationship between sermon note-taking and catechesis. Evangelically minded men and women took notes on sermons to serve as an *aide memoire* in subsequently recreating the sermon independently, either for their own edification or for the benefit of the godly community.[29] But as Arnold Hunt has argued, the process of note-taking also helped early modern women (and men) to understand rhetorical structures. It was "a way for them to appropriate what they had heard: to take a lengthy and complex body of religious teaching and to make it their own through a process of mental sorting and filtering."[30] When taking notes on a sermon, listeners were forced to understand its structure and to break it down to its constituent parts. As significantly, when a note-taker repeated a sermon from these notes, she was, in a sense, recreating it, either by finding new applications for the doctrine or by challenging herself to articulate the relation between a scriptural proof and its claims – a process that is also required in some more advanced forms of catechesis.[31]

Lady Fitzwilliam's notes are on a sermon preached on 2 Peter 1:10: "Wherefore, brethren, give rather diligence to make your calling and election sure: for if yee doe these things, ye shall never fall." Even a brief examination of the notes reveals their similarity to her catechetical compositions. Fitzwilliam visually represents the sermon's logic, placing the phrase "2 thinges" underneath the scriptural reference. She then connects this phrase with a bracket, with the words "1. An Exhortation" at the top; and the phrase "2. A reason" at the bottom. The top phrase is further subdivided with a bracket that branches out as follows: "1. The manner of propounding the exhortation: Brethren"; the second, "2. Exhortation it selfe." This diagram conveys Fitzwilliam's understanding of Ramist rhetorical structure, and just as significantly, her ability to represent this structure visually.[32] The sermon notes are occasionally in question-and-answer form. On the second page of her notes, she writes, "2. What is meant by Callinge." After transcribing a brief prose answer to this question, she includes two scriptural references, each of which contains a particular understanding of "calling": 2 Thessalonians 2:13–14 and 2 Timothy 1:9.

I have argued in Chapter 1 that elementary catechesis was believed to provide the intellectual groundwork for hearing sermons. But we need to be mindful of gradations in catechetical practice, since, as even this brief discussion indicates, advanced catechesis and sermon-repetition appear to have been closely related and (perhaps) mutually reinforcing activities. As Ian Green remarks, "By the late sixteenth or early seventeenth centuries, 'catechizing' was not a single operation but a whole range of overlapping and interlocking activities."[33] The existence of catechisms and sermon notes in FH 246 provides a valuable reminder that advanced catechesis often took place within the household as part of a constellation of literacy practices, all of which were designed to increase the scriptural and doctrinal knowledge of the godly.

Authorship and Audience

The four catechisms in Lady Fitzwilliam's manuscript miscellany vary in difficulty, suggesting that she tailored her questions to the abilities of her audiences. This is in accordance with what we know about maternal catechesis in the seventeenth century. Robert Abbot, for example, includes three different catechisms in *Milk For Babes* and specifies that the "first, briefer catechism" is to be "opened first." To see how Lady Fitzwilliam modulates her instruction, we may consider the catechism entitled, *A Child's First Lesson*. Fitzwilliam includes questions and answers that address the nature of the divine will, the centrality of Scripture, and the punishment of the damned. Interestingly, Calvin's theories of individual election and predestination are not covered, perhaps because Fitzwilliam judges these subjects too complex (or frightening) for the very young child. (In this, she compares favorably to Mrs. J.C. who, in her *The Mother's Catechism*, has the mother respond to the child's question why God damns some people to hell and not others with a theologically accurate but (at least to my mind) chilling answer: "His mere good pleasure.")[34] By contrast, *A Child's First Lesson* opens with a series of simple questions:

> Q. How came you into the worlde.
> Q. Who preserveth you in the worlde.
> Q. Who gives you your meat and drinke here.
> Q. Who makes you well againe when ye be sick.

These questions focus on basic human needs – safety, food, and health – that even a young child could appreciate. Because the answer to all questions is "God," the questions reinforce divine omnipotence and divine providence, central points of Calvin's theology. Because the catechism begins with these questions, form follows function; in both *A Child's First Lesson* and Calvinist theology, God comes first.

A Child's First Lesson also reveals Lady Fitzwilliam's pedagogical skill in employing a simple vocabulary and phrasing appropriate to her young audience. We can see that this is a deliberate choice by glancing at the first catechism in this manuscript miscellany, *Can It Be Otherwise*. Here, in a catechism designed for a more religiously advanced audience, Fitzwilliam answers the question, "Q. Be there not other warrants in the Scripture for men to beleeve" as follows:

> A. yes. 1. Christs calling and bidding men beleve in him. Mathew 11.28. Come unto me all ye that are heavie laden and weary and I will ease you.2. Christ exhorting men to beleve in him John 14.1 Ye beleve in god, beleve

also in me.3. His beseeching of men by his messengers. 2 Corinthians 5.20 We being embassadours for Christ as though God did beseech you by us, we pray you in Christ's steed to be reconciled to God.[35]

Fitzwilliam provides not one, but three scriptural warrants for her answers. This exchange also reveals Fitzwilliam's sense of argument – she first provides the reason for her belief, then the scriptural proof texts that ground her belief. In so doing, she follows the practice characteristic of catechesis. The Protestant minister John Ball urges catechists to clarify the relationship between scripture and doctrine in order to illustrate the scriptural basis of religious truth: "Take the pains to search into the proofs which are alleged for confirmation of the matter ... This wee commend, because it is a course behovefull for the obtaining of well-grounded knowledge, the getting of stedfast and assured faith and comfort, and growing to be familiarly acquainted with the word."[36] Lady Fitzwilliam also displays a developed sense of language, differentiating among modes of entreaty: Christ calls, exhorts, and beseeches. It is possible to view this exchange as a merely mechanical exercise, but I would argue that it more closely resembles a game in which questioner and respondent display their ability to make multiple responses, demonstrate their scriptural knowledge, and apply linguistic precision.[37]

By contrast, in *A Child's First Lesson* the questions and answers are brief and to the point.

> Q. How will God reprove them
> A. God hath diverse waies of reproving bad ones
>
> Q. Which is the first waie.
> A. He will sett their sins in order before them. Psalm 50.21
>
> Q. And what will followe upon that.
> A. They shalbe taken with a feare and secret terrour. Psalm 14.5

The sequence of the questions makes the logic transparent: "God has diverse ways, so let's discuss the first one first." The child can rely upon this logical structure as she learns the theological principles. As in Fitzwilliam's other catechisms, the answers in this exchange are mainly scriptural passages, but here they are neither glossed nor interpreted. The purpose of the exchange seems not to teach scriptural analysis but to get the child to learn tenets of belief and memorize scriptural verses – appropriate goals for the very young believer.

Perhaps the best evidence that Fitzwilliam carefully designed her catechisms for audiences of varying abilities can be found in the brief catechetical exchange that ends *Can It Be Otherwise*. Here, the advanced student (who by this point has presumably completed the rest of this first catechism) is challenged to construe or "reckon" the relation between a religious topic and a scriptural passage.

> Q. Reckon up some of these particularly.
> A. Knowledg of god and his worde. Colossians 1. 9.10
>   Faith in Christ. Colossians 2. 6.7.
>   Peace joy and hope. Romans. 15.13
>   Brother love. 1 Thessalonians 4.9.10
>   Patience. Colossians 2.11
>   Holines. 2 Thessalonians 3.13
>
> Q. Be these few all. A. Not so.[38]

Fitzwilliam here invites the catechumen to apply on her own what she has learned by reading these qualities and relating them to the accompanying scriptural verse – a process that, as we have seen, resembles that of sermon repetition. So for example, the first question asks the student to recall Colossians 1:9–10 from memory, unlike in *A Child's First Lesson*, where the scriptural citation itself constitutes the answer. These two verses comprise a long set of verb phrases:

> For this cause we also, since the day that we heard of it, cease not to pray for you, and to desire that ye might be fulfilled with knowledge of his will in all wisdome and spirituall understanding. That ye might walke worthy of the Lord, and please him in all things, being fruitfull in all good workes, and increasing in the knowledge of God.

Next, the student is enjoined to articulate the relation between these verb phrases and the virtue of knowledge of God and his word. Published catechists urge instructors to test the logical ability of their more advanced students similarly. The godly minister Robert Cawdry urges that students be challenged by requiring them to articulate the points of doctrine that can be deduced from a given scriptural citation:

> Or rather, first to make a choice of a place of scripture, where is contained a principle of Religion and when he hath discoursed and handled the question therein, to ask some of his hearers the point and questions that are specially intreated of in that text and so orderly from time to time to goe through the chiefe points of Christian religion.[39]

Such reversals present an intellectual challenge for more advanced students. Fitzwilliam here employs a similar method: she provides both the passage and the topic but requires the student to construe the relationship between them.

A similar method undergirds Fitzwilliam's responses earlier in this catechism. For example, the question-and-answer series that begins "Be there not other warrants in the Scripture for men to beleeve" could be easily rephrased as: "Reckon up this particularly: Warrants in scripture for belief. Matthew 11.28, John 14.1, 2. Corinthians 5.20." The topics of this final series arguably get more difficult as the list develops; the final topic, "Holiness" requires the student to "reckon" an answer to the question based solely upon a brief passage from 2 Thessalonians 3:13: "And ye, brethren, be not wearie in well doing." Thus, in contrast to the simple phrasing and monosyllabic answers in *A Child's First Lesson*, Fitzwilliam ends her most advanced lesson with an invitation for the student to emulate the teacher in pursuing further analysis: "Q. Be these few all. A. Not so." This exchange models a real-life conversation between a mother and child in which the child, having successfully "reckoned" the connection between abstract religious doctrines and scriptural texts, asks the mother if she has finished. The tone of this exchange is admittedly difficult to determine, but it is possible to read the child's response "Be these few all" as tonally similar to the American slang, "Is that all you got?," a playful phrase that simultaneously registers a delight in personal accomplishment and a sense of mastery. The mother's response "Not so" lightly corrects the child's outspokenness while not discounting her very real accomplishment.

The Worde of Faith: Fitzwilliam's Delight in Scripture Phraseology

The practice of maternal catechesis did not only develop Fitzwilliam's sense of audience. It also encouraged the development of her linguistic ability and textual skills. Protestant ministers had long recognized that biblical language and imagery required interpretation. As early as 1560, the editors of the Geneva Bible admitted, "A hard thing it is to understand the holy Scriptures."[40] But here godly ministers confronted a problem: how do you teach textual interpretation to mothers who lack a formal education? Most catechetical authors rely upon a pedagogy of imitation: in their texts they provide a model of scriptural interpretation and urge their readers to replicate it. Josias Nichols published *An Order of Houshold Instruction* in order to help parents catechize children within the home. He provides multiple models of scriptural interpretation, each keyed to a different developmental stage. In one example designed for intermediate students, he shows how a mother might teach Isaiah 53:11: "By his knowledge shall my righteous servant justifie many: for he shall beare their inequities." Nichols comments upon this passage:

> These words are evidently a prophecy of Christ Jesus, wherein the master must teach his familie to consider the persons. First, if he that speake this is God; then the persons of whom he speaketh are two. 1. Christ, whom he calls his rightous servant. 2. All believers, which are many men and women whose sins hee beareth.[41]

Nichols begins by underscoring the importance of genre: Isaiah 53:11 is a prophecy or prediction of future events. By focusing upon genre, he establishes an interpretive framework for viewing the passage. Nichols then directs the parent to what we might term the personae – the speaker and those spoken about. He explains that "In person, he is called a servant, God's servant, and a just servant. A servant, because being God he became a man, which is called the [f] form of a servant: god's servant, because he came to do [t] God's will." Nichols then adduces multiple instances when the term "servant" is used to refer to Christ in the Bible, and he provides scriptural support for each of these variations: the superscript designation [f], for example, directs the reader to Philippians 2:6–7: "Who, being in the forme of God thought it no robbery to be equall with God: but hee made himself of no reputation and tooke on him the forme of a servant." Nichols here demonstrates how a mother or father might focus upon the "words and sense" of a scriptural passage: first, pay attention to genre and characters, then note other instances in scripture where the same term is used and relate these terms to the passage under discussion.[42]

The minister John Fiske similarly models textual interpretation in *The Watering of an Olive Plant*, a catechism published after he used it among his Chelmsford congregation. When Fiske discusses The Lord's Prayer (Mathew 6:9–13), for example, he (like Nichols) begins by noting its genre: it is, he explains, a "pattern prayer."[43] He then proceeds to lead his reader step by step through its interpretation. So, for example, in discussing the phrase, "Hallowed be thy name," he includes first a very general scriptural citation (Peter 1) that invites the reader to compare this phrase with other scriptural phrases. He then provides a question and answer sequence: "what are we taught to beg in this petition in general? What in particular?" Answer: "The [p] enabling of us by his Grace, to become every way in our Times, instrumental of His Glory." The superscript [p] provides the catechumen with additional scriptural support for this doctrinal conclusion: 1 Peter 3:15, Psalm 23, 50, 2 Thessalonians 1:10–12, and 1 Peter 2:9, 12 and 4:10–11, 14, and 16.[44] Like Nichols, Fiske foregrounds genre and personae and invites catechumens to deepen their analysis by comparing the "words and phrase" of the passage to similar ones in scripture. At one point, Fiske remarks laconically that this process may be better suited for readers "with such capacities are allready entered, than such as but are in their enterance," but the impact of such instruction should not be underestimated: advanced catechesis could provide attentive mothers with training in argument and textual analysis, skills typically associated with ministerial training and considered necessary to authorship. That at least some early modern women applied these skills in composing original texts can be demonstrated by Sarah Symmes Fiske, Fiske's daughter-in-law, who composed a *Confession of Faith* demonstrating her mastery of scriptural citation and analysis; it was published after her death for use in domestic religious instruction.[45]

Lady Fitzwilliam demonstrates her ability to interpret scripture throughout her catechism. In one exchange she expounds the Pauline understanding of the relation between the law and gospel, whereby Christ's imputed righteousness saves the godly from slavish obedience to the law.

> Q. What worde of God.
> A. Not the worde of the lawe but the worde of faith Romans 10.8. that is the Gospell. as Ephesians 1. 13 in whom also ye trusted, after that ye heard the worde of truth, even the Gospell of your salvation.[46]

Fitzwilliam conflates two passages from the Pauline epistles: Romans 10:8: "But what saith it? The word is neere thee, even in thy mouth, and in thine heart: this is, the word of faith, which we preach" and Ephesians 1:13: "In whom also ye have trusted, after that ye heard the worde of trueth, even the Gospel of your salvation: wherein also after that yee believed, ye were sealed with that holy Spirit of promise." Although Fitzwilliam adopts the phrase "worde of faith" from Romans, the rest of the answer follows the passage from Ephesians. The two passages, however, are linked in Fitzwilliam's mind (and on the page) through parallel phrasing – "worde of truth" and "worde of faith" – and context; in each passage, Paul is outlining what Luther would term the freedom of a Christian man – that is, the way in which Christ's sacrifice frees the believer from strict observance of the law. She draws the two scriptural passages together by echoing the term "gospel" from Ephesians before introducing the quotation, so that the three phrases are conflated as functional equivalents: the word of faith, which is the word of truth, which is the gospel. We should note as well that Lady Fitzwilliam begins her answer with a negative definition, "not the worde of the lawe," which she then redefines while using the same phrase pattern, "but the worde of faith," a stylistic pattern that echoes Hebraic sense parallelism and thus supports Janel Mueller's arguments concerning the importance of vernacular scripture to the development of fifteenth- and sixteenth-century English prose.[47] Fitzwilliam's literary and theological sophistication is evident; the conflation is possible only because she was aware of the similar phrasings in different Pauline epistles at the same time that she recognized the contextual equivalence of the terms. The result is a theologically accurate but elegant understanding of the relationship between the law and the gospel.

Fitzwilliam's scriptural knowledge is certainly extensive, but she does not believe that scripture is so self-evident as to need no interpretation. So, for example, when she addresses a question concerning Christ's satisfaction of our sins, "Q. How or in what respect are we delivered from our ^sinnes by his suffrings on the crosse," she answers with an Old Testament quotation: "A. Isaiah sheweth Chapter 53.5 He was wounded for our transgressions, he was broken for our iniquities, the chasticement of our peace was upon him and with his strypes we were healed." But Fitzwilliam then recognizes that the connection between Isaiah and her claim is not self-evident – what precisely does "the chastisement of our peace was upon him" mean? She next provides a gloss that indicates her reliance upon the standard typological reading of Isaiah as foreshadowing Christ: "by which words," she explains "he shewes that Christ beare the punishment which our sins had deserved, and so saved us from the same." Similarly, Fitzwilliam sometimes offers her own summary of particular verses: when she answers a theologically difficult question concerning Christ's imputed righteousness, "Q. What warrant have we that god will accept of the bloud of Christ as a satisfaction for our sins," her answer is direct: "A. This: that God ^himself hath set him forth as a meanes of pacifying him for our sins by his blood. Romans 3.25."[48] The verse from Romans that Fitzwilliam cites in support of her answer, however, is complicated: "whom God hath set forth to be a reconciliation through faith in his blood to declare his righteousness by the forgiveness of sins that are passed." Fitzwilliam's answer replaces the word "reconciliation" with "pacifying," a choice that reveals her Calvinist understanding of God the Father as a judge who requires "satisfaction" for human transgressions; at the same time, she gestures to the initial phrase of Romans 3:26, "through the patience of God," which indicates that forgiveness of sins requires divine forbearance.

The catechumen is also required to practice copia, a rhetorical technique of amplification typically taught through education in classical rhetoric, and one which Lisa Gordis argues reflects appreciation for God's "loving fullness, indeed of almost overwhelming abundance."[49] One of Fitzwilliam's questions asks the catechumen to provide another term for the spiritual experience of being born again:

> Q. By what other termes is this dying to sin and quickening called in the scripture
> A. Repentaunce from dead workes Hebrews 6.1 and turning to God, to serve the living and true god. 1. Thessalonians 1. 9. This worke of Christ in the faithfull is called a new creation. He that is in Christ is a new creature 2 Corinthians 5. 17.[50]

Fitzwilliam invokes not just one, but four terms central to Protestant theology: repentance, turning to God, new creation, and new creature. She offers scriptural support for each and her phrase structure suggests the relations among them: when one repents and turns to God, one becomes a new creation or a new creature. Her facility with doctrine and scriptural texts is evident.

This catechism also reveals her understanding of figurative language in scripture – an understanding nearly all published catechisms, including maternally directed ones, insist is necessary for proper understanding. Responding to the question, "Q. And whence commeth this quickening of us into this new life," Fitzwilliam conjoins references to Romans, Ephesians, and Galatians to articulate the theology of justification:

> A. St. Paule shewes by saying. If we be planted with him into the similitude of his death, So shall we bee into the Similitude of his resurrection Romans 6.5 and Christ dwels in our harts by faith Ephesians 3.17. and now that we are crucified with Christ, we live yet not soe any more but Christ liveth in us Galatians 2. 20.[51]

These Pauline passages combine to expound the central point: it is because we "grow" with Christ that he can share in our death (by dying on the cross) just as we hope to share in his resurrection (by rising again on the last day). The image conveys a sense that the reciprocal growth of Christ and the believer ends in union. That Fitzwilliam understands the centrality of this image reveals how domestic catechesis encouraged the development of textual and linguistic abilities traditionally associated with ordained ministers.

Fitzwilliam's scriptural citations in this exchange reveal that she used a post 1576 quarto edition of the Geneva Bible. The 1560 Geneva translation of Romans 6:5 uses the horticultural concept of grafting to explain the Christian's life in Christ: "For if we be [c] grafted with him [d] to the similitude of his death, even so shal we be to the similitude of his resurrection." The editors of this edition explain the word's signification in superscript note [c]: "The Greke worde meaneth, that we growe up together with Christ, as we se mosse, yvie, mistletoe or such like growe up by a tre and are nourished with the joyse [juice] thereof." Lawrence Tomson changed the phrasing in his translation of the New Testament to make the passage's meaning more comprehensible, substituting "planted" for "ingrafted" and stressing that the relation is one of growing in likeness (similitude). "(4) For if we bee planted with him to the similitude of his death, even so shall we be to the [f] similitude of his resurrection."[52] In superscript note [4] to this edition, Tomson attempts to make the theological import of the "similitude" evident while echoing the language of the 1560 translation: "The death of sinne and the life of righteousness, or our ingrafting unto Christ, and growing up into one with him, cannot be separated by any meanes, neither in death nor in life." Fitzwilliam's concluding citation to Galatians 2:20 – "I live yet not I anymore but Christ liveth in me" – picks up on the concluding phrase of Tomson's note 4, suggesting that she may have read the note, recognized its significance, and sought to elaborate upon it. At the same time, Lady Fitzwilliam was not afraid to personalize scripture to reflect her own experience as a wife and mother. She changes the pronouns in Galatians 2:20 to reflect a communal focus: in her version, "Christ liveth" not "in me" but "in us."

"He asks counsel of others": Lady Fitzwilliam's Redaction of Rogers' *Seven Treatises* (1603)

Fitzwilliam composed her second catechism, *The First Treatise Teacheth*, which is based upon her reading of Richard Rogers' *Seven Treatises*, with the evident intent of using it within her household so that her children (and perhaps her servants) could benefit from the treatise's insights without reading the whole text. This kind of redaction may not have been uncommon within godly circles: Andrew Cambers describes how John Bruen similarly "abridged" *Seven Treatises*, "perhaps for the use of his family and godly boarders."[53] Two blank pages separate *The First Treatise Teacheth* from the first catechism; on the third page are three quotations headed, "Certaine Speaches in M R booke to be deeply weighed." This is the only attribution that Fitzwilliam provides.

> Untill we knowe that we are
> the Lords tis in vaine to
> goe about a godly life.
>
> No one man's state by nature
> ~~seing they~~ better then ano
> ther seing they be all sub
> ject to god's wrath
>
> He that knoweth not his mi
> sery cannot but goe on in
> depe securitie

Rogers was a respected Puritan minister in Wetherfield, Essex; his *Seven Treatises* was recognized as a thoroughgoing compendium of Calvinist theology, but Rogers' carefully drawn theological distinctions are contained within nearly 700 pages of expatiating prose.[54] He begins the first chapter of the First Treatise by addressing "who be the true children of God?" and continues in the second treatise to discuss "what the life of the true beleever is and the conversation of such as have assured hope of salvation." Only in Treatises 4 and 5 does Rogers undertake to offer his readers advice on "the daily practise of the Christian life"; he discusses, for example, "Satan's hindering the continuance of Faith" and emphasizes that "the Lord will deliver them (and that of very favour) out of many troubles."[55] It was also quite expensive. Ian Green remarks that if one were to look for a typical reader of Rogers' *Seven Treatises* and similar Calvinist devotional works, "it would be someone with an unusual degree of time and motivation as well as a fairly deep pocket."[56]

What godly readers needed, then, was an abbreviated account of *Seven Treatises*, one that respected its theological sophistication but repackaged its insights into a more accessible format like the catechism. At least two Protestant ministers recognized this need: the evangelically minded minister Thomas Cooper published *The Christian's Daily Sacrifice* in 1608; the title page advertises it as a prose summary "expressing the scope of the *Seven Treatises* of Master Rogers." Stephen Egerton published *The Practice of Christianitie*, a catechism based upon Rogers' *Seven Treatises* in 1618.[57] Egerton was a minister at St. Ann Blackfriars and he dedicated the work to his congregation. William Gouge, Egerton's successor at Blackfriars, wrote a preface to the reader of the 1623 edition in which he praises Egerton's work for those readers "who either cannot find leisure enough to read or afford money enough to buy the forenamed large volume." Gouge urges that *The Practice*, unlike *The Seven Treatises*, could be read by a beginning reader, since to help "the weaker sort, he hath also an Epitome of his Epitome by noting the summe of every answer in the margin." Gouge also insists that Egerton's redaction has lost nothing of the original in its substance: "Though the letter and words in this epitome be more than seven times fewer than in that volume, yet not a dram of the substance is lost."[58] Published by Thomas Man (and in its third edition in 1623), Egerton's *Practice* aimed at a moderately literate rather than a deeply informed reader, minimizing the theological analysis that made Rogers' work valuable to more religiously advanced readers. For example, where Rogers spends four pages explaining how God provides men and women with knowledge of their assurance of salvation, Egerton says simply that God does so "by giving to them, first, a clear sight, and lively feeling of their own heavie estate; and secondly, of their redemption and deliverance out of the same."[59]

In his address "To the Christian Reader," Egerton explains that he first wrote this catechism for his own private use and for manuscript circulation among his friends; it was only because it proved so popular that he determined to publish it. D. F. McKenzie suggests that many seventeenth-century authors decided to print their works for similar reasons, remarking that "such explanations, or excuses, abound."[60] Egerton writes,

> Understand, Christian reader, that having read over (some fourteen years ago) Master Rogers Seven Treatises of the Practice of Christianity, I made this abridgement of them which thou now seest, for the use of my self and some private friends, not having any the least cogitation of permitting it to come into print. But finding of late that I could not call in the copies I had given and lent abroad; and fearing lest some (which is a common practice in these days) might have thrust it forth, with wrong to me and to the author I gave way (not without much conflict and doubting to the publishing thereof).[61]

Like her ministerial counterpart, Fitzwilliam recognized the need for a catechetical version of Rogers' treatise. That she determined to compose one herself testifies to her intellectual confidence and her authorial competence – skills that, I argue, she gained from domestic catechesis.

Fitzwilliam deliberately shapes her catechetical redaction of Rogers' text so that it reflects her interests as a devout mother and noblewoman. She skips, for example, one of Rogers' longer digressions bewailing those benighted human beings who remain unmindful of their own sinfulness – a specifically ministerial concern. She also downplays the strident anti-Catholicism that characterizes both Rogers' and Egerton's texts. Rogers admits in his preface that he wrote *Seven Treatises* as an alternative to

Catholic devotionals such as Robert Parsons's popular *Christian Exercises*, which have "only a pretended shew of godlinessse," offering "poyson in a golden cup." Throughout his text, he laments the error of Catholics who think that "it is more easy to believe as we ought than live as we should," preferring "good deeds before faith." He excoriates Catholic authors for making "the world believe that the Popish religion is the only religion ... when yet the Anti-Christ is their captaine, and head."[62] Egerton displays a similar anti-Catholicism; one of the first questions in his catechism asks, "How are the Papists deceived?"[63] By contrast, Fitzwilliam includes no anti-Catholic remarks; she instead expends her rhetorical energy in providing a sophisticated distillation of Calvinist theology. Fitzwilliam's catechism reflects differences between print and manuscript publication: unlike her male counterparts, Fitzwilliam does not need to define her religion polemically and can assume that her domestic audience shares her Calvinist religious beliefs.

Throughout her redaction, Fitzwilliam consistently condenses Rogers' prose while maintaining the complexity of his theological analysis. We can see this most clearly by comparing the first sentence of Fitzwilliam's text with its corresponding sentence in Rogers' treatise:

ROGERS: First, to shew how a man may attaine to this, to know that he is the childe of God, and how God worketh it by his spirit in the hearts of those which are his.[64]

FITZWILLIAM: How God works in a man to make him his child. And how he brings him to know that he is soe.

Fitzwilliam cuts the metadiscursive phrases, "may attaine to this, to know that he is" while reworking Rogers' infinitive "to shew" to emphasize God's direct authority over man's salvation. In Fitzwilliam's revision, men do not "attaine" but rather "God works in a man." In her second independent clause, Fitzwilliam appropriates Rogers' pithy phrasing on the preceding page, where he states his purpose as "First, to shew who are true beleevers, and the children of God, and how men are brought unto this estate, and thereby may knowe that they are so."[65] She thus offers an understanding of the Calvinist doctrine of individual assurance that is both stylistically taut and theologically precise.

As she begins her catechism, Fitzwilliam displays a similar sense of authorial control, consistently condensing Rogers' analysis and supplementing his scriptural references. Because she chooses not to include Rogers' extensive discussion of unrepentant sinners, Fitzwilliam must conflate three pages of Rogers' text in order to keep the logic of his analysis intact. She accomplishes this by beginning with a general question:

> Q. How must this knowledge worke.
> 1.A. When he doeth wisely apply to himself particularly thinges spoken in generall. By the law he is brought to see himself a greevous sinner and by the threateninges ^of the law^ to be under the curse and in danger of condemnation for hereuppon his hart is affected and troubled greatly. And he cannot rest in deluding conceipts.

In the left margin, Fitzwilliam inserts references to pages 9, 10, and 12 (although she never identifies *Seven Treatises* as her source text, listing only the page numbers). This generality of references masks her omission of material on page 11 that details the problems posed by men and women who have no real interest in religion (again, a specifically ministerial concern) at the same time that it accurately reflects the way in which Fitzwilliam's answer conflates ideas and even phrases from the neighboring pages. So, for example, her insertion of the phrase "of the law" represents her reworking of Rogers' remarks on page 10 where he comments upon the "denouncing the threats of the law." Similarly, her phrase "hereuppon his hart is affected and troubled greatly" adapts Rogers' point on page 12 that "they were pricked in their harts for their sinnes." Her concluding characterization of the sinner who can no longer rest in "deluding conceipts" – that is, conceptions or thoughts – precisely condenses Rogers' extended analysis on pages 9, 10, and 12.

When she adapts Rogers' extended discussion of conscience, Fitzwilliam begins with a general question: "Q. What els doeth his knowledge worke." This question is not found in Rogers; it is used by Fitzwilliam to lead the catechumen to the next step. Where Rogers discusses this topic for three pages, Fitzwilliam's answer is characteristically concise:

> A. He falls to consulting what to doe in extremitie, as in Luke 15.17 and 16.13. And if he be not able to counsell himself, he askes counsell of others as Acts 2.37.

These scriptural citations reveal Fitzwilliam's thoroughgoing knowledge of scripture. Rogers alludes to the parable of the prodigal son as an example of a person consulting within himself, placing the scriptural reference, Luke 15:17, to the story in the right margin. Fitzwilliam adds this as well as an additional scriptural reference to Luke 16.13. This is the source for Rogers' narration of the parable of the unjust steward that follows in his analysis but for which he provides no scriptural reference. Fitzwilliam's scriptural references thus amplify Rogers' points concerning the importance of "considering and deliberating within oneself which is best to do" while maintaining the brevity of her catechetical method.

Fitzwilliam next provides a reference to Acts 2:37, in which the crowd asks advice from the apostles: "When they heard it, they were pricked in their hearts and said unto Peter and the other apostles, 'men and brethren, what shall we doe?'" Rogers addresses this example briefly: "And S. Luke in the Acts commends the fruite of that doctrine so highly, even that they were pricked in their harts for their sinnes, without which they had neither repented nor obtained pardon of their sinnes." Later, Rogers omits the scriptural reference but writes, "Yet the Lord guides them to ask counsell of others, as the aforementioned example in the Acts and the woman of Samaria doth teach."[66] By combining the scattered references in Rogers' text with her presentation of his discussion of the importance of moral deliberation and by summarizing the passage from Acts, Fitzwilliam condenses Rogers' analysis in a characteristically precise and concise manner. Significantly, she departs from Rogers by equating asking others for advice with debating within oneself thus emphasizing the importance of community in moral analysis. This accords with her practice in *Can It Be Otherwise*, where, as we have seen, she alters the pronouns to emphasize inclusivity in the scriptural passages she quotes. It is tempting to see such changes as reflecting her status as a mother and mistress of a large estate; for Fitzwilliam, religious questions would almost always have been addressed in consultation with others, either through domestic catechesis or within a community of like-minded gentlewomen. Throughout her catechism, Fitzwilliam reworks Rogers' prose, condenses his analysis, and provides concise scriptural support for his narrative examples. In Fitzwilliam's capable authorial hands, Rogers' compendious treatise becomes an accessible yet rigorous account of the Calvinist doctrine of assurance.

A Tender Mother

We have seen that Lady Fitzwilliam tailored her catechisms to reflect her family's Calvinist religious beliefs and that she shaped them to reflect the intellectual abilities of her audience. In her third catechism, *A Larger Unfolding*, she makes what I believe to be an original contribution to the extensive Calvinist literature on affliction. The first line reads: "A Larger unfolding of the matters before sett downe touching Afflictions pag 35.36.37." The phrase, "A Larger unfolding" refers to the amplifying of material in her first catechism, specifically its pages 35,

36, and 37. This inclusion of page numbers referring the reader back to the first catechism demonstrates her intention of making her manuscript function as a cohesive whole; at the same time it confirms her intention that this text function not as a private meditation but as one for other readers. It also implies an order of composition: the cross references indicate that she composed this third catechism after the first. We can thus infer with reasonable certainty that the materials as they appear in FH 246 reflect their order of composition, not a subsequent authorial arrangement. This is in keeping with FH 246's status as a household devotional.

But why did Lady Fitzwilliam choose to add this material to her first catechism? She may have done so in response to physical suffering and childbirth, since the catechism follows three prayers for women "in travail." We know that she bore at least five children, three of them born between 1608 and 1614, likely years for the manuscript's composition. But a concern with affliction – the physical and psychological problems that affect the godly – is generally characteristic of late sixteenth- and early seventeenth-century Calvinist writing. Between 1580 and 1635, several works were published which address this subject at length – these include Jean Taffin's *Of the Markes of The Children of God* (translated by Anne Prowse and published in 1590), Ezekiel Culverwell's *A Treatise of Faith* (1623), and John Ball's *A Treatise of Faith* (1631).[67] Fitzwilliam's third catechism addresses many of the same topics that these works do, although she does not employ the same order or language.

A Larger Unfoulding elaborates two metaphors that occur frequently in the literature of affliction, but it does so in a way that indicates Lady Fitzwilliam's personal concerns. The idea of God as a physician occurs in this literature as a means of explaining why God allows the godly to experience affliction; like a physician, the reasoning goes, God gives strong medicine to improve our spiritual health. Although the metaphor has patristic origins, it was employed frequently by Calvinist writers. Culverwell provides a typical seventeenth-century interpretation in *A Treatise of Faith*: God is a superior physician, he writes, who "knoweth all circumstances ... and so dispenseth this spiritual Physicke as he seeth most fit for the good of the patient and quality of the disease."[68] Ball similarly describes God as a superior "spirituall physician of our souls" who, when he dispenses afflictions, so "exactly" knows "our temper and disease" that he doth "accurately mingle the maligne and poisonfull ingredients in our Physicke with correctors and allayes" so "that the confection shall be good and altogether shall and must worke for the best."[69] The French theologian Jean Taffin glosses the metaphor succinctly: "What bee these afflictions, but medicines of our soules?"[70] Fitzwilliam applies the metaphor similarly:

> Q: What other thing must we think of to alay the bitternes of afflictions.
> A: Thinke thus, I doe putt my bodie into the physitions hands because I know that he hath skill not onely to know my disease and the danger of it but also what is good for me better then myself and I beleve him to be so faithfull and honest that he will seeke to doe me good with his best skill, but hurt he will doe me none wittingly. Why then should I be loath to permitt my selfe to God's handling and disposing seing he is most wise to know what the estate of my soule requireth and he knoweth what is best for me, what would doe me most good and how best to cure my diseases and to prevent that which would be hurtfull unto me.

Fitzwilliam sharpens her analogy through parallelism. Just as a skilled doctor will cause a patient pain to effectuate a cure, so an omniscient and omnipotent God will send sufferings to the godly. But Fitzwilliam is not fully satisfied with this answer. Recognizing that abstract knowledge of divine benevolence differs from personal and faithful acceptance of tribulation, she returns to this question later in the catechism, asking: "Q. How cann we *trust* assuredly for this" (emphasis my own). Her initial answer draws upon scripture as the revealed will of God: "A. Upon the warrant of his holy word, wherein he hath promised so much to all his faithfull ones. Looke in the Scriptures. Psalm 72 and 20, 13. psalm 27 and 30." But the questioner remains unsatisfied. She raises another objection, one which may reflect personal (or at least familial) experience with physical suffering:

> Q. Yet we see some have such obstinate diseases as will never be cured, as the gout, the stone etc.
> A. Yet see the goodnes of god, he tempers his bitter potions of afflictions with manie sweet blessings, as wealth, daintie food, soft beds, lovinge frends such as can minister comfort and such like. 2. He gives some ease betweene fitts and sometymes freedome from such fitts a good while together.

God may not cure all of our afflictions, explains Fitzwilliam, but he allays our suffering with "lovinge frends" and bodily luxuries. This answer bolsters Fitzwilliam's conception of God as a caring physician who wants only to cure his patients and so attempts to alleviate suffering when he can. But it is also personally revealing: by detailing such creature comforts, Fitzwilliam reflects her life as a wealthy seventeenth-century gentlewoman and her appreciation of the satisfactions that such wealth can provide.[71]

The other image that occurs frequently in this literature of affliction is that of God as a parent who treats his children severely to make them better. This understanding of God also has patristic origins, but like the image of God as a physician it was revived by sixteenth-century Protestant theologians. In this metaphor, afflictions are a form of punishment – or more mildly, correction. John Ball describes God as "a tender Father, and fellow-feeling elder brother, who best knoweth, and can measure out exactly what is meeteth."[72] Ezekiel Culverwell develops the same idea more extensively: unlike earthly parents who correct their children "after their owne pleasure," "God our heavenly Father, in great wisdome considereth, with what correction, and when to chastise his, so as may bee most for their profit; yea the best profit, to repair his Image of holiness in them, which is a chief end and use of all afflictions, as we shall hereafter see."[73] Jean Taffin also develops this metaphor at length:

> It is well knowne that fathers and mothers take no pleasure to afflict their children and to make them weepe. And although they have power to beate them, to appoynt them their diet and to put them abroad, either to school or to serve some other, yet when they doo this... it is for the benefite of the children, whose duetie also it is to well like of it and to render unto them willing obedience... What injury doo we to this onlie true father that we, being afflicted by his hand, after what manner soever, doo not sanctifie his name, conforming our selves to his will, thinking and confessing that all proceedeth from his goodnes and love, to his glorie and our benefite and salvation?[74]

Like Taffin, Fitzwilliam argues that God is a good parent who punishes human beings only because he loves them, a conclusion that she characteristically supports with a scriptural reference "Whom the Lord loveth, he chasteneth" (Hebrews 12:6). But Fitzwilliam's use of catechetical method allows her to personalize her analysis, so that her next question addresses her reader's (or auditor's) potential objection: "Q: Call ye that love, to scourge and vex and put to much smart and misery." In her answer, Fitzwilliam compares God to "tender mothers" who punish their children out of love:

> A. To scourge and afflict is not to love, but it may be out of love, as when tender mothers see their children given to some of ill tricks as lying or sullenness they take the rod in handes to whipp them. who will say this is done of hatred, and not rather of love and care of their good? If parents then chastice their children of love, why should we doubt, but when God chasticeth his, it is out of pure love, and good will, because he desyreth and is carefull of their good and salvation, and would not have them perishe with the worlde.

Although other writers describe God as a mother, Fitzwilliam's particular metaphor arguably reflects her own experience as the loving, disciplining mother of five children. Taffin, by contrast, compares God to a nursing mother who puts wormwood on her breast to wean her children.[75] Culverwell likens divine compassion to generalized maternal love: "even as the bowels of a tender hearted mother are mooved within her, when she seethe her childe in any peril; so is the Lord troubled to see his children in any extremity."[76] Fitzwilliam, for her part, specifies particular childish faults – "lying" and "sullenness." As in her references to "gout" and "stones" as potentially incurable diseases, the specificity of the vocabulary suggests a source in her lived experience. What we find, then, in Fitzwilliam's third catechism, is evidence of a personal engagement with Calvinist theology, drawing upon her experience as a mother and mistress of a large estate to make the theology both relevant and comprehensible.

Conclusion

Through catechizing her children, Fitzwilliam gained an appreciation of catechetical method, developed her sense of audience, and acquired experience in explaining the relation between scriptural text and doctrinal principle. From Rogers' compendious treatise, she created a focused and concise catechism, one which reflected her own concerns as wife and mother. This suggests that the importance accorded to mothers as domestic religious instructors made their role a culturally sanctioned source of female intellectual activity – and textual production – in early modern England.

Fitzwilliam's catechisms also suggest an alternative relation between ministerial and domestic authority in early modern England. As we have seen, when Protestant ministers urged fathers and mothers to catechize their children at home, they did so out of the belief that if Protestantism was to take lasting hold in England, the common people needed to be educated in the fundamentals of their faith. Because they could not personally undertake a wide-scale educational program, they urged it upon fathers and mothers, with the result that religious instruction was no longer the exclusive preserve of an educated clergy. Like the godly minister Stephen Egerton, Fitzwilliam composed a catechetical redaction of Rogers' *Seven Treatises*. The most important difference between the two redactions is the mode of circulation: Egerton's manuscript was published in print and went into at least three editions in five years.

Fitzwilliam composed her catechism in manuscript for use in the home and went without scholarly notice for four centuries.

Notes

1. Kate Narveson discusses FH 246 in *Bible Readers and Lay Writers in Early Modern England* (Aldershot: Ashgate Press, 2012), 139. She comments, "Taken as a whole, the volume suggests that the range and focus of the topics that concerned this woman embraced practical religion, whether devotional exercises, household instruction, or sermon-going. Her particular concerns with child-bearing and the instruction of children exist alongside a concern for doctrinal understanding more generally and she took careful notes on treatises that explain the central experiences of the faithful."
2. We know the birth dates of three of Fitzwilliam's children: Winifred (1608) Anna (1610) and John (1614) from *Familysearch.org*. The birth dates of her other children, William and Katherine, are unknown.
3. Much of the preceding biographical information is derived from Mary Finch, *Five Northamptonshire Families* (Winchester: Wykeham Press, 1966), 100–32. Mildred Cooke was the granddaughter of the older William Fitzwilliam through his daughter Ann, wife of Anthony Cooke of Gidea Hall, Essex (102). On kinship and friendship among the godly gentry, see Jacqueline Eales, *Puritans and Roundheads: The Harleys of Brampton Bryan* (Cambridge: Cambridge University Press, 1991), 8. Micheline White demonstrates the importance of regional connections among seventeenth-century Puritan gentlewomen in "Women Writers and Literary-Religious Circles in the Elizabethan West Country: Anne Dowriche, Anne Lock Prowse, Anne Lock Moyle, Elizabeth Rous and Ursula Fulford" *Modern Philology* 103.2 (2005): 187–214.
4. Ian Green, *Print and Protestantism in Early Modern England* (Oxford: Oxford University Press, 2000), 311.
5. The first catechism contains page numbers; the rest do not. I cite page numbers when quoting from the first catechism.
6. Lady Fitzwilliam did not date any of her compositions. We know that she began her household devotional sometime after she married William Fitzwilliam and moved to Milton, because her married name appears on the volume's title page. We also know that Fitzwilliam compiled her second catechism based upon her reading of Richard Rogers' *Seven Treatises* (1603), so the book must have originated sometime after that date. I assert 1603–23 as the likeliest period for the composition of the work, because Fitzwilliam's children were small then, and it is probable that she composed the manuscript for domestic religious instruction. Theoretically, composition could have occurred any time between 1603–43.
7. On the rivalry between ministerial and lay writing culture, see Narveson, *Bible Readers and Lay Writers*, 22: "Along with the concern about lay ability was an

unspoken concern about maintaining professional standards . . . How did the ministry's call for lay Bible reading cohere with their sense of exegesis as a specialized professional skill?" Green, *Print and Protestantism*, 106–7, remarks that arch-conformists and godly ministers agreed that "while everybody should study the scripture, the soundest interpreters were those with knowledge of the original languages in which the Bible was written, which in practice usually meant the best-educated ministers of the day."

8. Green, *Print and Protestantism*, 151
9. Information about these catechisms, as well as the subjects they cover, can be found in Green's invaluable "A Finding List of English Catechisms," in *The Christian's ABC: Catechisms and Catechizing in England*, Appendix 1 (Oxford: Oxford University Press, 1996), 573–751. For examples of catechisms in which the answers consist largely of scriptural citations, see Green, *The Christian's ABC*, 52, 92, 253.
10. Ian Green observes that "in Protestant England, most members of the royal family, many members of the aristocracy, and some of the gentry had a resident chaplain on hand to help lead the household devotions and offer guidance on private prayer." "Varieties of Domestic Devotion in Protestantism," in *Private and Domestic Devotion in Early Modern Britain*, ed. Jessica Martin and Alec Ryrie (Aldershot: Ashgate, 2012), 10–31, 15. See also J.T. Cliffe, *The Puritan Gentry* (London: Routledge, 1984), 24–42.
11. Robert Abbot, *Milk for Babes*, in *Catechisms for Mothers, Schoolmistresses, and Children*, ed. Paula McQuade (Aldershot: Ashgate, 2008), Sig. aa1r–aa2v.
12. Green, "Varieties," 23.
13. Susan Felch, "Halff a Scripture Woman": Heteroglossia and Female Authorial Agency in Prayers by Lady Elizabeth Tyrwhit, Anne Lock, and Anne Wheathill," in *English Women, Religion, and Textual Production, 1500–1635*, ed. Micheline White (Aldershot: Ashgate, 2012), 147–66, 157.
14. For example, Fitzwilliam's catechism is remarkable in the attention it pays to the duties appropriate to a person's station in life. The Puritan minister Samuel Hieron also addresses duties and similarly supports each answer with a scriptural quotation in *The Doctrine of the Beginning of Christ* (London, 1620). But each author phrases the questions and answers differently. For example, Hieron asks: "Q. What is the rich man's duty? A. To honour God with his riches Proverbs 3.9" (Sig. C6r). Fitzwilliam addresses a similar question in *Can It Be Otherwise*, but she gives a more complex and religiously advanced answer supported by a different scriptural quotation: "Q. Thus much for dutie or respect of sex and age. What duties for such as be in prosperitie? A. To use our prosperitie and lawful liberties so as we neither be puffed up therewith nor joy therein of which evil Job cleared himself Chapter 31. 25" (33).
15. Bailey Collection A.2. 125. Commonplace Book and Catechetical Instructions on Sabbath Evenings, Chetham's Library, Manchester, UK.
16. Dorothy Burch, *A Catechisme of the Severall Heads of the Christian Religion*, in *Catechisms for Mothers, Schoolmistresses, and Children*, ed. Paula McQuade (Aldershot: Ashgate, 2008), Sig. A3v.

17. On Grace Mildmay's writings, see Green, "Varieties of Domestic Devotion," 18; Narveson, *Bible Readers and Lay Writers*, 153 and Retha Warnicke, "Lady Mildmay's Journal: A Study in Autobiography," *Sixteenth Century Journal* 20 (1989): 55–68.
18. Unlike his father, William Fitzwilliam spent most of his life at Milton; although he became Baron Fitzwilliam in 1620, he held no public office and did not associate with court circles. Under his tenure as head of household, the Fitzwilliam family plunged deeply into debt in large part due to the loss of revenue from court-appointed offices. Finch, *Five Northhamptonshire Families*, 129–34.
19. Andrew Cambers identifies tables of contents, along with indexes and title pages, as features borrowed from printed books that "were designed to steer readers" through texts. "Reading, the Godly, and Self-Writing, circa 1580–1720," *Journal of British Studies* 46 (2007): 796–825, 810.
20. Narveson, *Bible Readers and Lay Writers*, 151–76.
21. Cambers has convincingly argued that in early modern England, "the primary venue for shared reading was in the family." "Reading, The Godly, and Self-Writing," 819; see also Cambers and Michelle Wolfe, "Reading, Family Religion, and Evangelical Identity," *The Historical Journal* 47 (2004): 875–96.
22. George Webber, "A Short Exercise," in *A Garden of Spiritual Flowers* (London, 1687), 74.
23. Bailey Collection A.2. 125, Commonplace Book and Catechetical Instructions on Sabbath Evenings; Bailey Collection A.2.126, Commonplace Book; Scriptural Questions.
24. Narveson, *Bible Readers and Lay Writers*, 69–70.
25. Quoted in Cliffe, *The Puritan Gentry*, 27.
26. Samuel Clark, *The Lives of Sundry Eminent Persons in This Later Age* (London, 1683), 203.
27. Clark, *The Lives*, 154.
28. Femke Molekamp, *Women and the Bible in Early Modern England* (Oxford: Oxford University Press, 2013), 56.
29. Arnold Hunt, *The Art of Hearing: English Preachers and Their Audiences, 1590–1640* (Cambridge: Cambridge University Press, 2010), 98.
30. Hunt, *The Art of Hearing*, 63.
31. Hunt discusses Ignatius Jurdain as an example of "the mental dexterity that resulted from the constant practice of note-taking and repetition." "For an experienced hearer such as Jurdain, it was a relatively simple matter to pick out a few valuable points from an otherwise indifferent sermon, store them in a mental filing system (or physically, in a commonplace book) under an appropriate subject heading, and retrieve them later in order to apply them in a new context." Hunt concludes, "At this level of attainment, sermon repetition was anything but a passive exercise." *The Art of Hearing*, 102.
32. Lady Fitzwilliam's inspiration for this spatial representation may be the diagram, "Howe to Take Profite in Reading of the Holy Scriptures" which, as Molekamp remarks in *Women and the Bible*, "appeared in most editions of

the Geneva Bible" (25). Protestant divines also included similar diagrams in their published treatises. See, for example, the diagram, "The Resolution of the Creede" included in the prefatory material to William Perkins' *An Exposition of the Symbole* (London, 1595).

33. Green, *The Christian's ABC*, 5.
34. Mrs. J.C., *The Mother's Catechism*, in *Catechisms for Mothers, Schoolmistresses, and Children*, ed. Paula McQuade (Aldershot: Ashgate, 2008), 18.
35. Fitzwilliam, *Can It Be Otherwise*, 12.
36. John Ball, *A Short Treatise Contayning All the Principall Grounds of the Christian Religion* (London, 1617), Sig. A5r. Writing over a century later, Isaac Watts makes the same point: "Let there be one or more well chosen texts of scripture added to support almost every answer and to prove the several parts of it. This will show the child that we own the scripture or Word of God to be the Divine and Supreme Rule of our belief and practice." *A Discourse on the Way of Instruction by Catechisms* (London, 1786), 56.
37. The exchange provides a type of "intertextual pleasure" that Lisa Gordis, drawing upon Roland Barthes, compares to "the children's game of topping hands." *Opening Scripture: Bible Reading and Interpretive Authority in Puritan New England* (Chicago: University of Chicago Press, 2003), 108.
38. Fitzwilliam, *Can It Be Otherwise*, 43.
39. Robert Cawdry, "To the Godly Reader," *A Short and Fruitfull Treatise of the Profit and Necessitie of Catechising* (London, 1604), Early English Books Online (1599:12), Sig. A7v–A7r.
40. "To Our Beloved in the Lord," in *The Geneva Bible: A Facsimile of the 1560 Edition* (Peabody, MA: Hendrickson Publishing, 2007). Watts echoes this belief in 1786: "Scripture was written for men rather than children, since it abounds in metaphorical expressions and Eastern idioms of speech." *A Discourse*, 42.
41. Josias Nichols, *An Order of Houshold Instruction* (London, 1596), Sig. D1v.
42. Nichols, *An Order of Houshold Instruction*, Sig. D1r.
43. John Fiske, *The Watering of an Olive Plant in Christ's Garden* (Cambridge, Massachusetts Bay Colony, 1657), 16.
44. Fiske, *The Watering*, 20.
45. Fiske, *The Watering*, 4. On Sarah Symmes Fiske, see Paula McQuade, "Household Religious Instruction in Seventeenth-Century England and America: The Case of Sarah Symmes Fiske's *A Confession of Faith* (Composed 1672)," *ANQ* 24 (2011): 108–17.
46. Fitzwilliam, *Can It Be Otherwise*, 11.
47. Janel Mueller defines scripturalism as "a writer's molding of his thought and language after a recognizable mode or model from the Old or New Testament." *The Native Tongue and the Word* (Chicago: University of Chicago Press, 1984), 245.
48. Fitzwilliam, *Can It Be Otherwise*, 5.
49. Gordis, *Opening Scripture*, 108.
50. Fitzwilliam, *Can It Be Otherwise*, 18.

51. Fitzwilliam, *Can It Be Otherwise*, 17. Ephesians 3:17: "That Christ may dwell in your hearts by faith." Galatians 2:20: "I am crucified with Christ, but I live, yet not I any more, but Christ liveth in me; and in that I now live in the flesh, I live by the faith in the Sonne of God, who hath loved me, and given himselfe for me."
52. We can compare this translation of Romans 6:5 with that provided in the Authorized Bible (1611): "For if we have been planted together in the likenesse of his death: wee shalbe also in the likenesse of his resurrection." *The Holy Bible, 1611 edition, King James Version* (Peabody, MA: Hendrickson Publishers, 2010).
53. Cambers, "Reading," 813.
54. Green remarks that "six editions in twenty eight years" renders Rogers' *Seven Treatises* a "steady seller" rather than a "runaway best seller," *Print and Protestantism*, 316, 318.
55. Richard Rogers, *Seven Treatises* (London, 1603), 1, 72, 422, 535.
56. Green, *Print and Protestantism*, 318.
57. Thomas Cooper, *The Christian's Daily Sacrifice* (London, 1608); Stephen Egerton, *The Practice of Christianitie* (London, 1618), Early English Books Online (1609:13). All subsequent references to this text will be to this edition unless otherwise noted.
58. William Gouge, "To the Christian Reader," in *The Practice of Christianitie* (London, 1623), Sig. A6v–A6r.
59. Egerton, *The Practice*, 10.
60. D. K. McKenzie, "Speech, Manuscript, Print," in *Making Meaning: Printers of the Mind and Other Essays*, ed. Peter D. MacDonald and Michael F. Suarez, S.J. (Amherst: University of Massachusetts Press, 2003), 249.
61. Egerton, *The Practice*, Sig. A4r.
62. Rogers, *Seven Treatises*, Sig. B1r, B2v, B1r, B1v.
63. Egerton, *The Practice*, 8.
64. Rogers, *Seven Treatises*, 2.
65. Rogers, *Seven Treatises*, 1.
66. Rogers, *Seven Treatises*, 11–12, 14.
67. Jean Taffin, *Of the Markes of the Children of God, and of Their Comforts in Affliction* (1590), in *The Collected Works of Anne Vaughn Lock*, trans. Anne Prowse, ed. Susan M. Felch (Tempe, AZ: Renaissance English Text Society, 1999), 74–190; Ezekiel Culverwell, *A Treatise of Faith* (London, 1623); John Ball, *A Treatise of Faith* (London, 1637).
68. Culverwell, *A Treatise of Faith*, 389.
69. Ball, *A Treatise of Faith*, 324.
70. Taffin, *Of the Markes*, 147.
71. Finch remarks upon the "impression of luxury" conveyed by a 1618 inventory of the personal estate of Katherine Fitzwilliam's father-in-law, Sir William Fitzwilliam IV: "an unduly large proportion of his wealth was in the form of unrenumerative effects, such as rich furnishings and plate." *Five Northhamptonshire Families*, 129.

72. Ball, *A Treatise of Faith*, 323.
73. Culverwell, *A Treatise of Faith*, 390–1.
74. Taffin, *Of the Markes*, 151–2.
75. Taffin, *Of the Markes*, 148–9.
76. Culverwell, *A Treatise of Faith*, 405.

PART II

Female Witness and Inter-Confessional Dialogue

Part II highlights the writings of two Protestant conformist women who drew upon their experience with maternal catechesis to engage sympathetically with Catholic devotional writings. Katherine Thomas, studied in Chapter 3, based upon her reading of a Catholic devotional work, composed a catechism that imaginatively underscores the importance of women as resurrection witnesses and gospel teachers. Because she represents this catechism as an extension of the historical catechism she designed for her children, Thomas creatively connects her experience as a maternal catechist with her interest in women's role as teachers of religious truth. In Chapter 4, we turn our attention to another late-seventeenth-century woman, Barbara Slingsby Talbot, who redacted her late father's Catholic devotional book in 1686/7, seeking to engage in the ongoing public debate concerning the status of English Catholics. Long devalued as a "personal catechism" and "transcription," her manuscript in actuality constitutes a vibrant contribution by a woman to the late seventeenth-century debate concerning the toleration of English Catholics.

CHAPTER 3

"At Magdalin's House"
Maternal Catechesis and Female Witness in the Manuscript Miscellany of Katherine Thomas (b. 1637)

> Her of your name, whose fair inheritance
> Bethina was, and jointure Magdalo
> An active faith so highly did advance
> That she once knew, more than the Church did know,
> The Resurrection.
> John Donne, "To Mrs. Magdalen Herbert: Of Saint Mary Magdalen"[1]

Introduction

Little in the extant biographical information about Katherine Thomas would suggest that she would compose an original catechism that daringly revises male-dominated Christian ecclesiology. A member of the country gentry who lived in Michaelchurch Escley, a village in Herefordshire near the Welsh border, Thomas married Edmund Thomas, a local gentleman farmer; they had five children, three of whom died young. Edmund died intestate when Katherine was thirty-three; she wrangled control of the estate and managed it with considerable success for at least twenty-five years while raising her two surviving children, Humphrey (1665/6–1732) and Anne (b. 1667).[2] Were it not for the survival of her manuscript miscellany, Katherine Thomas would be yet another statistic: a wealthy country gentlewoman who experienced a slightly higher than average rate of child mortality and who died in her late fifties after an extended widowhood.

But her manuscript miscellany affords a different picture. Compiled over a thirty-year period, it reveals that Thomas spent her days practicing a schedule of daily devotional reading, educating her children, visiting with friends and family, and superintending the operation of a large working estate. It resembles other seventeenth-century manuscript miscellanies composed by women both in the kinds of text it includes (prayers, sermons, elegies, passages from popular devotional works) and in its juxtaposition of original and transcribed texts. Although she lacked a formal education and was geographically isolated, Thomas was well read; her manuscript miscellany contains excerpts from the best-known seventeenth-century Protestant conformist theologians.[3] Its generic and topical diversity confirms recent work suggesting that rural Englishwomen had access to an extraordinary range of printed materials. Like other seventeenth-century gentlewomen, Thomas composed her manuscript miscellany to showcase her taste and wide-ranging devotional reading.[4]

Because Thomas' manuscript miscellany is largely conventional, it is easy to overlook its inclusion of a catechism that explores women's ability to teach within the church. We have seen in Chapter 1 that Thomas includes a historical catechism, *Places of Scripture*, in her manuscript miscellany. Thomas' second catechism, which I call *An Old Book*, is different: like Fitzwilliam's *The First Treatise*, it redacts a devotional treatise into catechetical form as it narrates the order of Christ's post-resurrection appearances. As we will see, the gospels contain two different accounts of Christ's Easter appearances: Luke describes how Christ first appeared to Peter, but John declares that Mary Magdalene was the first person to encounter the risen Jesus, leading some subsequent theologians to designate her as *Apostolorum Apostola*, or Apostle to the Apostles.[5] Feminist critics recognize that these differing accounts have important implications. "Since the resurrection appearances are taken 'to establish the structure of community leadership,'" writes Elaine Pagels, "Luke's theory necessarily restricts the circle of apostles – and hence, of authoritative leaders – to that small, specifically named group." Patristic theologians invoked the Lucan narrative to exclude women from positions of authority within the church, as Elizabeth Schussler-Fiorenza explains, "Patristic Christianity ... attempted to play down the significance of women disciples and their leader Mary Magdalene and concentrate on apostolic figures like Peter and Paul and the twelve."[6] In *An Old Book*, Thomas challenges this patristic slant: she insists that Christ appears first to his female disciples and that he eats a final meal "at Magdalin's house." Because Christ's Easter appearances were traditionally linked with witnessing the truth of Christ's resurrection and because Christ's resurrection meals were interpreted as Eucharistic symbols, Thomas' catechism offers an alternative history of women's participation in the church, one that combines her reading and her scriptural knowledge to affirm women's ability to teach others the "good news" of Christ's resurrection. I argue that Thomas creates this representation because of her experience as a domestic catechist, and

I make the larger claim that women's catechetical experience emboldened them to produce texts that emulated ministerial practices.

Because Thomas' catechism insists upon the centrality of women to the educational mission and sacramental practices of Christianity, it can benefit from being read alongside Amelia Lanyer's *Salve Deus Rex Judaeorum*, a verse account of Christ's passion that similarly seeks to "reimagine women's relationship to the sacred in provocative ways."[7] In the past three decades, feminist theologians have recovered a history of women's rejection of male-dominated ecclesiology, demonstrating how some women enacted alternative visions of Christian community in which women played a central role.[8] As a catechism, *An Old Book* offers a generically distinct representation of women's role within the church. Thomas bases her text on the Catholic publisher John Heigham's *The Life of Our Lord and Savior Jesus Christ, Gathered Out of the Famous Doctor Bonaventure* (hereafter, *Life of Christ*) which is, in turn, his translation and adaptation of St. Bonaventure's classic devotional *Vita Christi*. Working at the behest of the Poor Clares at Gravelines and reflecting the values of this female Catholic community, Heigham's *Life of Christ* portrays women as the primary resurrection witnesses and depicts Christ as surrounded by a nurturing female community during his time on earth. Thomas appropriates and extends Heigham's women-centered depiction. Her catechism records the importance of women, especially wealthy widows like herself, to the establishment and continuation of Christian community.

What is more, Thomas' catechism contributes to our understanding of inter-confessional relations in early modern England. All of the other items in her devotional suggest that Thomas was a practicing member of the Church of England; she records her attendance at local services and includes passages from (mostly) Church of England loyalist devotional works. Yet Thomas bases her catechism on a Catholic devotional text that had been smuggled into England at least fifty years previously. Her possession of this work suggests that prohibited Catholic books sometimes circulated among Protestant conformist readers and that at least some of these readers read such books sympathetically.[9] As we will see, Thomas lived in an area where Catholics and Church of England loyalists lived side by side: she is likely to have had Catholic friends, neighbors, and perhaps even family members. This area of Herefordshire was also home to a Jesuit seminary at Cwm that distributed devotional manuals and catechisms among local Catholics. Such an environment could well have fostered the development of a religious eclecticism. Towards the end of her catechism, Thomas offers a remarkable model of interested but tolerant reading: one can engage with alternative ideas, she suggests, without abandoning one's own beliefs. *An Old Book* provides evidence of one late seventeenth-century Englishwoman's ability to engage substantively and affectively with alternative religious perspectives.

Thomas' Manuscript Miscellany

Katherine Thomas (née Bridges) was born in 1637, the second daughter of William Bridges, gentleman of Tibburton Hall in Bosbury, Herefordshire. She married Edmund Thomas of nearby Michaelchurch Escley sometime before 1660, probably in 1658/9. Edmund's family is listed in a visitation of 1683 as possessing a coat-of-arms, and Katherine and Edmund were large local landowners. Their manor, Michaelchurch Court, was the largest house in the community and included several working farms. Thomas was an able property manager, conscious of her duties both to her children and to the community. In a prayer which she composed for "private use" after the unexpected death of her husband, Thomas petitions, "Bless O Lord and prosper that littell substance which thou hast bestowed one me, that I may have soeficient to paye my dept's truly, relive the pore willingly, and live in my famaly chearefully." She used the legal system effectively, gaining control of the estate after her husband's death and transferring it to her son before her death to avoid estate taxes.[10]

Michaelchurch Escley is one of a small cluster of villages (including Cusop, Hay-on Wye, Craswell, and Newton) located in the southeastern corner of Herefordshire; it is likely that residents of the individual villages considered themselves to be members of a larger regional community. We know, for example, that Katherine attended services on February 26, 1671, (two days after the death of her husband) at St. Mary's Church in Cusop. She notes with approval the sermon preached on that day by Mr. Rawlings on Luke 24:38: "and Christ said unto them, why are ye trubled, and why doe thoughts arise in your hearts."

Thomas' social circle most likely conformed to the characteristic pattern in which gentry maintained connections with members of their extended family and those of like social class across a considerable area.[11] We know that Thomas deliberately kept up connections with her brother and sisters after her marriage: her manuscript miscellany contains "Heavenly Meditations on Affliction" copied from a book of her "Sister Kings." Siobhan Keenan has determined that this sister "married a Mr. Peter King" and remarks that "this suggests that they continued to socialize with each other after marriage, occasionally discussing religion and exchanging literature." "Thomas' use of her sister's book," observes Keenan, "confirms the existence of literary networks between regionally based gentlewoman."[12] Thomas' manuscript miscellany also includes an elegy written by nineteen-year-old Elizabeth Pierce of Bath sometime before her death in 1671, which was engraved upon Pierce's tombstone in 1694. It further includes two verses, "both wretten on grave stons or tombs" which Thomas notes are taken "out of the history of Saint paules Cathedrall pag.119," as well as verses "written upon a wall in St. Edmund's Church in Lumbart Streete, Londan." The book to which she refers is William Dugdale's *The History of St. Paul's Cathedral in London from Its Foundations Untill These Times* (1658), a large, expensive volume, with numerous highly detailed engravings of the interior and the exterior of the old Cathedral, as well as transcriptions of its epitaphs on funeral monuments. St. Edmund's was destroyed in the great fire of London and rebuilt by Christopher Wren.[13] That Thomas included verses from Dugdale, verses written upon the walls of an otherwise unremarkable London church, and an elegy written upon the death of a teenage girl from Bath in her manuscript miscellany suggests how the circulation of books among early modern women could counter their geographical isolation.

When Thomas composed her manuscript miscellany is uncertain. The editor of the Perdita edition suggests that Thomas compiled it during the 1690s, noting the inscription on the inside cover, "Katherine Thomas, 1691." But certain portions of Thomas' text concern events that occurred much earlier; her elegy expressing her grief over the death of her daughter, for example, is dated 1665. Rather than pinpointing a single date of compilation, I regard it instead as a record of Thomas' religious and spiritual readings over as much as three decades. As I will discuss in more detail, there is some evidence in the manuscript miscellany that Thomas revised earlier material in the context of subsequent reading.

Thomas composed her text as both a private devotional manual and an exemplification of her taste, piety, and maternal devotion. Of course, these aims are not mutually exclusive.[14] But this does mean that Thomas' manuscript miscellany differs from Lady Fitzwilliam's household devotional, designed as we have seen, primarily for the education of her children and servants. One way to register the difference is to look at the contents of the two collections: where Lady Fitzwilliam includes mostly catechisms and sermon notes, Thomas juxtaposes prose devotional treatises, prayers, elegies, catechisms, and a maternal legacy, genres popular among early modern women readers, compilers, and transcribers. This generic diversity provides some clues regarding Thomas' interests: she seems to have thought about texts in terms of genre, juxtaposing, for example, transcribed elegies with three original elegies. Thomas thereby memorializes her role as wife and mother, and participates more broadly in early modern manuscript culture.

The range of Thomas' devotional reading is suggestive. She excerpts materials from important Protestant conformist theologians of the seventeenth century: "verses out of Bishop" John Cosin's "Book," "a prayer for patience out of Doct [Simon] Patrick's book," and selections from the popular devotional manual *Crummes of Comfort*. As a Church of England loyalist, Thomas displays a developed awareness of larger Christian tradition, noting with approval when authors cite Augustine and Jerome. Much of this excerpted material is devotional in nature and reflects her practice of structuring her day around regular prayer: the manuscript miscellany includes "a Morning prayer," and "an evening prayer" as well as more general prayers "for protection" and "against sensuality," as well as numerous scriptural verses, especially from the Psalms. Polemical works are absent, as are works of formal theology.

Thomas' literary interests and religious eclecticism are remarkable in view of her lack of a formal education. While she writes a clear italic hand, her knowledge of grammar and syntax is less secure; her spelling is idiosyncratic even by early modern standards. Thomas possesses more than functional literacy, but she cannot compare with a university-educated male writer. Early modern women recognized that their lack of university education was a hindrance to certain levels of literary achievement: Lady Grace Mildmay, for example, admonished her daughter to read her 900-page manuscript "not looking for Eloquence, exact Method, or learning which could not proceed from me, who have not been raised up in universitie learning."[15] While such humility is conventional in part, it also accurately reflects the difficulties that women faced in undertaking to write original works. Thomas offers notes defining colons, semi-colons, and parentheses, as well as the proper use of commas and hyphens, on the back page of her manuscript. That Thomas was able to move from reading catechisms to writing them suggests that the role of catechetical instructor furnished some early modern women with the generic awareness necessary for original composition.

Thomas offers a dedication to her surviving children in the beginning of the manuscript miscellany. This is a highly conventional legacy: she urges her surviving children to get along with another, avoid drinking and fornication, and keep the Sabbath day holy. Andrew Cambers has demonstrated that works like Thomas' manuscript miscellany were often treasured heirlooms within godly families, with subsequent generations often signing a work as a testament to the memory of the deceased.[16] Children treasured these textual witnesses to a parent's or grandparent's spiritual growth. The Protestant emphasis upon exemplarity led subsequent generations to believe that they could benefit from the experience of their elders.[17] Thomas herself urges the importance of godly examples. But such manuscripts were also treasured because of their representations of loving motherhood – which Thomas cultivated by formatting *An Old Book* as a continuation of *Places of Scripture*, a catechism that she may have used with her children.

Whether Thomas composed her book for circulation outside of the household is unclear. It contains the type of texts typically included in manuscript miscellanies intended for circulation outside the household, but it lacks an address to extra-familial readers, a preface, additional ownership marks, or any other evidence of readership. If we had evidence of the manuscript's circulation, it would amplify Thomas' proto-feminist representation of women's ability to serve as resurrection witnesses, just as Amelia Lanyer's alternative vision of the sacred is strengthened by her multiple dedications praising female community. But without additional evidence, we can, unfortunately, note this only as a possibility.

Seventeenth-Century Catholic Lives

We know that Thomas wrote *An Old Book* sometime after transcribing *Places of Scripture*, the historical catechism I discussed in Chapter 1. Thomas' original title read: "Places of Scriptures to Ask children; and are remarkable out of the ould and new testament." She subsequently added the following: "and Som out of other Books." She proceeds to identify this other book as "an ould Book called the Life of Jesus," but as I have suggested, this is the only identification she provides. (This deviates from Thomas' practice elsewhere in her manual: she carefully notes the author of nearly all of the texts she excerpts, for example, a prayer excerpted from "Bishop Andrew's [Launcelot Andrewe's] Day Devotions," and another "out of [Edward]Kemp's book." She even identifies lay authors, including, for example, "A short prayer" composed by "E. T. my daughter.") Many such lives, modeled on medieval vitae, were published by conformist Protestant clerics between 1650 and 1680. These lives are all similarly titled (*The Life of Christ, The Life of Jesus*), and most are large, expensive books with intricate engravings.[18] Unlike catechisms, these works did not aim to teach fundamentals of the faith. Instead, they provided an account of the life, passion, death, and resurrection of Jesus. The goal was to encourage readers to meditate upon Christ's life and then model their lives accordingly.

But Thomas is not citing any of these texts – which might explain her uncharacteristic failure to indicate its authorship. *An Old Book* is based upon Thomas' reading of a text translated, augmented, and published by John Heigham in 1622 (third edition, 1634): *The Life of Our Lord and Savior Jesus Christ*.[19] Heigham was an English Catholic who went into exile first at Douai and later at St. Omer, France, where he played a central role in the publication and dissemination of English versions of the Primer and the Tridentine Mass, as well as translations of popular Catholic polemical and devotional works. Over sixty works bearing his imprint survive. As A. F. Allison observes, Heigham was "an organizer and a man of action ... an able controversialist ... widely read, dexterous in argument, forceful in expression, and tireless in defense of the Church to whose cause he devoted his life." His wife, Maria, played a central role in smuggling these books into England. The "apostate and informer" William Udall remarked "there hath not any boke of state, or ortherwyse bin brought into England or printed beyond the seas but it hath been performed by one ... Heigham or his wife."[20]

Heigham's *Life of Christ* is not a literal translation of Bonaventure's *Life of Christ*. He "augmented and enriched" his medieval model by revising its chapters and by adding a considerable amount of material. (I estimate that at least 30 percent of Heigham's text is new.) He also inserts editorializing comments at the conclusion of each chapter. Heigham does not rely exclusively upon canonical scripture to recreate his narratives but additionally draws upon extra-biblical sources. This practice reflects in part the genre's purpose: authors drew upon multiple sources so as to create the most inspiring devotional narrative. But the practice also reflects its confessional affiliation: Catholics believe that both scriptural and non-scriptural texts can be sources of religious truth. In the first 200 pages of *The Life of Christ*, Heigham includes references to such well-known sources as Anselm, Origen, Jerome, and Eusebius, as well as lesser luminaries such as Palladius, Athanasius, and Balaam, "Prophet of the Gentills."[21] He utilizes apocryphal texts such as the *Protoevangelium of St. James* (second century) to narrate the infancy and adolescence of Mary the mother of Jesus; throughout, he also ranges freely among the canonical gospels, choosing passages in Jesus' life to exemplify particular moral lessons or collating multiple accounts to craft the most compelling narrative. For example, in his presentation of Jesus' teaching at the temple while a child, Heigham draws upon Luke 2:42, but in his account of the passion, he collates accounts found in Mark 15, Luke 23–32, and John 19:33. He also utilizes cultural details found in the Hebrew Scriptures to amplify his representations of events in Christ's life, perhaps drawing upon Numbers 3:47, for example, in his depiction of Mary's presentation of Christ in the temple.[22]

Heigham designed his text to appeal specifically to women readers. We can see this from his preface: he dedicates his translation of *The Life of Christ* "to the reverend and religious Mother Clare Marianna, abbess of the English Poor Clares at Gravelines and all of her devout and religious daughters."[23] In this he self-consciously models himself upon Bonaventure, who addressed the original *Life of Christ* to a Poor Clare.[24] The Poor Clares at Gravelines were a religious community located not far from the Jesuit College at St. Omer. (Gravelines is midway between St. Omer and Calais, so Heigham would have had multiple occasions to visit the convent as he oversaw the shipping of his books at Calais.) Founded by Mary Ward, the convent was variously associated with the Franciscans and the Jesuits. The prolific translator Elizabeth Evelinge was a sister at Gravelines. Jamie Goodrich argues that although the order did not cultivate the conspicuous intellectualism of the Benedictine nuns at the English convent of Cambrai, it was nonetheless a center of female intellectual activity.[25] A copy of the 1632 edition of Heigham's *Life of Christ* held in the Huntington Library, is dedicated to a Poor Clare, Ellinor / Helen More, attesting the book's centrality within female religious communities: the dedication reads, "To the Religious reverend, and Holy virgin, Eleanora Mooriana, we wisheth health, happiness, and prosperity in this world and eternal happiness in the world to come."[26]

Heigham explains that he has dedicated his work to the female religious at Gravelines because they have chosen to live in female community; taking vows of obedience, chastity, and poverty, they possess a holiness that Heigham as a married man cannot emulate. "Who more willingly protect it," writes Heigham, "than those who in their owne lives so strictly observe it, that to behold the same, sensuall libertines stand amazed, lazie heretiques are quite confounded, virtuous Catholiques are marvelously edified, and God himself is greatly glorified."[27] They are thus the fitting dedicatees of a text detailing the life of Christ. Heigham relates that he has dedicated the book to the Abbess Clara Marianna because he recognizes the female religious at Gravelines as her spiritual daughters, at whose request he has written this book: "I have now at last brought to an end, the Treatise of the

Life of Christ which as is well known to some of your Religious daughters, when I had but newly begun and imparting to their view the survey of some imperfect sheetes they greatly besought me to go forward therein ... so far did their most pious desires prevayle with me, depending much (next after God) upon the assistance of their holy prayers, that I promised them to employ therein, all the little talent which God hath lent me."[28] The dedicatory letter, then, sets out an important context within which to understand Heigham's *Life of Christ*.

Heigham's text appeals to the values of the female community to which it is dedicated. Not only are the principal characters (exclusive of Jesus) women, but Heigham selects events in the various gospels in which women played a central role and then foregrounds them. So in addition to "the excellent sermon made by our Lord Jesus on the mountaine (Matthew 5.3)" – he includes accounts of Mary's nativity (drawn from the *Protoevangelium*), her espousal to Joseph, the conversion of Mary Magdalene (Luke 7:37), and the hospitality provided by Martha and Mary (Luke 19:38). In Heigham's retelling, women sustain Jesus during the most difficult moments of his life. Thus when Heigham narrates the crucifixion, he draws upon John 19:33 to emphasize that the Virgin Mary and Mary Magdalene remained at the foot of the cross; the male disciples (except for the unnamed "disciple that Jesus loved") are absent.

In this narrative, the male disciples consistently fail to support Christ: Heigham narrates "how his own disciple did betray him" and "How Peter sunk a little" while Christ walked on water. By contrast, he expends considerable narrative energy urging the reader to imagine how it must have felt for Mary to watch her son die.[29] Women are also central to many of Christ's miracles. There are chapters entitled, "The Mother of St. Peter Delivered of an Ague by Our Lord (Matthew 8:14)," "The Widows Sonne Raised to Life by our Lord Jesus and Restored to His Mother (Luke 11.7)," "The Woman Healed of a Bloody Flux (Luke 8.40)," and "The Woman of Canaan Whose Daughter was Possessed by a Devil (Matthew 15:21)." Of the eight "healing" miracles that Heigham includes, five are performed for women or at their behest.[30]

Resurrection Witnesses in the Gospels

We can perhaps best see how Heigham shaped his narrative to reflect the interests of a female readership by examining his treatment of Christ's Easter appearances – the same subject that, as we will see, Thomas chooses to explore in her catechism. In the early Christian communities, men and women who had encountered the risen Christ were regarded as "witnesses": that is, they were Christians who could testify about their experience to others. In the words of Gerald O'Collins and Daniel Kendall, "the early witnesses of Christ were the ones who got Christianity going."[31] Without them, Christianity would have probably remained a small sect within rabbinic Judaism. In all of the accounts of Christ's post-resurrection appearances, the men and women who meet Jesus are transformed into teachers who instruct others about the good news of Christ's resurrection. A resurrection witness, then, becomes one who is authorized to teach others – a position of considerable authority in the early church.

The role of women as Easter witnesses was widely debated in the first centuries of Christianity in part because, as we have seen, the canonical gospels contain different narratives. There are six different accounts of Christ's post-resurrection appearances in the gospels; four of these indicate that Christ first appeared to women. Joseph Fitzmeyer provides a concise summary of these appearances and the varying importance accorded to Mary Magdalene in them.[32] Contemporary scriptural scholars argue that these accounts differ because the gospel authors composed their narratives to reflect the interests of different communities.[33] They have identified two distinct theologies underpinning these narratives. The first (and dominant) tradition, exemplified by Luke 23:56–24:53, emphasizes the importance of Peter while downplaying the testimony of female witnesses to the resurrection. As Elizabeth Schussler-Fiorenza remarks, "Mary Magdalene is mentioned in all four canonical gospels as the primary witness to the Easter faith-event. However, Luke's gospel already attempts to play down her role as primary witness by stressing that the resurrected Lord appeared to Peter on the one hand and by omitting a resurrection appearance to the woman disciples."[34] Luke first narrates how Mary Magdalene, along with Johanna, and Mary, the mother of James, go to Christ's tomb, where they are told of Christ's resurrection by two angels. He juxtaposes this account with a narration of the risen Christ's unmediated revelation to Peter, describing how the two disciples, returning from Emmaus, journeyed "to Jerusalem, and found the eleven gathered together, and them that were with them, which said, The Lord is risen in deede, and hath appeared to Simon" (Luke 24:33–34). This account contrasts Christ's prioritizing of Peter (and implicit validation of an all male leadership, exemplified by the two disciples who encounter Christ on the road to Emmaus) with women who are informed of the resurrection through intermediaries.

An alternative tradition, exemplified in the Gospel of John (but also reflected in Mark's Gospel) presents Mary Magdalene as the primary witness of the resurrection. John presents Mary Magdalene as a wealthy widow and one of Christ's closest companions. He pointedly contrasts Peter's failure to see the risen Christ with Mary Magdalene's personal encounter with the risen Lord, narrating how Peter and another disciple visit the empty tomb, see the "linen wrapping lying there" but do not go in. The passage ends with the two male disciples returning to their homes (John 20:10). As Raymond Brown comments on John 20:10, "The real purpose of this verse is to get the disciples off the scene and give the stage to the Magdalene."[35] John 20:11–18 then narrates Mary Magdalene's encounter with her risen Lord:

> But Mary stood without at the sepulchre weeping: and as she wept, she bowed her selfe in to the sepulchre, And saw two Angels in white, sitting, the one at the heade, and the other at the feete where the body of Jesus had layen. And they sayd unto her, Woman, why weepest thou? She said unto them, They have taken away my Lord, and I knowe not where they have laid him. When she had thus said, shee turned her selfe back, and saw Jesus standing, and knew not that it was Jesus. Jesus sayeth unto her, Woman, why weepest thou? Whome seekest thou? Shee supposing that hee had beene the gardener, sayd unto him, Sir, if thou has borne him hence, tell mee where thou hast laide him, and I will take him away. Jesus saith unto her, Marie. She turned her self, and said unto him Rabboni, which is to say, Master. Jesus saith unto her, Touch me not: for I am not yet ascended to my Father: but goe to my brethren, and say unto them, I ascende unto my father and to your Father, and to my God, and to your God. Mary Magdalene came and told the disciples that she had seene the Lord, and that hee had spoken these things unto her.

This dramatic narration recalls earlier comments (John 10:3) in which Jesus is the good shepherd who "calleth his owne sheep by name, and leadeth them out." Mary Magdalene recognizes Jesus only when he names her; her response, "Rabboni" acknowledges his authority. The effect of this exchange is to set Mary up as a paradigmatic disciple, personally called by the risen Christ. Her affirmation, I have "sene the Lord" is, as Raymond Brown remarks, "the standard apostolic announcement of the resurrection." It insists upon her womanly ability to testify to the truth of Christ's resurrection, even to men. In the sonnet that serves as a prelude to this chapter, "To the Lady Magdalen Herbert," John Donne enlarges this understanding, writing of Mary Magdalene that "An active faith so highly did advance/ That she once knew, more than the Church did know/The Resurrection."[36]

Implicit in the canonical gospels, then, are two distinct accounts of Christ's post-resurrection appearances that assign differing importance to the role of women. Scholars generally agree that patristic theologians drew upon Luke to justify an all male priesthood, although they disagree as to whether this constitutes a deliberate strategy of exclusion.[37] Second- and third-century Gnostic writings reflect the gendered difference: *The Gospel of Mary*, for example, depicts an argument between Peter and Mary Magdalene as to whether a woman can witness the truth of Christ's resurrection to the male disciples.[38] But by the sixth century, Luke's account had become dominant. The importance accorded to women as Christian witnesses in the gospel of John was downplayed, although, as we shall see, it continued to serve as a residual cultural model.

Women as Resurrection Witnesses in *The Life of Christ*

Heigham's *Life of Christ* purposefully interweaves events from the gospels of John and Mark and suppresses the Lucan narrative in order to highlight women's ability to teach others the good news of Christ's resurrection. Heigham's Jesus first appears to his mother Mary, an incident without scriptural basis but reflective of Catholic pastoral tradition.[39] Heigham then draws upon John 20:11–18 to narrate how Jesus appeared to Mary Magdalene, and thereafter to the "three Maries," and then to Joseph of Arimathea. Both these appearances lack support within the canonical scriptures; the appearance to Joseph is detailed in the Gospel of Nicodemus. Heigham then draws upon 1 Corinthians 15:7 to explain how Jesus next appeared to "James the less"; only then does Heigham draw upon Luke to explain how Jesus appeared to Peter and the disciples on the way to Emmaus (Luke: 24:13–35). Heigham concludes his account with a description of Jesus' final appearance to all of his disciples, as well as his mother, Mary Magdalene, and the three Maries, so women are described as both the first and last resurrection witnesses (John 20:11–30) and (John 21:1–23).

In Heigham's account, Mary the mother of God and Mary Magdalene are the most significant witnesses of the resurrection. Following John 20: 11–18, Heigham contrasts Mary Magdalene's acknowledgment of the risen Christ with Christ's withholding his appearance from Peter and John: "The two disciples came to see the sepulcher, but they did not tarry there, and therefore for that tyme, deserved not to see Christ. But Magdalene persevered, though the disciples departed, whence she deserved before the rest to see our Lord God."[40] Heigham concludes that the persevering Magdalene "deserves" to be the first person among Christ's associates to witness the risen Christ. Fidelity to gospel truth, whatever one's gender, is the primary determinant of Christian witness.

Heigham also follows John 20:11–18 closely in portraying Mary Magdalene as recognizing Christ only when he calls her by "familiarly by her name," again recalling Christ as the good shepherd (John 10:16). Heigham gives Mary's response in Aramaic, "Rabboni," which many modern Bibles translate as "teacher," but which Heigham glosses as "master" in keeping with early modern exegetical practice. Following John 20:17, Heigham then narrates how Christ commands Mary to tell the good news of his resurrection to the male apostles: "Go and tell my brethren that I ascend to your father, and to my father, to your God, and to my God."[41] Heigham's *Life of Christ* demonstrates that long after the official precedence given to Luke's narrative, the Gospel of John continued to be a source for an alternative understanding of the centrality of women to Christ's life, death, and resurrection, and for an emphasis on the importance of women, especially Mary Magdalene, as witnesses to Christ's resurrection.

Women as Witnesses to the Resurrection in *An Old Book*

Thomas read Heigham's *Life of Christ* attentively, copying multiple passages from it into her manuscript miscellany. But she also read Heigham's text selectively, transcribing passages that detail Mary's betrothal, the Magi's vision of a cross of gold, the presentation of Jesus in the temple, and the flight into Egypt – all areas of obvious personal relevance to Thomas as a wife and mother.[42] These passages contain idiosyncratic historical and cultural details characteristic of Counter-Reformation biblical scholarship.[43] Thomas appreciated these details, recording for example, how Joseph, "according to the Custom of the hebrwes gave a ring too the Blesed virgin, to this day keept in the city of perusia [Perugia] in Iatalie with great respect and veneration (Saith the Life of Jesus)" and how "when Jesus was ofred by the Blessed virgin and presented on the alter he was Bought againe or redeemed for 5 pence= or 5 pieeces of mony, which ware Called Sicles."

Thomas augments Heigham's account of the order of Christ's Easter appearances, thus engaging with a topic with demonstrable implications for the role of women within the church. As already noted, *An Old Book* is a continuation of Thomas' first catechism, *Places of Scripture*. Its status as a continuation is indicated both by its title – which she adds on to the title of her first catechism – and its layout. Like *Places of Scripture, An Old Book* aligns the questions on the left-hand side of the page and answers on the right, connecting them with a horizontal line. Thomas has admittedly not mastered the formal, mechanical presentation of a catechism and so sometimes includes the answer within the question itself – as she occasionally does in *Places of Scripture*. But by recasting material from the last 200 pages of Heigham's 800 page text into a catechetical format, *An Old Book* reshapes Heigham's *Life of Christ* so that a less-than-attentive reader is able to grasp the implications of Heigham's representation of the order of Christ's Easter appearances.

She begins by placing a topic sentence – "and that Book Saith that our Saviour appered first to his Blessed Mother" – on the left. She places the completion of that sentence, "The virgin Mary" on the right, connecting them with a horizontal pen stroke. She then continues to underscore the importance of women, linking the second topic to the first with "and Next_____to Mary Magdalin." The remainder of the catechism is structured by these "next" and "then" sequences, a principle that highlights the order of Christ's appearances. Thomas locates Christ's appearances to his male disciples in the middle of the catechism: "Then to St. Jams the Less," "Next to St. petter by himself a Lone," "Next to the 2 disiples in the way to Emaus." Thomas concludes the catechism as she began: by underscoring the priority of women among the Easter witnesses. In her final topic statement, Thomas records that Christ appeared "then to all, St. tho. being present," a statement that she emphasizes in the corresponding phrase on the right: "to all the twelve apostles." Within this framing, however, she inscribes the continued presence of the women who witnessed the resurrection: "and our B. Lady Magdalin and the other Marys." Amplifying the direction taken in her source text, Thomas' catechism foregrounds Christ as surrounded by a nurturing female community during his time on earth. It is tempting to relate this insistent focus on female community to Thomas' own life, since we know that she exchanged books and ideas with female kin (and perhaps neighbors) and so would likely have recognized the value of female friendships in the cultivation of one's spiritual well-being.

By using the catechetical format and linking this catechism with one designed specifically for children, Thomas imaginatively connects the role of women as Easter witnesses with the role of mothers in religious instruction. It is possible that at least one other seventeenth-century woman did as well.[44] This connection never reaches the level of argument in Thomas' catechism, but it is highly suggestive of her self-understanding. It indicates that she may have understood her maternal instruction within the larger historical and religious context of women as religious teachers and witnesses.

"At Magdalin's House"

Thomas concludes her catechism with a purported meal that Christ shared with his male and female associates before ascending into heaven. Drawing on all four gospels, Heigham narrates at least six meals that Christ shared with his followers during his forty days on earth after his resurrection from the dead. At least from the first century, exegetes have interpreted these meals as Eucharistic symbols, recognizing that the gospel narrators repeat and remember the paschal supper by means of these meals. So, for example, in Luke 24:13–35, the two disciples on the road to Emmaus recognize Jesus only when they eat with him. Most agree that this narration is a theological lesson, designed to show that Christ's divinity can only be fully recognized through the sacrifice of his body (symbolized by the breaking of the bread).[45]

Thomas does not incorporate any of these meals in her catechism. As we have seen, she includes Christ's appearance to the disciples on the road to Emmaus, but not the meal he shared with them. The one post-resurrection meal that Thomas includes in her catechism specifies that women were present. For this intentional deviation from Heigham's text and the Gospels, there can be only one explanation: Thomas' belief that both men and women were among Christ's associates when he established the Eucharist. Let me be clear: I am not claiming that Thomas asserts women's ability to serve as priests within the Church of England. Unlike Amelia Lanyer, Thomas does not use priestly vocabulary when discussing the women's role at this last meal. She does, however, depict their engaged participation in the central sacrament of the church. Thomas specifies that Christ "Blessed them," a phrase which could refer to all those present but one that more naturally applies to its immediate antecedent "and our B. Lady Magdalin and The other Marys." Christ himself welcomed women's participation in Eucharistic celebration. While such a representation does not subvert official Church doctrine, it does register an important shift in emphasis. It indicates Thomas' belief that Christ affirmed the spiritual equality of men and women and invited all to share in the Church's central sacrament.

Thomas' catechism concludes by stating that this final communal meal was eaten "at Magdalin's house," thus again highlighting the importance of Mary Magdalene as a witness of Christ's resurrection as well as suggesting that she was so close to Christ that he was a guest at her home. This meal is Thomas' original recreation of a signally important event in the history of the early Church: it has no analogue in either the Gospels or Heigham. Heigham describes Christ's final meal with the disciples as taking place "in the supping chamber at Mount Sion."[46] John 21:7–15 narrates a final meal of broiled fish on the beach. Thomas' representation may be indebted to popular early modern accounts of Mary Magdalene, which describe her as a wealthy widow who provided support for the gospel ministry – a narrative which was arguably as popular in the early modern period as the narrative of the penitent Magdalene, derived by her association with the prostitute in Luke 37: 36–50. This positive conception of Mary Magdalene rests upon the conflation of her with Mary, sister of Lazarus and Martha in Luke 10: 38–42. John Donne plays upon this positive conception of Mary Magdalene in his poem to Magdalen Herbert, in which he describes Mary Magdalene as, "Her of your name, whose fair inheritance / Bethina was, and jointure Magdalo."[47]

Although Thomas' understanding of Mary Magdalene as an affluent widow most likely reflects an early modern tendency, it can also be seen to reflect the role of wealthy widows in the early church. As we have seen in Chapter 1, Thomas possessed a thorough knowledge of the Bible, composing a historical catechism for her children based upon her reading of the Old and New Testaments. In her prefatory letter to her children, Thomas urges them to get along with one another by providing the scriptural examples of Joseph and his brothers, Abraham and Lot, and Jesus and the disciples. She observes, "I hope these holy examples are soeficient, althoe there are many more which you may make good use of . . . " (124). Thomas would have known that throughout the Acts of the Apostles and the Pauline epistles, Paul's ministry is assisted by wealthy widows, such as Lydia and Prisca, who provide financial support and allow their homes to be used as house churches for the apostles. Feminist scholars contend that these women were integral members of the early church community, as significant as the male preachers in spreading Christianity. These women are shown as practicing diakonia, or the "true leadership demanded of the followers of Jesus." Roughly translated as "service," diakonia does not refer only to table service but also to "the service and love" that Mark and John see "at the core of Jesus' ministry and as the central demand of apostleship."[48] In Raymond Brown's view, such diakonia or service may have had the status of an ordained ministry through the laying on hands by the time that John composed his gospel.[49]

Drawing upon these cultural and scriptural models, Thomas amplifies and integrates disparate source materials to recreate a signally important event in Jesus' resurrection. She thus emulates Heigham's narrative method in *The Life of Christ*, although whether this was intentional is uncertain. At the same time, Thomas' representation suggests the extent to which she saw Mary Magdalene as a model for her own participation in Christian community. Thomas underscores the importance of Mary Magdalene in *Places of Scripture* as well, when she queries "To whom did Christ apeare to first after he was risen from the dead" and then responds, "Mary Magdalin." Extending and elaborating upon this representation, Thomas represents Mary Magdalene in *An Old Book* as a woman a lot like her: a wealthy widow who communicates in the central sacraments of the church and is active as a head of household in sharing the central truths of Christianity.

Religious Eclecticism in Herefordshire

Besides her marked interest in and identification with the women like Mary Magdalene who were among the first witnesses to Christianity, the Church of England loyalist Thomas is notable for her engagement with and appreciation of a Catholic devotional text. In her sole comment on the character of Heigham's *Life*, Thomas observes "and many other things are written in that Book, larger than our Bible declares it." The backdrop to her remark was the distinction between Catholic and Protestant exegetical traditions: as we have seen, while godly Protestants attempted to reconcile various scriptural passages, Catholics selected certain narratives and augmented them with extra-scriptural sources and popular traditions. Thomas registers Heigham's amplification of scriptural material in her description of it as containing material "larger than our Bible declares." By incorporating material from this Catholic text within her Protestant conformist devotional, Thomas transposes a traditional Catholic respect for non-scriptural traditions into a Protestant household context. Thomas reads Heigham's *Life of Christ* generously – and wishes for her readers to do so as well. This generous model of reading indicates that Thomas possessed the ability to recognize the value of differing beliefs while continuing to hold her own – an eclectic model of cross confessional dialogue.

How did Thomas obtain Heigham's text, which she describes as "very old" when she read it? In the seventeenth century, Herefordshire was a rural, farming community – as it still is today. One wouldn't immediately think of it as a thriving market for contraband books. But seventeenth-century Herefordshire was also a Catholic stronghold, where the religion could be practiced with only occasional governmental intervention.[50] In 1622, the Jesuits founded the College of St. Francis Xavier, at Cwm, a small village near Welsh Newton, approximately nineteen miles from Thomas' home in Michaelchurch Escley. Cwm played an active role in the training of Jesuit missionaries and the dissemination of Jesuit texts. The pamphlet *A Short Narrative of the Discovery of a College of Jesuits at a Place Called the Come in the County of Hereford* (1679) makes clear the size of the operation: "There are One and twenty Chimnies in both Houses, and a great many Doors to go in and out at; and likewise many private Passages from one room to the other."[51]

John Kemble, a Jesuit priest who had trained at Douai in the 1620s, lived at his brother's Pembridge castle less than twenty miles from Michaelchurch Escley. He actively ministered to Herefordshire Catholics for over fifty years. In 1678, this apparent toleration was interrupted by the Popish Plot. While most contemporaries recognized that there was little danger to Charles II, Titus Oates succeeded in stirring up anti-Catholic prejudice in Herefordshire. Father Kemble, who was nearly eighty years old at the time, was arrested, interrogated, and eventually put to death as a traitor in 1679.[52] The same year, government agents invaded the Jesuit College at Cwm. The priests must have had advanced notice of the attack, since no priests were discovered at the college. Government raiders discovered mostly Catholic books – lots of them.

> In one of these Houses there was a Study found, the Door therof very hardly to be discovered, being placed behind a Bed, and plaistered over like the Wall adjoining in which was found great store of Divinity Books, and others, in Folio and Quarto, and many other lesser books... many whereof are written by the principal learned Jesuits.[53]

The discovery of so many books (and no priests) at a house in the isolated Herefordshire countryside supports the claim of Alexandra Walsham that the Catholic Church in the late seventeenth century increasingly relied upon books to nourish and support the Catholic faithful.[54]

We know from the official government account of the raid at Cwm that many of these books were devotional aids. It describes how raiders found "several books lately printed against the Protestant religion," "small popish Catechisms, printed and tyed up in a bundle," "some popish manuscripts, fairly and lately written" and some lives of Ignatius Loyola.[55] After the raid, these books were transferred to the Hereford Cathedral Library. Hannah Thomas has recently catalogued these books; she has discovered over 150 titles, including several works written or translated by John Heigham. Dr. Thomas has found notations on some of the pages of the books that indicate that the library at Cwm served as a lending library for Catholics.[56] None of these notations refer to Katherine Thomas, so no direct connection between Thomas and the library at Cwm can be established. But the existence of this library so close to her home suggests that Katherine Thomas certainly had ample opportunity to read prohibited Catholic devotional texts.

Conclusion

By recasting a Catholic devotional text into a catechism, Thomas takes on the role of a witness to the good news of women's participation in the educational mission and sacramental practices of early Christianity. When she encountered a Catholic book that provocatively challenged the tradition of male dominance in the Church, she adapted her source text to create an alternative to dominant cultural understandings. Her brief catechism affirms the ability of women to serve as Christian witnesses, to participate in the Eucharistic celebration, and to contribute to the Christian mission by using their power and authority within the home. This is an original and imaginative theological vision. What we find, then, in the manuscript miscellany of Katherine Thomas is evidence suggesting how one early modern woman drew on her experience as a mother both to legitimize her authorial practices and to emulate ministerial activity. Even more significantly, Thomas may have recognized – and exploited – the relationship between catechetical form and content: as a catechism, *An Old Book* lodges forceful implications concerning the ability of women to teach the basic truths of Christianity both within the household and outside of it.

An Old Book also urges us to think more deeply about the variegated religious landscape of early modern England, where Catholics, Protestant conformists, puritans, and sectarians might live in proximity. Alexandra Walsham has proposed that religious toleration emerged out of the everyday experiences of early modern men and women who interacted with husbands, wives, family members, friends, and neighbors who possessed different religious beliefs.[57] At the very least, Thomas' catechism suggests that sympathetic inter-confessional engagement was not the exclusive prerogative of an educated, urban, male elite.[58]

Notes

1. "To Mrs. Magdalen Herbert: Of Saint Mary Magdalen," in *The Complete Poems of John Donne*, ed. Robin Robbins (London: Longman, 2010), 489.
2. Siobhan Keenan's " Embracing Submission? Motherhood, Marriage, and Mourning in Katherine Thomas' Seventeenth-Century Commonplace Book," *Women's Writing* 15.1 (2008): 69–85, explores the tension between maternal grief and religious belief in Thomas' elegies. I am indebted to Keenan's essay, as well as to Nina Wedell and Bob Steele, members of the Ewyas Lacy Study Group and creators of the website www.ewyaslacy.org.uk, for biographical information about Katherine Thomas. Kate Chedgzoy cogently discusses Thomas's manuscript in *Women's Writing in the British Atlantic World: Memory, Place, History, 1550–1700* (Cambridge: Cambridge University Press, 2007), 41–7.
3. National Library of Wales, MS 4340A. Katherine Thomas' Commonplace Book. Perdita Manuscripts, 1500–1700. The section of the manuscript containing the catechism is unpaginated.
4. On the variety of print and manuscript materials found in early modern women's manuscript writing and what this variety can tell us about women's access to literary and religious culture, see Victoria Burke, "Seventeenth-Century Women's Manuscript Writing," in *The History of British Women's Writing, 1610–1690*, ed. Mihoko Suzuki (Basingstoke: Palgrave Macmillan, 2011), 99–112, as well as her "Manuscript Miscellanies," in *The Cambridge Companion to Early Modern Women's Writing*, ed. Laura Lunger Knoppers (Cambridge: Cambridge University Press, 2009), 54–67. On women's religious manuscripts, see Burke's "'My Poor Returns': Devotional Manuscripts by Seventeenth-Century Women," *Parergon: Journal of the Australian and New Zealand Association for Medieval and Early Modern Studies* 29.2 (2012): 47–68. Special issue: *Early Modern Women and the Apparatus of Authorship*, ed. Sarah C.E. Ross, Rosalind Smith, and Patricia Pender. See also Margaret Ezell, *Social Authorship and the Advent of Print* (Baltimore: John Hopkins University Press, 1999), 27–8; and Kate Narveson, *Bible Readers and Lay Writers in Early Modern England* (Aldershot: Ashgate Press, 2012), 131–76.
5. Katherine Ludwig Jansen, "Maria Magdalena: Apostolorum Apostola," in *Women Preachers and Prophets through Two Millennia of Christianity*, ed. Beverly Kienzle and Pamela Walker (Berkeley: University of California Press, 1998), 57–96, especially 57–9.
6. Elaine Pagels, "Visions, Appearances, and Apostolic Authority," in *Gnosis: Fetzschrift for Hans Jonas* (Gottingen: Vandenhoeck and Ruprecht, 1978), 416–27, 417. Elizabeth Schussler-Fiorenza, "Patriarchal Household of God and the Ekklesia of Women," in *In Memory of Her: A Feminist Theological Reconstruction of Christian Origins* (New York: Crossroad Publishing, 1987), 285–333, 304. Raymond Brown, "Roles of Women in the Fourth Gospel," in *The Community of the Beloved Disciple* (New York: Paulist Press, 1979), 183–98, summarizes as follows: "A key to Peter's importance in the Apostolate was the

tradition that he was the first to see the risen Jesus." Brown continues, "The tradition that Jesus appeared first to Mary Magdalene has a good chance of being historical ... The secondary place given to the tradition of an appearance to a woman or women probably reflects the fact that women did not serve at first as official preachers of the Church" (189–90).

7. Micheline White, "A Woman with St. Peter's Keys," *Criticism* 45.3 (Summer 2003): 323–41, 323. The scholarship on Lanyer is extensive. See, especially, Erica Longfellow, "Ecce Homo: The Spectacle of Christ's Passion in *Salve Deus Rex Judaeorum*," in *Women and Religious Writing in Early Modern England* (Cambridge: Cambridge University Press, 2004); Janel Mueller, "The Feminist Poetics of *Salve Deus Rex Judaeorum*," in *Aemilia Lanyer: Gender, Genre, and the Canon* (Lexington, KY: University of Kentucky Press, 1998), 99–127; Femke Molekamp, "Reading Christ the Book in Aemilia Lanyer's *Salve Deus Rex Judaeorum* (1611)," *Studies in Philology* 109.3 (2012): 311–32. Also, Susanne Woods, ed. *The Poems of Aemilia Lanyer: Salve Deus Rex Judaeorum* (Oxford: Oxford University Press, 1993).

8. See, for example, the following essays in *Women Preachers and Prophets through Two Millennia of Christianity*: Linda Lierheimer, "Preaching or Teaching, Defining the Ursuline Mission in Seventeenth-Century France," 212–26; Peter Voght, "A Voice for Themselves: Women as Participants in Congregational Discourse in the Eighteenth-Century Moravian Movement," 227–47; Phyllis Mack, "In a Female Voice: Preaching and Politics in Eighteenth-Century British Quakerism," 248–63.

9. On the continued popularity of Catholic devotional books among Protestants in seventeenth-century England, see Alec Ryrie, *Being Protestant in Reformation Britain* (Oxford: Oxford University Press, 2013), 284–92.

10. Keenan, "Embracing Submission," 71, 82; Bob Steele, "The History of Michaelchurch Court and its Estate" (www.ewyaslacy.org.uk/-/The-History-of-Michaelchurch-Court-and-its-Estate).

11. Lawrence Stone, *Love, Sex, Marriage, and the Family in England* (New York: Harper and Row, 1979), 69–80. See also Jacqueline Eales, *Puritans and Roundheads: The Harleys of Brampton Bryan* (Cambridge: Cambridge University Press, 1991), 11.

12. Keenan, "Embracing Submission," 71.

13. William Dugdale, *The History of St. Paul's Cathedral* (London, 1658). On women's interest in funerary monuments, see Patricia Phillippy, "Living Stones: Lady Elizabeth Russell and the Art of Sacred Conversation," in *English Women, Religion, and Textual Production, 1500–1625*, ed. Micheline White (Aldershot: Ashgate, 2012), 17–37. On epitaphs in late seventeenth-century English culture, see Joshua K. Scodel, *The English Poetic Epitaph* (Ithaca: Cornell University Press, 1991).

14. Here I differ slightly from Keenan, "Embracing Submission," 74, who sees it as a "didactic miscellany for her household" and a "private devotional manual tailored to her concerns." Andrew Cambers suggests that even what we might

think of as private spiritual journals were designed to be circulated within and read by a select community of like-minded men and women. "Reading, the Godly, and Self-Writing in England, circa 1580–1720," *Journal of British Studies* 46 (2007): 796–825, 796.
15. Cited in Kate Narveson, *Bible Readers and Lay Writers in Early Modern England* (Aldershot: Ashgate Press, 2012), 19.
16. Cambers, "Reading, the Godly, and Self-Writing," 821.
17. Narveson, *Bible Readers and Lay Writers*, 72–3.
18. See, for example, Samuel Clark, *The Blessed Life and Meritorious Death of Our Lord and Saviour Jesus Christ* (London, 1664); Joseph Hall, *Contemplations Upon the Remarkable Passages in the Life of the Holy Jesus* (London, 1679); Jeremy Taylor, *Antiquitates Christianae: or The History of the Life and Death of the Holy Jesus* (London, 1678). Many were frequently reprinted.
19. All subsequent citations will be from the Newberry Library's copy of *The Life of Our Lord and Savior Jesus Christ* (St. Omer, 1634).
20. A. F. Allison, "John Heigham of St. Omer," *Recusant History* 4 (1959): 226–42, 236, 231.
21. Heigham, *Life of Christ*, 146.
22. Heigham writes that the infant Jesus was redeemed "for five Sicles," *Life of Christ*, 176–7, a detail not included in his gospel source text (Luke 2:23–39), but found in Numbers 3:47: "Thou shalt also take five shekels for every person: after the weight of the Sanctuarie shalt thou take it."
23. Heigham, *Life of Christ*, Sig. A2r.
24. *Meditations on the Life of Christ, An Illustrated Manuscript of the Fourteenth Century*, trans. Isa Ragusa (Princeton: Princeton University Press, 1961), xxvii.
25. Jaime Goodrich, "'Ensigne-Bearers of Saint Claire': Elizabeth Evelinge's Early Translations and the Restoration of English Franciscanism," in *English Women, Religion, and Textual Production, 1500–1625*, ed. White, 83–101, 85.
26. An Aire choir nun, Ellinor / Helen More professed in 1681, aged 22. In religion, she was Clare Magdalen. Biographical information obtained from the "Who Were the Nuns? Database," www.history.qmul.ac.uk. The Newberry Library copy also indicates the book's role within female community: it contains an inscription, "Margret Harris her book to pray for heer godmother, 1657."
27. Heigham, *Life of Christ*, Sig. A4r.
28. Heigham, *Life of Christ*, Sig. A3r.
29. Heigham, *Life of Christ*, 504, 405, 603–12.
30. The male-centered miracles that Heigham includes are 1) Christ's healing of the bedridden man (John 5:5); 2) Jesus's healing of the Centurion's son (Matthew 8:5) and 3) Christ's healing of a man "sick of palsy" (Matthew 9:2). I do not include Christ's raising of Lazarus from the dead in this tally, since Heigham stresses equally the sickness of Lazarus and the agency of his sisters Mary and Martha: "Lazarus, the brother of Martha and Mary, falling sorely sick, his sisters sent a messenger to the Lord" (464).

31. Gerald O'Collins, S. J., and Daniel Kendall, S. J., "Mary Magdalene As Major Witness to Jesus' Resurrection," *Theological Studies* 48 (1987): 631–46, 632.
32. Joseph Fitzmeyer, *The Gospel According to Luke (X-XXIV)* (Garden City, New Jersey: Doubleday, 1985): 1535–7.
33. Raymond Brown, *The Community of the Beloved Disciple* (New Jersey: Paulist Press, 1979), 18–22; and *An Introduction to the New Testament* (New Haven: Yale University Press, 1997), 7–15.
34. Schussler-Fiorenza, "Patriarchal Household of God," 304–5.
35. Raymond Brown, *The Gospel According to St. John* (New York: Doubleday), 988, quoted in O'Collins and Kendall, 634.
36. Brown, "Roles of Women," 189; "To Mrs. Magdalen Herbert: Of Saint Mary Magdalen," in *The Complete Poems of John Donne*, 489.
37. Brown, "Roles of Women," Pagels, "Visions, Appearances, and Apostolic Authority," and Schussler-Fiorenza, "Patriarchal Household of God," argue for the intentional devaluation of women's authority; O'Collins and Kendall, in "Mary Magdalene," conclude that the historical record is mixed as to whether such suppression was deliberate: "Popes Leo the Great and Gregory the Great could pay remarkable tribute to the person of Mary Magdalene as late as the fourth century" (642).
38. Karen King, *The Gospel of Mary of Magdala: Jesus and the First Woman Apostle* (Santa Rosa, California: Polebridge Press, 2003), 17; and "Prophetic Power and Women's Authority: The Case of the Gospel of Mary (Magdalene)," in *Women Preachers and Prophets*, ed. Beverly Kienzle and Pamela J. Walker, 21–41, 27.
39. Katherine Ludwig Jansen relates that when popular preachers departed from scripture in the late medieval period by insisting that Christ appeared first to his mother, they did so in order to please the laity. "Maria Magdalena: Apostolorum Apostola," in *Women Preachers and Prophets*, ed. Beverly Kienzle and Pamela J. Walker, 69–70.
40. Heigham, *Life of Christ*, 716.
41. Heigham, *Life of Christ*, 720–1.
42. It is on the basis of these passages that I have been able to identify Heigham's *Life of Christ* as Thomas' source text. For these passages, many of them Heigham's additions to Bonaventure's text, see 63, 148, 179, and 191 of his *Life of Christ*.
43. Debora Shuger, *The Renaissance Bible: Scholarship, Sacrifice, and Subjectivity* (Berkeley: University of California Press, 1994), 11–54.
44. Femke Molekamp observes that a 1639 Geneva Bible, held by the Morgan Library, has a carefully embroidered back cover depicting the resurrected Christ appearing to Mary Magdalene in the garden as described in John 20: 11–18. She remarks that inscriptions on the front pastedown suggest that "this Bible with its carefully wrought cover was passed from mother to daughter." *Women and the Bible in Early Modern England* (Oxford: Oxford University Press, 2013), 47–8. Did the embroiderer envision a connection between her representation of the risen Christ's revelation to a woman and her own role as

a maternal religious instructor? We cannot know with certainty that she did, but the needlework and inscription are suggestive of her interest in women's role as religious teachers.

45. We can see this tradition expressed in Caravaggio's painting, *The Road to Emmaus* (1601), which simultaneously represents Christ's breaking of the bread and the disciples' sudden recognition of his divinity.
46. Heigham, *Life of Christ*, 768.
47. Jansen, "Maria Magdalena, Apostolorum Apostola," 77–8; Donne, "To Mrs. Magdalen Herbert," 489.
48. Schussler-Fiorenza, "Patriarchal Household," 320, 317.
49. Raymond Brown remarks concerning the representation of Martha in John 12:2 as "serving at table": although "on the story-level of Jesus' ministry this might not seem significant . . . the evangelist is writing in the 90's when the church office of diakonos already existed in the post-Pauline churches and the task of waiting on tables was a specific function to which the community or its leaders appointed individuals by laying on hands." "Roles of Women," 187. On the history of women deacons within the Catholic Church, see Phyllis Zagano, *Holy Saturday: An Argument for the Restoration of the Female Diaconate in the Catholic Church* (New York: Crossroads Publishing, 2000), 86–92.
50. Roland Mathias writes that Herefordshire was a region "open to the suspicion, that it was . . . for various reasons, known to be safe for Catholics" (4) and that "a few months after King James' accession about a hundred and forty people were discovered in the act of celebrating the Feast of the Purification of the Blessed Mary" (14). *Whitsun Riot: An Account of a Commotion amongst Catholics in Herefordshire and Monmouthshire in 1605* (London: Bowes and Bowes, 1963). To be sure, these events occurred approximately seventy-five years before Thomas composed her text, but when considered alongside the establishment of the Jesuit College at Cwm in 1622, and the Government raid of this College in 1679, they suggest the longstanding importance of Catholicism in the region.
51. Herbert Croft, *A Short Narrative of the Discovery of a College of Jesuits at a Place Called the Come in the County of Hereford* (London, 1679), 3.
52. Archibold, W. A., "John Kemble," in *Oxford Dictionary of National Biography* (Oxford: Oxford University Press, 2004), (www.oxforddnb.com.ezproxy.depaul.edu/view/article/15320).
53. Croft, *A Short Narrative*, 4
54. "To adapt a penetrating remark of John Bossy," writes Walsham, "I want to explore the possibility that as English Catholicism became more typographical, so it became less sacramental." "Domme Preachers: Post-Reformation Catholicism and the Culture of Print," *Past and Present* 168.1 (2000): 72–123, 81.
55. Croft, *A Short Narrative*, 6.
56. Thomas, "The Society of Jesus in Wales, c. 1600–1679: Reconstructing and Analyzing the Cwm Jesuit Library at Hereford Cathedral," paper presented at the conference, *What Is Early Modern Catholicism?* (June, 2013).

57. "Could it be," asks Alexandra Walsham, "that the parochial experience of confessional coexistence and social ecumenism helped not just to pave the way for the edicts and statutes that retrospectively licensed it, but also for the intellectual insights of those who mounted a case for toleration?" *Charitable Hatred: Tolerance and Intolerance in England, 1500–1700* (Manchester: Manchester University Press, 2006), 279.
58. On confessional coexistence in rural communities, see Bill Stevenson, "The Social Integration of Post-Restoration Dissenters, 1660–1725," in *The World of Rural Dissenters*, ed. Margaret Spufford (Cambridge: Cambridge University Press, 1995), 360–87.

CHAPTER 4

Catholicism, Catechesis, and Coterie Circulation
The Manuscript of Barbara Slingsby Talbot (b. 1633)

Introduction

In a portrait painted by the school of Peter Lely in 1660, Barbara Slingsby Talbot, wearing a red dress and pearl earrings with a brocade green shawl, gazes confidently at the viewer. The resemblance to her mother, Barbara Bellasis Slingsby, who had posed for a portrait in a red dress and pearl earrings at about the same age, is striking – and likely to have been intentional. Talbot's daughters Barbara (1670–1763) and Gilberta (d. 1746) would also have their portraits painted in red dresses and pearls, as would Talbot's granddaughter.[1] These portraits suggest that the raven-haired women of the Talbot family identified with their maternal line, a cultured Yorkshire family with a longstanding tradition of female manuscript compilation and circulation.

Twenty-seven years after sitting for her portrait, Barbara Talbot drew upon this tradition in preparing a manuscript for circulation among her friends and family. Talbot's manuscript, held at the Huntington Library as HM 43213, is a small, handwritten text (4 inches by 6 inches) that has been carefully designed and formatted to resemble a print devotional manual. Talbot explains that this is a copy she has made of a book sent to her by her father, Henry Slingsby, a Royalist executed by Oliver Cromwell in 1658. "Most of the contents of this litle booke," Talbot writes, "was taken out of one, sent to me by my father, when hee was upon the scafold ready to be executed." Talbot explains that she has copied her father's book "principlely to presarve in memorie the last Legacie he left mee."[2] Despite this striking account of its origin, HM 43213 has been overlooked both by scholars of early modern women's writing and seventeenth-century historians. It is not mentioned in contemporary histories of women's writing nor is it discussed by any of her father's biographers.[3] *The Guide to British Historical Manuscripts in the Huntington Library* lists the manuscript under the name "Henry Slingsby" and describes it as "a personal catechism, transcribed in the hand of and with a preface by Lady Barbara (Slingsby) Talbot, the author's daughter in 1687."[4] This description of Talbot's manuscript implicitly denies it any public significance and thus minimizes its interest for scholars. An equally significant difficulty is the label "transcribed." Transcription conventionally connotes the mechanical copying of words and phrases; it is considered a low-level literary activity. It is time to rethink this value judgment. We have seen in Chapter 1 that Lady Ann Montagu includes a carefully transcribed copy of Joseph Hall's *A Briefe Summe of the Principles of Religion* in her loose papers. I have argued that we need to see Montagu's transcription as a form of authorship: she transcribes Hall's catechism to demonstrate her taste, religious piety, and maternal devotion.

Other sixteenth- and seventeenth-century transcriptions, like Talbot's, are not precise replications, but thoughtful engagements with printed texts. These transcriptions are often composite texts, in which an author recasts words and phrases from her source and adds some of her own. How can we characterize the mixture of authorial agency and multiple voices evinced by such texts? Jaime Goodrich has recently shown how some early modern female translators exploited the multiple voices inherent in translation, advancing "their doctrinal views by drawing on the authority of their source texts." A transcriber similarly adopts (and adapts) another's words to express her ideas, relying upon strategies of indirection to advance her intentions. This allows her to speak publicly without declaring independence. Although some early modern women may have been drawn to transcription because it allowed them to conform to social restrictions on female authorship, others may have made this choice because they desired to take advantage of the multiple voices inherent in transcription. Like translation, transcription allowed early modern women to cultivate what Goodrich describes as the "intertextuality essential to developing literary authority in early modern England."[5] Rather than deride transcription as mindless copying, we should see it as the savvy manipulation of inherited texts for one's own purposes.

In a brief preface, Talbot admits that her manuscript is not an exact copy; she first states that she has transcribed "most" of her father's book; later, after acknowledging that some of the content was "contrary to the faith and Doctrien of the church of Ingland," she claims that she has included "the best of itt."[6] Her father's book, in turn, was not a "personal" catechism of his, but a Catholic devotional text, *The Key of Paradise*, that had been published abroad and smuggled into England. Talbot, herself a Church of England loyalist, was catechized and taught to read by her mother; she spent her adolescence among her mother's cultivated family where she is likely to have gained an appreciation for coterie manuscript circulation. When she copied, redacted, and circulated her late father's Catholic devotional manual, Talbot was not acting exclusively out of filial piety. Nor was she mechanically transcribing her late father's book. Instead, Talbot was availing herself of her maternal inheritance of domestic catechesis and coterie manuscript circulation in an attempt to retrieve her late father's reputation – and perhaps to reinforce public perceptions of her own Church of England loyalism – by intervening in ongoing public debates about the political status of English Catholics. Talbot transcribes, redacts, and circulates her father's book to appeal implicitly for the toleration of English Catholics while nonetheless conforming to the cultural restrictions on female speech.

A Loyal Gentleman of Singular Worth

Throughout the seventeenth century, Henry Slingsby was known as a man of conscience who chose to die rather than compromise his Royalist beliefs. Born in 1601/2 into an aristocratic Yorkshire family, Slingsby was educated at Cambridge. He married Barbara Bellasis, daughter of the wealthy and cultured Thomas Bellasis, Viscount Fauconberg. Well read and literate, Slingsby produced a diary of his life between 1638–49 modeled on Montaigne's *Essays*.[7] He also worked tirelessly for the restoration of Charles II and fought at the battle of Marston Moor. After the Royalist defeat there, he retired to his family home at Redhouse, approximately four miles from York. In 1655, Slingsby joined the Duke of Rochester in an abortive attempt to seize Hull, after which Slingsby was placed under house arrest at Hull and then at York. Cromwell was reluctant to execute Slingsby, in large part because Cromwell's daughter Mary was married to Slingsby's nephew (Barbara's first cousin) Thomas Bellasis.[8] But when Slingsby continued to plot on behalf of Charles II, Cromwell charged him with treason. Slingsby was tried, condemned, and executed in 1658. Even on the scaffold, Slingsby described his death as a sacrifice to the Royalist cause, stating that "he was to die for being an honest man, of which he was very glad but sorry that it was not for some more effectual service to His Majesty."[9]

Talbot's 1686 transcription was surely motivated in part by a desire to secure her father's reputation as a martyr of conscience, a reputation bolstered by multiple print and artistic representations in the late 1680s and sustained into the twentieth century.[10] Slingsby himself had contributed to a heroic image of himself in print, composing a letter of advice to his sons, Henry and Thomas, while he was in prison awaiting execution. It was published in London in 1658 immediately after Slingsby's execution as *"A Father's Legacy. Sir Henry Slingsbey's Instructions to His Sonnes."* Slingsby projects his death as a Christ-like sacrifice, remarking with wry understatement that he "retaines a slight memorie, of his patience and dolorous passion, who forgave his own death." "We cannot share in a crown," Slingsby concludes, "if we have no part in the cross."[11]

Although Slingsby's contemporary reputation was inextricably associated with his Christian faith, his confessional affiliation is unclear. Most modern scholars believe that Slingsby was a Church of England loyalist, noting that his Cambridge tutor was the Protestant divine John Preston and that Slingsby articulates theological beliefs consonant with Prayer Book Protestantism throughout his diary. To take but one example, when debating whether to consecrate his family chapel at Redhouse, Slingsby admits that while "it is not amiss to have a place consecrated for devotion," he fears that by so doing he "draws near to the superstition of the Church of Rome, who do suffer such external devotion to efface and wear out the inward devotion of the heart." He insists that he wants to avoid turning "devotion into superstition."[12] David Scott concludes that Slingsby's "approach to religion appears to have combined something of the 'painful' earnestness of the godly with reverence for the order and decency of the Arminians."[13]

But multiple seventeenth- and eighteenth-century sources attest to Slingsby's Catholicism. The *Humble Apology of the English Catholicks* (1666) includes Slingsby among a list of the "names of such Catholics whose estates (both Real and Personal) were sold ... for their pretended delinquency; that is, adhering to their king" and as one nineteenth-century scholar remarked, "this list was published during the lifetime of his children." The claim is repeated in the *Kalendarium Catholicum* (1686).[14] The eighteenth-century historian Mark Noble remarked that "Sir Henry Slingsby was a loyal roman catholic, universally beloved, and his death greatly as lamented." Another nineteenth-century antiquarian, F. C. H., observes that Charles Dodd's *Church History of England* (1737–42) includes Slingsby among Roman Catholic knights, describing him as "a loyal gentleman of singular worth and honor."[15]

Which interpretation should we believe? It is possible that Slingsby was a Church of England Protestant. To be sure, many of the Catholic sources written after the Restoration have a vested interest in claiming Slingsby, a determined Royalist plotter, as one of their own. Moreover, the

Kalendarium Catholicum quotes *A Humble Apology* nearly verbatim, suggesting that it relied upon it as its source. Dodd similarly cited *A Humble Apology* in support of his claims, so it is possible that many of the later attestations of Slingsby's Catholicism rely upon a single text.[16] But even if we conclude that these sources are partial, we still have to account for Barbara Slingsby Talbot's manuscript, which indicates that her about-to-be executed father sent her a book containing doctrine contrary to the Church of England, as well as my determination that this book was, in fact, a popular Catholic devotional. Most contemporary historians have not examined Slingsby Talbot's manuscript, so they are unaware of its implications for Slingsby's confessional identity.

Another possibility is that Slingsby was a church Papist who conformed outwardly to the Church of England in order to preserve his family estate. Multiple eldest sons, especially among the Yorkshire elite, acted similarly. But this conclusion does not account for the multiple attestations of Protestant belief expressed throughout Slingsby's diary. These attestations indicate a developed understanding of the differences between Church of England and Catholic theology – and Slingsby's approval of the Church of England position.[17] Nor does it address the fact that in 1641, Slingsby was named as one of the persons "for the speedy disarming of popish recusants and other dangerous persons" for North Riding. Remarking upon the eighteenth-century description of Slingsby as Catholic, David Scott notes that Slingsby "as late as 1651 . . . professed allegiance to the Church of England."[18]

A final possibility is that Slingsby was a Protestant throughout much of his life, but converted to Catholicism sometime before his death, perhaps while he was in prison awaiting execution. D. P., a nineteenth-century scholar, believed similarly, remarking: "During his life, till the very last, it is, I think, quite certain that Sir Henry Slingsby was a Protestant . . . But I think that in the Tower, when under sentence, Sir Henry Slingsby was by some means reconciled to the Catholic church."[19] This interpretation accords with what we know about many conversions to Catholicism in seventeenth-century England: Peter Lake and Michael Questier have shown that prisons were widely known as incubators of Jesuit spirituality in seventeenth-century England.[20] Applicants to the Catholic seminary at Douai describe converting while imprisoned on various offenses, and they affirm the importance of prohibited Catholic devotional works, like *The Key of Paradise*. Gaspard Rudd, S.J., explains that he was "reconciled" to the Catholic faith "by Father William Ford, at that time a prisoner in chains for the Catholic faith, in York." Francis Cater similarly explains that he "followed his father to the Protestant Church" until the age of twelve when his uncle sent him to York prison, "where, brought up among Catholics in that prison, I learnt, together with grammar, the precepts of the Catholic Church."[21]

I find this interpretation the most plausible. End-of-life conversions to Catholicism were not uncommon among the Yorkshire gentry in late seventeenth-century England: to take but one example, Slingsby's father-in-law, Viscount Fauconberg, was a conforming member of the Church of England for much of his life but publicly converted to Catholicism shortly before his death in 1653 – a conversion that may have been witnessed by his granddaughter Barbara. A late-in-life conversion also provides a useful context for understanding Slingsby's decision to bequeath his Catholic devotional book to his daughter. In *A Father's Legacy*, which Slingsby likely composed for publication, he does not comment upon the specifics of his faith, urging his sons only to avoid "novellisme," "whose pernicious seed has spread so many dangerous Sects, Schismes, and Heresies."[22] In contrast, when Slingsby sent his Catholic devotional book to his daughter from the scaffold, he was entrusting to her a "legacie" that ensured her recognition of his status as a loyal follower of the King and a committed Catholic.

A Maternal Inheritance

We know that Barbara Talbot was catechized and taught to read by her mother before she was five years old. In 1638, Henry Slingsby described his wife, Barbara Bellasis Slingsby, as "very tender and careful over her children having yet but two and now with child; she has so taught her daughter Barbara, who was born the 14th of May in year 1633 that she is able already to say all her prayers, answer to her catechisme, read and wright a little."[23] Like the accounts of childhood catechesis examined in Chapter 1, this narrative represents domestic catechesis as the responsibility of the mother and links it with learning to read and write. We know that Talbot valued her mother's catechetical education, since she purposefully inserts the catechism in a list of things required to be known by every Christian in her transcription of her father's devotional manual. When, in *A Father's Legacy*, Henry Slingsby mentions Barbara, he associates her with her mother and the family tradition of female piety, urging his sons Tom and Harry to "Return my blessing to your sister my dear Bab: and tell her from her dying father, that she needs no other example than her vertuous Mother for her directory: in whose steps, I am confident, she will walk religiously. Her modesty and blameless demean can promise nothing less."[24]

Unfortunately, Barbara Bellasis Slingsby died only three years after catechizing her daughter. Slingsby sent eight-year-old Barbara to live with her mother's brother, John Bellasis, at Coxwold, part of the Newborough Priory estate. John Bellasis was a committed Catholic who would subsequently be imprisoned upon the (false) accusation of Titus Oates that he was the leader of a nascent Catholic army.[25] (Slingsby sent his son Thomas to live with his sister, Mary Bethell, attesting a gendered affiliation pattern in which sons associate with the paternal line and daughters with the maternal.)[26] Talbot spent much of her adolescence at the Bellasis family home. Although Talbot's grandmother, aunt, and uncle were practicing Catholics, the family were not rigid dogmatists: Talbot's first cousin, Thomas Bellasis, was Protestant and, as we have seen, married Cromwell's daughter. The Bellasis family was in this sense representative of the educated, Northern elite – a religiously mixed family in which relations between Catholics and Protestants were characterized by toleration.

While resident at Newborough Priory, Talbot would almost certainly have continued her catechetical education. She would also have been likely to participate in coterie manuscript circulation, for the women of the Bellasis family were learned, cosmopolitan women. Talbot's maternal grandmother was born into the Cholmley family, well-known recusants and manuscript compilers in Yorkshire;[27] Talbot's aunt, Margaret Bellasis, may have had a scribal manuscript prepared for her which included poems by Donne, Jonson, and Corbett, as well as erotic verse by Nashe.[28] In Jerome de Groot's words, the available evidence suggests that the Bellasis family was part of "an educated and cosmopolitan Yorkshire community, interested in manuscripts, learning, and communication, with a relatively forward-thinking set of matriarchs."[29]

We can get a sense of the intellectual and literary sophistication that characterized Talbot's adolescence by looking at a collection of French exercises composed by Barbara Talbot in 1642 when she was living at Newborough Priory. In this manuscript, discovered by de Groot, the ten-year-old Barbara was asked by her tutor to respond to a series of wishful exclamations in French.

> Would to god thou wouldest love thy booke so well as thou doeth play
> But would to god the King should love me so well as thou lovest wine

I would we all should love that which we ought to love
And if I should love play more, what oughteth thou to care[30]

Once again, we see the importance placed upon a dialogic interchange in female domestic education. As in maternal catechesis, this conversational mode of instruction can be intellectually and linguistically demanding. The conversation focuses on Talbot's translation of the substantive or optative forms of the verb "to love" and the process of translating this verb demands that Talbot pay attention to the meaning of words and phrases – just as in catechetical exercise. Perhaps even more remarkable is the sense of verbal play and self-confidence that this excerpt conveys. The young Barbara first exclaims over her lack of royal favor, then proceeds to tease her tutor about his love of wine and gently reprimand him for criticizing her! From her mother (and her mother's family) Barbara Talbot inherited a thoroughgoing knowledge of Protestant doctrine and an appreciation for religious toleration, as well as intellectual confidence and literary sophistication. She activated this maternal inheritance in her transcription of her late father's Catholic devotional book.

The Key of Paradise

As we have seen, HM 43213 was a recast version of *The Key of Paradise*, a devotional manual compiled and published by John Wilson, a Jesuit priest and director of the Catholic Press at St. Omer.[31] Wilson was an early advocate of the usefulness of print in the Catholic mission to England, remarking in a letter to Henry Garnet, S.J.: "Books penetrate where the priest and religious cannot enter and serve as precursors to undeceive many."[32] Wilson saw his publications and editorial activities as a conservative response to the impact of the English Reformation on traditional devotional practices. "I do not here offer unto you," he reminds his readers, "any new thing ... Only this that I have heere gathered together and restored unto you againe that which the injury of tymes had violently taken from you and sought to abolish all memory thereof."[33] *The Key* was conceived as a primer for English Catholics who were "young beginners in virtue." Like the *Primer* and the Catholic *Manual*, it contained established Catholic prayers as "The Lord's Prayer" and "An Examination of Conscience."[34]

The Key also included productions of Spanish and Italian spirituality, such as *A Dialogue Concerning Contrition and Attrition* and *A Dialogue Concerning Contemplation or Mental Prayer*. The popularity of *The Key* can probably be explained in part by its collection of Italian and Spanish spirituality for the use of English Catholics. Its 1675 edition contained the following sequence of fifteen texts, as well as other offices and prayers:

> A Daily Exercise
> An Introduction to the Christian Faith
> The Beginning of the Gospel According to St. John
> A Godly Dialogue Concerning Contrition and Attrition
> An Act of Contrition
> A Dialogue of Meditation
> An Entertainment of the Good Thoughts
> A Brief Exhortation to the Often Frequenting of the Sacrament of Penance
> A Prayer to Be said Before We Go to Confession
> Instructions for Examining Our Conscience
> An Examen of Conscience
> A Shorter Method of Confession
> A Treatise of Indulgences
> A Brief Preparation for Receiving the Blessed Sacrament
> A Prayer After Receiving

To determine what Talbot considered to be "the best of itt," we can compare her transcription to the 1675 edition of *The Key of Paradise*. Talbot omits the first section, *A Daily Exercise*, and adopts the title of the second section, *An Introduction to the Christian Faith*, as the title for her manuscript as a whole. This section, containing basic prayers and serial listings of such concepts as "The Cardinal Works of Mercy," originates within late medieval piety, as does *The Key of Paradise's* inclusion of the opening verses of St. John's Gospel. These verses were, as Eamon Duffy observes, frequently included in printed Books of Hours.[35] In varied combinations, these texts also appear in other seventeenth-century Catholic devotional collections, such as Peter Canisius' *An Introduction to the Catholick Faith* and John Wilson's *The Treasury of Devotion*.[36] In her transcription, Talbot excises the "Angelical Salutation" or "Hail Mary," as well as numerical listings such as "Six Sins Against the Holy Ghost," "Four Sins Crying to Heaven for Vengeance," and "Three Evangelical Counsels (Voluntary Poverty, Perpetual Chastity, and Entire Obedience)." We can easily infer why Talbot excises these items: from a Protestant perspective, they either venerate Mary, or focus too much on categorizing sin and privileging the cloistered life.

It is surprising how much of her father's Catholic text Talbot retains. This first section of *The Key of Paradise* contains twenty-one items; Talbot includes (in some form) all but five of these, or approximately 77 percent. She includes its listings of the "Cardinal Virtues," "The Fruits of the Holy Ghost," "The Eight Beatitudes" and the "Spiritual Works of Mercy," as well as its selection from the Gospel of John. In her Protestant text, just like *The Key of Paradise*, the devout believer is urged to the following "Corporal Works of Mercy": (For ease of comparison, I have stricken through the phrases that Talbot excises and have set her substitute wording in boldface, a practice that I continue throughout this chapter.)[37]

> To feed the hungry
> To give drinke to the thirsty
> ~~To~~ harbour the ~~stranger~~ **harborless**
> To clothe the naked
> To visit the sicke ~~and those that be in prison~~
> To **visit the prisoners and** redeeme the captives
> To bury the dead[38]

Seventeenth-century Catholics and Protestants agreed that it was good to do such works of mercy; they disagreed only over their efficacy with regard to one's salvation. That Talbot, a Church of England loyalist, is able to include three-fourths of her father's Catholic devotional text suggests a fairly extensive common ground between Catholics and Church of England Protestants in the late seventeenth century.

Most interesting are those items that Talbot keeps, but changes to reflect her Protestant faith. *The Key of Paradise* lists the "Ten Commandments," then "The Seven Sacraments of the Catholic Church: Baptisme, Confirmation, the Eucharist, Pennance, Extreme Unction, Order, and Matrimony." It follows immediately with the "The Theological Virtues." Talbot's text contains the same listings in the same order, changing only *The Key's* listing of "The Seven Sacraments" to "The 2 Sacrements," under which she writes "Baptisme and The Lord's Super." She leaves the other headings – "The Ten Commandments" and "The Theological Virtues" – intact. Talbot's changes to "The Precepts of the Church" are equally revealing. At first glance, one might assume that little of this list would be acceptable to a Church of England Protestant because it features such Catholic terminology as "festivall days of the Church," "sacred office of the Mass," and "fasting." But in fact she manages to include a substantial amount of the original text.

> To selebrate the appointed ~~festival days of the Church~~ **festivalls** in abstaining from servill ~~workes~~

Catholicism, Catechesis, and Coterie Circulation 127

> To here reverently ~~the sacred office of the mass on Sunday, and Holy-Days~~ praiers and sermons on Sundais and holy dais
> ~~To fast the lent, the four Ember weeks, and the Eves according to the custom of the church and Friday and Saturday to abstain from flesh.~~
> To confes thy sins ~~to an approved Priest~~ and receive the ~~Holy Eucharist at the feast of Easter: and to do these things, at least, once in the year.~~ holy sacrament at att least thrice a yeare
> Not to ~~solemenize~~ selebrate maryage ~~on the days~~ in times forbiden by the church.[39]

Talbot's alterations reveal her keen awareness of religious differences: she appropriately cuts the third precept, concerning fasting, entirely, because it does not accord with Church of England doctrine. She also cuts the insistence that one confess "to a priest" and increases the number of times that one should receive the holy sacrament from once a year to three. But I am more interested in how much of her father's text Talbot retains: "festival days" becomes "festivalls," "the sacred office of the mass" transforms to "praiers and sermons," "holy Eucharist" to "holy sacrement," "solemnize" becomes "selebrate." Yet the list, "Precepts of the Church," remains.

When we turn to Talbot's transcription of the prose texts and dialogues in *The Key of Paradise*, we can see how she drew upon the doctrinal lessons provided by childhood catechesis when adapting her source. For example, when she transcribes the title "Instructions for examining our Conscience and for Confession," Talbot omits "and for Confession."[40] She includes, however, an account of the Catholic mission to Japan, presumably because it reflects historical fact. She alters the wording in a description of a Japanese convert's joy at receiving absolution; her source text reads, "By the effect of the sacrament which he greatly admired," but she reads, "by the efect of this practis which hee greatly admired."[41] She omits entirely (without comment) *The Key's* twenty-page *A Treatise of Indulgences* and silently replaces an overtly Catholic "Act of Contrition" with an orthodox Protestant version. Underpinning all of Talbot's redactions is her appreciation of the doctrinal differences between Catholicism and Protestantism – which, I would suggest, Talbot developed in part from her maternal catechetical training and in part from her experience of growing up in a family that included Catholics and Protestants.

This appreciation is evident in Talbot's alterations to *The Examination of Conscience Upon the Ten Commandments*. *The ABC with the Catechism*, the most popular early modern catechism, stipulates that one should examine one's conscience before receiving the Lord's Supper, so Talbot was not obligated to reject this text, which was included in multiple Catholic devotional works throughout the seventeenth century. *The Examination of Conscience* is structured as preparation for the sacrament of penance. Under "the first commandment; that is, of honouring God above all things," the believer is urged to ask himself the following questions.

~~Of the First Commandment: Of honouring God above all things.~~

The First
Concerning faith: if he hath beleeved ~~whatsover~~ the doctrin of the holy ~~Roman~~ catholicke church ~~believes~~; or ~~to~~ on the contrary hath had any erronious ~~opinions~~ or ~~with words or exterior signs has~~ made shew of ~~any~~ Heresie, or Infidelity, ~~or committed~~ in committing any act contrary to the true honor and adoration of God.
    2 If he hath been over-curious in searching into ~~matters~~ the misteries of faith ~~measuring them with humane reason.~~ or douting of any artickle thereof.
    ~~3 if he hath read or kept Books, either written by Heretics, or for any other respect, forbidden by the Church.~~
    4 If he hath learned the praiers ~~and other necessary things, which~~ and caticism that every Christian is bound to ~~know~~ learne ~~as are~~ and the Commandments and the principal misteries of our faith.[42]

Talbot signals her appreciation for a Church of England "middle way": she cuts, for example, the phrase "measuring them with human reason" as well as the prohibition on keeping books "forbidden by the Church." Talbot also consistently deletes any passage that reflects what she considers Popish prescriptivism. At the same time, she reflects the importance of catechesis within Protestantism – and perhaps her own experience – by inserting the "caticism" among the works that "every Christian is bound to learne."

Talbot's text includes two works closely associated with post-Tridentine Catholicism: *A Godly Dialogue Between Contrition and Attrition* and *A Dialogue of Mental Prayer*. The scholastic distinction between contrition and attrition was rejected by early Protestant reformers because they considered it a product of a theology of works. Luther derisively described attrition as "gallows sorrow."[43] The distinction took on increasing importance after the Council of Trent, where Catholic theologians encouraged the development of the position that attrition alone was a "sufficient disposition for the forgiveness of sins in the sacrament."[44] Protestant theologians unanimously rejected this determination, both because it emphasized the sacramental efficacy of confession and because it could be construed as downplaying the importance of grace. The Protestant theologian Jeremy Taylor's dismissal of the Tridentine determination is representative: "From these premises it follows, that if the priest can absolve him that is attrite, he may pardon him who hath affections to sin still remaining; that is, one who fears hell, but does not love God."[45]

Talbot's alterations to *A Godly Dialogue Between Contrition and Attrition* reflect both the complexity of the subject and her developed understanding of the theological issues at stake. While she accepts the traditional Catholic distinction between contrition and attrition, arguably on grounds of its pastoral utility, she denies both that confession is a sacrament and that it is efficacious in producing true contrition.

> ~~DEMANDE~~ / Q: if one should confesse himselfe ~~actually and Sacramentally~~ sincerely and receive the blessed sacrament with Atrition ~~alone~~, only, should not hee obtaine pardon of his sins and ~~should he~~ be putt therby into the grace of god againe?
>
> ~~ANSWERE~~ / A. Yes, by the vertue of **repentance and** the sacrament, the siner of Attrite becomes contrite, and therfore ~~among other reasons~~ it imports much to ~~go often for confession~~ confes and repent oftne ~~for as much as what Attrition cannot effect it self, it effecteth by the virtue of the sacrament of confession~~ that you may bring your selfe to perfitt contrition.[46]

Talbot first alters her source's "actually and sacramentally" to "sincerely and receive the blessed sacrament," thus shifting the referent "sacramentally" from confession (not a sacrament in the Church of England) to the Lord's Supper (a sacrament in the Church of England.) She also adds language affirming the importance of "repentance" in confessing one's sins – reflecting doctrine presented in basic catechesis. Talbot's alterations thus emphasize confession and self-examination – penitential practices shared by both Protestants and Catholics.

Perhaps drawing upon her maternal catechetical training, Talbot reformats *A Godly Dialogue* to makes it resemble a Protestant catechism. Its title, as given in *The Key*, reads *A Godly Dialogue Between Contrition and Attrition*. Talbot changes the title to *A Dialogue Concerning Contrition and Attrition*. The small change is significant. Although in the early sixteenth century the distinction between the genres of dialogue and catechism was unclear, Ian Green contends that by the 1570s "there is a case for a measure of separation, with the term dialogue being reserved for those instructive or disputatious works of the type which had been used in the middle ages . . . to impart information or ideas in an engaging manner to those who could read."[47] No longer does the title lead the reader to expect a conversation between personified abstractions, a genre characteristic of early sixteenth-century Catholic practice; instead, it signals an exchange between two speakers on matters of religion – in short, a catechism. As presented in *The Key of Paradise*, *A Dialogue Between Contrition and Attrition* employs the question-and-answer format marking the two sides with the words "Demand and Answer." Talbot, for her part, uses the identifiers "question" and "answer" and imposes catechetical formatting by using the abbreviations "Q" and "A" in her left margin to denote them after a few pages – a paratextual feature we recognize as common to Protestant print catechisms. The earliest published edition of the *ABC with the Catechism* employs this format, as does the catechism included in the 1633 edition of *The Book of Common Prayer*.

Talbot encountered greater difficulty in adapting *A Dialogue of Mental Prayer*, a treatise on four kinds: natural, doctrinal, supernatural, and mixed. Talbot includes only the first two. She transcribes *A Dialogue's* presentation of the second type of prayer almost verbatim. Doctrinal prayer directs the believer to contemplate an event in Christ's life or death and "ponder" the following:

> As if you **If I** should weigh in the balance the labours of this life with the everlasting joyes of heaven, the eternall paines of hell with the momentary pleasures of sin, the favor of God or his anger, with the frindshipe or ofence of a mortall prince, the noble and everlasting riches prepared for **of** my soule with the transitory pleasures **commodities** of any **my** body or trifles of the world.[48]

The emphases of this passage are recognizably Catholic in the devaluation of the body and the world. But significantly, there is nothing in this passage that counters Protestant doctrine. So Talbot largely retains it.

Talbot's redactions to *A Dialogue's* presentation of "natural prayer" are more extensive. Natural prayer is

> to think upon some good things and to speak to God by that occasion; **for that occation** you may helpe your selfe with some spiritual **good** booke, as the following *Of Christ* by T. A kempis or the like For example, I read a sentence or too or more till I find something that moves my soul to affection. For God speaks to us by all his creatures. but especially by **his word** by good books. Then, I shutt my **the** booke and thinke upon that which **what** I **you** have read as long, or longer than I have been reading: as when a friend, or any person of respect speaks to me, I **and** consider with attention what hee saith.[49]

That Talbot replaces *The Key's* reference to Thomas à Kempis' *Life of Christ* with one to the Bible is not surprising. But she also eliminates her source text's suggestion that one might relate to that (non-scriptural) book as one might relate to a friend. Talbot makes this alteration presumably because she has changed the referent. These excisions reflect Talbot's theological understanding: Church of England Protestants held to *sola scriptura* (the Bible as the sole authority in matters of faith) at the same time that they recognized that devotional reading could deepen one's faith life.

By transcribing selectively and recasting portions of *The Key of Paradise*, Talbot emulates the literate activity of male Protestant writers and clergymen. In his study of the Protestant minister Edmund Bunny's redaction of Robert Parsons' *Christian Exercises*, Brad Gregory affirms the two authors shared a commitment to "rigorous religion," concluding that "Bunny could identify and strip away a Catholic veneer from Parson's treatise while retaining its world view and imperatives for Christian conduct."[50] The comparison to Talbot's recasting is not exact; *The Key* was intended as an introduction to the Catholic faith and so devotes more attention to Catholic doctrine than Parson's text does. But Talbot's reworkings suggest that Catholicism and Prayer Book Protestantism share a belief in the need for personal repentance, the importance of self-examination, and the value of both doctrinal and natural prayer. Although they differ in the number of sacraments they allow and in their understanding of these sacraments, both strains of Christianity recognize the centrality of the Lord's Supper and Baptism. Talbot's text thus offers a powerful attestation of the shared beliefs and practices of Protestants and Catholics in late seventeenth-century England.

The Last Legacie

Why did Talbot decide to recast her late father's Catholic devotional manual in 1686/7? James II, a Catholic convert, had ascended to the English throne in 1685. Unlike his brother Charles II, who converted to Catholicism immediately before his death, James II openly practiced his faith. James' conversion, remarks Steven Pincus, "was deeply felt and well informed."[51] The evident sincerity of his religious convictions initially made the King sympathetic to high-ranking Tories who admired his refusal to equivocate concerning his beliefs. Soon after his accession, however, James II's authority was challenged by a rebellion in which Charles, Duke of Monmouth (the illegitimate son of Charles II) attempted to raise an armed force against his uncle. The rebellion was quickly put down, and James II took advantage of the popular support it engendered to relax restrictions on English Catholics.[52] One of James II's early actions was to appoint John Bellasis, Talbot's maternal uncle (and surrogate father), to a commission to safeguard Catholic interests. James II subsequently appointed Bellasis to the Privy Council and eventually made him the first Lord High Commissioner of the Treasury. These promotions occasioned considerable public debate: James had elevated a Catholic to the third highest position in the realm. Pincus observes that revisionist historians like Mark Goldie and Tim Harris suggest that the revolution of 1688 was partly a consequence of the growing dissatisfaction among Anglican-Tories with James II's pro-Catholic political and religious agenda.[53]

We know that Talbot and her husband actively supported James II in the aftermath of the Monmouth rebellion. Barbara Talbot had married her husband Sir John Talbot (1630–1714) in 1660; the portrait by the school of Peter Lely may have been painted in honor of their engagement. Like his father-in-law, John Talbot was a staunch Royalist who was known for his "evident sincerity and the consistency of his political convictions." He was also a conforming member of the Church of England, described by a French ambassador as "Protestant but very Royalist." Talbot raised a regiment of horse in support of the King and camped with the King at Hounslow Heath in September of 1685. Talbot was subsequently named Colonel of the Queen Dowager's Regiment of the Horse and was a steady supporter of the monarch until James II's defeat, at which point John Talbot retired from political life.[54]

It is possible that by circulating a revised copy of her late father's devotional manual, Slingsby Talbot sought to counter claims that Henry Slingsby was a Catholic convert. We have seen that she consistently excises evidence of *The Key's* Catholicism. A reader who was unaware that her manuscript was a transcription of a Catholic text could assume that it was a Protestant devotional manual and thus conclude that Slingsby was a Church of England loyalist. When considered in this context, her manuscript attests to her paternal legacy of royalism and Church of England loyalism. Underscoring her own Protestant conformity, it contrasts her paternal legacy with her maternal Uncle's Catholicism.

But there is another interpretation of Talbot's motivations for revising her late father's manual: Talbot copied and circulated her reworked version of her late father's Catholic devotional manual in order to advocate for inter-confessional concord. I find this interpretation, which assumes that most readers would have recognized her father's book as Catholic, slightly more persuasive, in part because it takes into account Talbot's observation that the original manual did not fully conform to Protestant doctrine, and in part because it acknowledges the lived experience of so many religiously mixed Northern families. Talbot remarks upon her motivations in her preface:

> And whereas some things in itt are contrary to the faith and Doctrien of the church of Ingland (which I profes) and by the grace of god alwais intend to doe, therefore I have transcrib'd the best of itt not only because I thinke itt very pious and usefull but principlely to presarve in memorie the last Legacie he left mee.[55]

Identifying herself as a "profess [ing]" member of the Church of England, Talbot insists that she nonetheless finds her father's devotional book "very pious and usefull." This is qualified approbation, to be sure. But it lodges forceful implications concerning relations between Protestants and Catholics in late seventeenth-century England. Talbot reaches across confessional boundaries to acknowledge the piety and utility of other faith traditions, just as her revisions to her father's devotional manual underscore the considerable doctrinal and devotional ground they share.

When considered in this light, Talbot's manuscript constitutes a valuable contribution to the ongoing public discussion concerning English Catholicism in late seventeenth-century England.[56] Mark Knights has ably documented the contours of this public discussion in print.[57] But as I have argued in my introduction, manuscript circulation was a vibrant medium for the dissemination of ideas in this period, especially among women. Aware of the cultural importance of manuscript circulation, especially among the Northern gentry, we need to see HM 43213 as more than a "transcribed," "personal catechism": it is a contribution to the public debate concerning the toleration of English Catholics in late seventeenth-century England.

Conclusion

Scholars have been slow to recognize Talbot's contribution to the contemporary political debate concerning English Catholics, in part because her work has been characterized as a "personal catechism" and "transcription," and in part because she circulated her work in manuscript. That Talbot, a wealthy gentlewoman, wife, and mother, might want to avoid what has been called the "social stigma" of print would not be surprising. But an even more compelling reason for Talbot's decision to compose in manuscript can be found in her sense of audience: she wrote primarily to Yorkshire Royalist men and women like herself, who would likely have been familiar with her father's reputation as a committed Royalist and perhaps aware of the rumors of his conversion. Manuscript composition, which sought to address a select, coterie readership, was perhaps the most effective way to reach such an audience.

At the same time, the non-public character of manuscript circulation is perhaps the biggest obstacle to an understanding of its social and literary importance in early modern England. To grasp what Talbot was doing when she circulated her version of her late father's Catholic devotional book in 1686/7, I reconstructed much of her family history, especially the popular perceptions of Henry Slingsby's Catholicism. At the same time, I needed to locate Talbot's circulation of her manuscript within the contemporary political climate. To understand the political import of women's manuscript circulation, then, requires considerable knowledge of what has been termed "local" or "micro" history.

Talbot's manuscript suggests the continuing importance of Catholic devotional works from the 1620s and 1630s in late seventeenth-century England. Put in slightly different terms, Catholic devotional works seem to have had a long shelf life; they were read differently by members of the same family (or community) at specific historical moments. When Henry Slingsby sent his Catholic devotional book to his daughter immediately prior to his execution, he intended it to be a textual witness of his religious devotion and personal integrity. Talbot's reworking of her father's book, approximately twenty-eight years later, suggests how she interpreted her father's "legacie" in the context of contemporary religious and political debates. Tracing the permutations of Catholic books within the context of a single family provides insight into the shifting status of Catholicism throughout the seventeenth century.

Notes

1. The location of the portrait of Barbara Bellasis Slingsby is presently unknown. It was previously held in the Wombwell Family Collection in Newborough Priory; a copy is included in Geoffrey Ridsdill Smith, *Without Touch of Dishonour: The Life and Death of Henry Slingsby, 1602–1658* (Kineton: The Roundwood Press, 1968), 29. The portraits of Barbara Talbot, her daughters Barbara and Gilberta, and her granddaughter are held by The National Trust, Lacock Abbey, Fox Talbot Museum and Village. Barbara Slingsby Talbot's granddaughter wears a red dress but not pearls. These portraits can be viewed online: www.bbc.co.uk/arts/yourpaintings.
2. Talbot, "Preface," HM 43213, n.p. Huntington Library, San Marino, California.

3. Slingsby's biographers include Daniel Parsons, "Preface," in *The Diary of Sir Henry Slingsby, of Scriven, Bart* (London, 1836), v–xxiii. Parson's edition also includes an account of Sir Henry Slingsby's trial, a copy of Slingsby's "A Father's Legacy" and extracts from family correspondence and papers. Ridsdill Smith, *Without Touch Of Dishonour*; David Scott, "Slingsby, Sir Henry, First Baronet (1602–1658)," in *Oxford Dictionary of National Biography* (Oxford: Oxford University Press, 2004): www.oxforddnb.com.ezproxy.depaul.edu/view/article/25727.
4. *The Guide to British Historical Manuscripts in the Huntington Library* (San Marino, California: Huntington Library and Art Gallery, 1982), 355.
5. Jaime Goodrich, *Faithful Translators: Authorship, Gender, and Religion in Early Modern England* (Evanston, IL: Northwestern University Press, 2013), 186, 192. I adopt the term "polyvocality" from Goodrich, 192, who observes "translation and other so-called derivative forms of authorship were at times attractive to early modern writers because of their polyvocality." Her chapter on the translations of Margaret Roper and Mary Basset, daughter and granddaughter of Thomas More, offers a useful prototype for my argument.
6. Talbot, "Preface," HM 43213, n.p.
7. Ridsdill Smith, *Without Touch*, 33, 55.
8. Ridsdill Smith, *Without Touch*, 76–82, 135–39.
9. Ridsdill Smith, *Without Touch*, 159–60.
10. In 1968, Brigadier Peter Young remarked of Ridsdill Smith's biography that "after reading these pages we see Sir Henry Slingsby as he really was, a man whose actions sprang from Conscience, Loyalty, and Honor." "Introduction," in *Without Touch of Dishonor*, xvii–xviii.
11. Henry Slingsby, *A Father's Legacy* (York, 1706), in Parsons, *The Diary of Sir Henry Slingsby, of Scriven, Bart*, 210–11.
12. Scott, "Slingsby, Sir Henry"; Parsons, *The Diary of Sir Henry Slingsby, of Scriven, Bart*, 20.
13. Scott, "Slingsby, Sir Henry." Ridsdill Smith, *Without Touch*, 43, refers bluntly to Slingsby's "Puritanical leanings."
14. Roger Castlemaine, *To All the Royalists that Suffered for His Majesty, and to the Rest of the Good People of England the Humble Apology of English Catholics* (London, 1666), Sig. B3r; D. P. "Priory of Robert Knaresborough and Sir Henry Slingsby," *Notes and Queries* SXI (Jan 19, 1867): 53–4, 54. Thomas Blount, *Kalendarium Catholicum for the Year 1686* (London, 1686), Sig. B6v.
15. Mark Noble, *Memoirs of the Protectoral House of Cromwell* (London, 1787), 2:394. Dodd is quoted in F. C. H., "Sir Henry Slingsby," *Notes and Queries* SXI (March 2, 1867): 183. Steven Pincus comments favorably upon Dodd's accuracy as a historian, noting that he, a Catholic, had access to "a range of Catholic manuscripts that are no longer extant." *1688: The First Modern Revolution* (New Haven: Yale University Press, 2009), 126.
16. F. C. H., "Sir Henry Slingsby," 183.
17. On recusant families in Yorkshire, see Alexandra Walsham, *Church Papists: Catholicism, Conformity, and Confessional Polemic in Early Modern England*

(Woodbridge: Boydell and Brewer, 1999), 76–81. Slingsby's theological knowledge is evident, for example, in his brief discussion of the lack of a need for priestly absolution in *The Diary of Sir Henry Slingsby*, 9–10.
18. On Slingsby's nomination to the committee for "the disarming of Popish recusants," see Parsons, "Preface," in *The Diary of Sir Henry Slingsby*, ix; also, Scott, "Sir Henry Slingsby."
19. D. P. "Priory of Robert Knaresborough and Sir Henry Slingsby," 54.
20. Peter Lake and Michael Questier, "Prisons, Priests, and People," in *England's Long Reformation 1500–1800*, ed. Nicholas Tyacke (London: University College London Press, 1998), 195–235.
21. Henry Foley, S.J., *Records of the English Province of the Society of Jesus*, Vol. 3 (London: Burns & Oates, 1878), 187, 189.
22. Slingsby, *A Father's Legacy*, in *The Diary of Henry Slingsby*, 203.
23. *The Diary of Sir Henry Slingsby*, 3.
24. Slingsby, *A Father's Legacy*, 218.
25. Andrew J. Hopper, "Belasyse, John, first Baron Belasyse of Worlaby," in *The Oxford Dictionary of National Biography* (Oxford: Oxford University Press, 2004): www.oxforddnb.com.ezproxy.depaul.edu/view/article/1977.
26. Ridsdill Smith, *Without Touch*, 61.
27. On the Chomley family commonplace book, see Jerome de Groot, "Coteries, Complications, and the Question of Female Agency," in *The 1630's: Interdisciplinary Essays on Culture and Politics in the Caroline Era*, ed. Ian Atherton and Julie Sanders (Manchester, Manchester University Press, 2006), 189–209, 196.
28. Jerome de Groot, "Every One Teacheth After Thyr Own Fantasie," in *Performing Pedagogy in Early Modern England*, ed. Kathryn Moncrief and Kathryn McPherson (Aldershot: Ashgate, 2011), 33–52.
29. de Groot, "Every One Teacheth," 40.
30. Quoted in de Groot, "Every One Teacheth," 43.
31. I have consulted the 1623 edition of *The Key of Paradise*, held by the Library of Mount Stuart Rothesay, in facsimile: *The Key of Paradise*, in *English Recusant Literature, 1558–1640*, Vol. 394 (Ilkley: Scolar Press, 1979). I quote from a 1675 edition, held by the Bodleian, *The Key of Paradise* (St. Omer, 1675), Early English Books Online (944:08). J. M. Blom remarks that subsequent editions had generally the same formatting as earlier editions. *The Post-Tridentine English Primer* (The Netherlands: Catholic Record Society, 1982), 139. I note, however, that a 1681 edition, published in Paris and advertised as "the last edition, most correct," differs somewhat. *The Key of Paradise* (Paris, 1681), Early English Books Online (1912:04). Slingsby Talbot's transcription most closely follows the 1675 edition.
32. Quoted in Alexander Walsham, "Domme Preachers: Post-Reformation Catholicism and the Culture of Print," *Past and Present* 168.1 (2000): 72–123, 102.
33. John Wilson, *The English Martryologe* (St. Omer, 1608), Sig. 3v.

34. Blom, *The Post-Tridentine English Primer*, 139, 142.
35. Eamon Duffy, *Marking the Hours* (New Haven: Yale University Press, 2006), 133.
36. Peter Canisius, *An Introduction to the Catholick Faith* (1633), in *English Recusant Literature, 1558–1640*, Vol. 134 (Ilkley: Scolar Press, 1973). John Wilson, *The Treasury of Devotion* (1622), in *English Recusant Literature, 1558–1640*, Vol. 346 (Ilkley: Scolar Press, 1977).
37. Slingsby Talbot's spelling differs from that of *The Key of Paradise*. I reproduce her spelling in the excerpts that I include in my text, with the exception of the excised words and phrases which (necessarily) reproduce the spelling of *The Key*.
38. *The Key*, 97–8; Talbot, HM 43213, 85–6.
39. *The Key*, 13–14; Talbot, HM 43213, 7.
40. *The Key*, 84; Talbot, HM 43213, 77.
41. *The Key*, 92; Talbot, HM 43213, 83.
42. *The Key*, 97–8; Talbot, HM 43213, 85–6.
43. Thomas Tentler, *Sin and Confession on the Eve of the Reformation* (Princeton: Princeton University Press, 1977), 351.
44. P. de Letter, "Two Concepts of Attrition and Contrition," *Theological Studies* (March, 1950): 3–33, 14.
45. Jeremy Taylor, *Unum Necessarium: or the Doctrine and Practice of Repentance* (London, 1655), 638.
46. *The Key*, 24–25; Talbot, HM 43213, 16–17.
47. Green, *The Christian's ABC*, 54.
48. *The Key*, 59; Talbot, HM 43213, 54.
49. *The Key*, 57; Talbot, HM 43213, 50–1.
50. Brad S. Gregory, "The True and Zealous Service of God: Robert Parsons, Edmund Bunny, and *The First Book of Christian Exercises*," *The Journal of Ecclesiastical History*, 45.2 (April, 1994): 238–68. Such devotional hybrids were not uncommon in seventeenth-century England. Alexandra Walsham observes that Francis Meres and Thomas Lodge adapted the works of Luis de Granada for a Protestant readership and that Christopher Sutton, canon of Westminster, produced an excised version of Henry Garnet's translation of Luca Pinelli's *Meditationi Brevi Del Santissimo Sacramento*, "Domme Preachers," 105–6. See also, Susannah Monta, "Uncommon Prayer? Robert Southwell's *Short Rule for a Good Life* and Catholic Domestic Devotion in Post-Reformation England," in *Redrawing the Map of Early Modern English Catholicism*, ed. Lowell Gallagher (Toronto: University of Toronto Press, 2012), 245–72.
51. Steven Pincus, *1688: The First Modern Revolution* (New Haven: Yale University Press, 2009), 122.
52. J. R. Western, *Monarchy and Revolution: The English State in the 1680's* (New Jersey: Rowan and Littlefield, 1972), 203.
53. Pincus, *1688: The First Modern Revolution*, 121.

54. "Talbot, John (1630–1714)," in *The History of Parliament: the House of Commons 1660–1690*, ed. B.D. Henning (Suffolk: Boydell and Brewer, 1983): www.historyofparliamentonline.org.
55. Talbot, "Preface," HM 43213, n.p.
56. Talbot dates her preface 2 Feb, 1686 (Feb 12, 1687 [New Style]) – the same day that James II published his *Declaration of Toleration of English Catholics for Scotland*. She may have finished her transcription on this date or she may have appended the date subsequently. Regardless, by specifying this date, Talbot alerts readers to consider her text in the context of James II's public calls for the toleration of Catholics.
57. Mark Knights, *Representation and Misrepresentation in Later Stuart Britain: Partisanship and Political Culture* (Oxford: Oxford University Press, 2005), 223–37.

PART III

Print and Polemic

In Part III we turn from women's manuscript compositions to their print publications. Chapters 5 and 6 highlight two mid-seventeenth-century women who drew upon the catechism's association with pious womanhood to intervene in Civil War–era religious and political disputes. Dorothy Burch, studied in Chapter 5, composed a manuscript catechism to demonstrate her religious and scriptural knowledge to a dismissive minister; she subsequently printed it, arguably in order to engage in ongoing debates concerning Laudian reforms. In Chapter 6, we examine Mary Cary's creative use of the catechetical form in *The Resurrection of the Witnesses* (1648; 1653). Like Burch, Cary participated in evangelical strains of piety and engaged in seventeenth-century politics. But where Burch's catechism arose from a local religious dispute, Mary Cary sought to intervene in broader Civil War debates. Unlike Burch, who composed a doctrinally orthodox catechism, Cary used the catechetical form to anchor her radical scriptural exegesis of Revelation 11:1–14 in which she predicts the success of Cromwell's New Model Army. As we will see, Cary activates the power and authority accorded to women as domestic and maternal catechists to energize her radically communitarian vision of Christian community.

CHAPTER 5

"A Knowing People"
Catechesis and Community in Dorothy Burch's A Catechisme of the Severall Heads of the Christian Religion *(1646)*

> At sermons, and Prayers men may sleep or wander;
> but when one is asked a question, he must discover what he is.
>
> George Herbert, *A Priest to the Temple* (1671)[1]

Introduction

In 1646, Dorothy Burch, a wife and mother living in a small village in Kent, published an instructional work designed to teach children the basic principles of the Protestant faith. She titled it *A Catechisme of the Severall Heads of the Christian Religion* and dedicated it to her children, "whose good," she wrote, "I must and will consider as my own."[2] Burch's catechism was not an early modern best seller: only one edition was published, and the work and its author faded from public view. Scholarship on early modern women authors has similarly overlooked her life and authorship: there are few critical assessments of her life or work, and she is not included in any of the recently published anthologies of early modern women writers.[3]

Up to this point in the present study, we have considered women of varied social classes who compiled original catechisms in manuscript. In this chapter, we turn our attention to the factors that encouraged Burch to publish her catechism. While there are some crucial exceptions, most early modern women writers who published their work were gentlewomen whose status enabled them to transcend the societal restrictions placed on female authorship.[4] Alternatively, they were separatists whose dissenting religious beliefs impelled them into print.[5] In contrast, Dorothy Burch belonged to neither category. In all likelihood, she was the wife of a tradesman or shopkeeper.[6] The publication of Burch's catechism thus bears out Nigel Smith's claim that the expansion of print culture during the Civil War created new publishing opportunities for non-aristocratic authors and women.[7] But Burch differs from most of these in her refusal of separatism. While her catechism certainly evinces the "hotter sort of piety" that Patrick Collinson calls characteristic of early modern English Puritanism, it teaches an orthodox version of English Calvinism, emphasizing such intellectually complex but widely accepted premises as salvation by faith alone and the imputation of Christ's righteousness to the faithful.[8] Burch's authorship thus raises questions crucial to our understanding of both print culture and women's writing in early modern England: how did a godly, working-class wife and mother living far from London, England's literary and cultural center, come to publish a text of religious instruction?[9]

In addressing these questions, this chapter confirms recent work that points to the importance of local history in understanding the work of early modern English women writers. This, in turn, demands the consideration of archival and documentary sources to retrieve the religious and textual communities in which these female authors composed and circulated their works. Here, I utilize county histories, public records, taxation lists, and churchwardens' accounts to reconstruct the religious and literary milieu that supported the publication of *A Catechisme*. I demonstrate that Dorothy Burch was connected through her parish to the London and the international godly community. Burch's sense of participation within the larger evangelical Protestant cause and her commitment to her local community were crucial factors in her emergence as a published author.

I will also be arguing that Burch's authorship of a theological work highlights our need to attend more closely to dominant literary and cultural forms in early modern English women's writing. When Burch composed her catechism, she was working within a genre that, as we have seen, had come to be associated with mothers and mistresses of households through the domestication of pious instruction; in publishing her text, Burch was putting into print a form of literary activity that ordinary Protestant women practiced in their home.

As a final consideration, I will show that the publication of Burch's catechism is involved in the religious upheavals of the English Civil War, particularly the public controversy in Kent over Archbishop Laud's clerical appointments. From the critical perspective of Christopher Durston and Judith Maltby, "Although some historians have argued that the Laudians managed to achieve some degree of popularity for their programs, the bulk of the evidence supports the view that they failed effectively to reform the religious sensibilities of the grassroots."[10] We know that Laudian reforms were being actively debated within Kent in the early 1640s.[11] Burch published her catechism in part to provide a public witness of her – and her community's – religious knowledge and thus to counter Laudian claims of lay ignorance.[12] In differing from "top-down narratives" of the English Civil War, Burch's story confirms the importance of "history from below" in efforts to recover the lives of less prominent early modern Englishwomen.[13] Undergirding Burch's authorship, then, is a complex mix of factors: a tradition of maternal catechizing, an advantageous cultural location, an evangelical Protestant community, and the social upheaval caused by the English Civil War.

National and International Protestantism: Strood and St. Nicks

When Dorothy Burch composed her text, she was living with her husband and small children in Strood, a community of approximately two hundred people in Kent, a region with a longstanding tradition of religious nonconformity.[14] Strood was not, however, an isolated country village. It was located only one and a half miles from Rochester, a cathedral city and episcopal seat with a population between 1,000 and 2,000 residents in the sixteenth century.[15] Moreover, the "High London Road" ran through Strood, giving residents access to London, which was approximately thirty miles to the east. Church records indicate that Strood's residents not infrequently traveled to London to purchase supplies, meet with friends, or consult about church business.[16] Dorothy and Peter Burch lived in "the little Borough in Strood, along the main Watling street (now A2) and the heart of the village."[17]

Residents could also travel to London via the River Medway, an inland tributary that connects Kent with the Thames estuary. Peter Clark has conjectured that easy access to London by this means brought Strood an outbreak of the bubonic plague in the 1630s. To the east, the River Medway connected Strood's residents with the North Sea. A wharf located at the foot of the Rochester Bridge in the town allowed entrance to colliers, barges, and other seafaring vessels. Throughout much of its history, Strood's residents have worked on the sea.[18] Parish records recount visitors from Holland and the Spanish Netherlands as well as Ireland. Strood's location lent the small village an international flavor and exposed its residents to Dutch customs and theology. In Clark's words, "Close continental ties led to a number of small but quite important settlements of foreigners in the county, especially Dutch and Frenchmen and ... immigration of this sort remained an important ingredient in Kentish life right up to 1640."[19]

The parish church of Strood was St. Nicholas. Like most seventeenth-century village churches, it served as the focal point of community life: not only did it baptize, marry, and bury its parishioners, but it also provided villagers with poor relief and entertainment. Hasted describes St. Nicholas as a "spacious building, consisting of a nave and two aisles and the great chancel with a tower steeple at the west end, in which is a clock and six bells ... In the south aisle is a small stone chapel built in 1607 by the Morelands." Augustine Moreland, son of the chapel builders, was a contemporary of Peeter and Dorothy Burch and an acquaintance: their names frequently appear together on church documents.[20]

During much of the time that Peeter and Dorothy Burch lived in Strood, the vicar of St. Nicholas was Robert Chamberlaine (1615–39). Chamberlaine appears to have practiced an evangelical strain of piety. In 1629 he initiated a program of poor relief which stipulated that "all of the monies previously collected and variously disbursed to the poor would be laid out upon some parcel or parcels of land whereby some good may come and rebound to the uses of the poor of this parish." Margo Todd has noted that programs such as this were characteristic of sixteenth- and seventeenth-century evangelical piety.[21] During Chamberlaine's tenure, itinerant preachers were invited to preach at St. Nicholas. Such invitations indicate both the vibrancy of parish life and the parish's connections to the larger evangelical community.

Further evidence of these connections emerges in the various special collections undertaken at St. Nicholas to assist Calvinist churches overseas. In 1603 and again in 1626, the parish took up special collections to help their "suffering brethren" in Geneva and the Palatinate. These collections reveal a commitment to what Patrick Collinson terms the "cause of international Protestantism;" that is, a belief that the welfare of the Protestant church in England was inextricably linked to the welfare of the church on the Continent. The 1626 collection was initiated by a group of influential London ministers, including John Davenport of St. Stephen's Coleman Street, William Gouge of Blackfriars, Richard Sibbes of Gray's Inn, and Thomas Taylor, lecturer at St. Mary Aldermanbury. "In a circular letter," explains Collinson, "addressed to all Godly Christians, these ministers dramatized the plight of their Palatinate brethren who would be 'very thankful' for coarse bread and drink if they could get it." St. Nicholas' response indicates the type of piety practiced at the parish: Gouge and especially Sibbes were eloquent, inspirational preachers, who, while theologically conservative, emphasized the transforming power of divine love for mankind.²² Burch's catechism too reflects this piety, as I shall indicate in more detail subsequently.

Evangelical Protestantism and Literacy: Peeter and Dorothy Burch

We can place Peeter Burch in the vicinity of Strood as early as 1629, when he was one of twenty-three men who signed the July petition to purchase a plot of land for the poor of the parish to farm.²³ Peeter probably married Dorothy sometime before 1628, because baptismal records indicate the birth of a son, Anthony Burch, in 1628 to Peeter Burch in Birling, Kent, a small village eight miles from Strood. Baptismal records indicate the birth of another son, George Burch, to Peeter Burch in Leybourne, a village one mile from Birling, in 1630. By 1632, Dorothy and Peeter Burch were living in Strood. Parish records then indicate the birth of at least four more Burch children: Mary in 1632, Peeter in 1634, Elizabeth in 1636, and John in 1638.²⁴ Mary survived to adulthood, but Elizabeth died at age five and John at age six, while Anthony, George, and Peter's deaths are not recorded. It is possible that Peeter and Dorothy Burch had other children, but there are no records of this.

Peeter and Dorothy Burch appear to have been moderately successful: in a 1645 assessment inventory of uncollected taxes, he and his wife were taxed at three shillings – an amount that places them in the upper middle of village residents unable or unwilling to pay the tax.²⁵ The tax was collected "for the repair of the church and churchyard," but I suspect that this "repair" may have been a delayed implementation of High Church measures, since many of the men and women who are cited for not paying the tax played an active role in parish life during Chamberlaine's tenure. Furthermore, we know that in 1650, Peeter Burch came to the attention of the authorities for his attempt to collect four pounds lent to an acquaintance. The circumstances surrounding this loan are unclear, but at a minimum it suggests that Peeter and Dorothy Burch had enough disposable income to lend money to others.²⁶

Perhaps Peeter Burch's most remarkable characteristic is his ability to read and write. In the mid-seventeenth century, Strood's literacy rates (measured by the ability to sign one's name) seem to have been around 60 percent: a level significantly below that of London and other urban areas, but higher than the average for non-urban areas.²⁷ "We know," writes Watt, "that by the 1640s roughly 30 percent of adult males in rural England could sign their name, with up to 78 percent fully literate in

London." Strood's better-than-average literacy rate could have resulted from its location near Rochester. Cressy suggests, "The highest degree of literacy may not have been found in the towns themselves but in their satellite villages... [which], like modern suburbs, could enjoy the fruits of urban endeavor while avoiding the costs of urban blight."[28]

Extant historical records suggest that Peeter Burch was highly literate. At least in part because of this ability, he was chosen to serve as a churchwarden of St. Nicholas in 1639. Because the congregation made the choice, Burch's religious views were evidently shared by a majority of the members. Among the more than two hundred years of churchwardens' accounts for St. Nicholas parish, the vast majority of entries are little more than lists of money received and money spent. Here, Burch's record stands out, so much so that Henry Plomer, the early twentieth-century editor of St. Nicholas' churchwardens' accounts, characterizes it as "very interesting."[29] Peeter Burch's assured literacy emerges in the following record of what he has given "in relief of poor strangers and our own poor:"

Two soldiers whose hands were shot off And came from the Palatinate	6 d
One Edmond Piercy and his wife who said that they had lost 700 at sea	6 d
To Anne Allen and her two sonnes which had their house burned at Castle Ryson [Rising] in Norfolk	4 d
To Mary Williams and her small children which came from Holland and were to travel to Cornwall	6 d

The internationalism of this small village in Kent is immediately apparent. But imagination and empathy are also evident throughout this narrative: whether we look at Burch's description of his gift "to five Irish people who were taken by the turkes" or his account of "Amy Shaw and Katherine Hancocke of Pickle herring [in Southwark] who had their houses consumed with fire," we find a degree of expressiveness which exceeds a simple ability to sign one's name.[30] Although literate proficiency was most typically obtained through formal education, it could also be acquired through an intense knowledge of scripture: as a number of scholars have demonstrated, early modern Protestantism's emphasis upon individual knowledge of the Bible promoted a high rate of literacy among its more committed believers, both male and female.[31] When all of these particulars are taken into account, a picture begins to emerge of Peeter and Dorothy

Burch: in all likelihood, they were highly literate evangelical Protestants who were deeply involved in their parish church and village.

"A Knowing People"

We are fortunate to know a good deal about the circumstances surrounding the composition of Dorothy Burch's catechism, in large part thanks to the letter "To the Christian Reader" that prefaces her text. Burch explains that her decision to publish her catechism originated in a dispute over church practices in St. Nicholas parish. When Robert Chamberlaine died on June 1, 1639, he had been the pastor of St. Nicholas for over twenty years. He was replaced by John Mann, a High Church curate, as part of Laud's attempt to enforce religious conformity in the Kentish countryside. Not surprisingly, Mann was not well liked by St. Nicholas' evangelically minded parishioners. When he was removed from his benefice sometime between 1642 and 1644, he was accused of being "a common drunkard and frequenter of Alehouses and Taverns, drawing others to the same excesses with him, and . . . a common swearer by bloudy oathes, and useth to curse and is a common quarreler and fighter."[32] *The Churchwardens' Accounts* registers this change in leadership. Unlike Chamberlaine, who had been active in all aspects of parish life, from organizing poor relief to arranging for itinerant preachers, Mann seems to have kept to himself. As Plomer laconically remarks, "Mann's name does not appear much in these records."[33] During Mann's tenure, *The Churchwardens' Accounts* records only the most basic purchases: there is no indication that outside preachers were invited to speak, and organized poor relief, which had long been a feature of the parish, ceased.

Mann's arrival seems to have split the parishioners of St. Nicholas into opposing factions. Political differences may have underlied this schism: it is likely that the majority of St. Nicholas' parishioners would have identified with the Parliamentarians, whereas Mann was a High Church Royalist who is reported to have said that "he scorned Parliament."[34] During Mann's tenure, the names of several St. Nicholas parishioners, such as Philemon Ewes, John Chambers, Henry Allen, and Peeter Burch, no longer appear in *The Churchwardens' Accounts*, despite the active role that many of these men had played in parish life for nearly two decades. They reappear only in the 1650s, under Mann's replacement, Daniel French. The newer lay leadership appears to have been both less literate and less socially engaged: James Branford, who served as churchwarden during Mann's tenure, could only sign his name with a mark. This suggests that either he held the position in name only, since the ability to read and write was generally a prerequisite for the position, or that perhaps that he was capable with numbers but not with written words. This discrepancy would not have been uncommon among men who worked on the sea, whose profession required them to calculate navigation charts and keep account books, but not to read or write. Another man, Augusten Punnet, signified his approval of the accounts by sketching a "quite well drawn" anchor, providing yet another indication of Strood's longstanding association with the sea.[35]

Burch never identifies Mann by name in "To the Christian Reader." She does, however, offer a first-hand account of the conflict:

> But by reason that the Minister of the Parish where I live, because myself and others will not honour him in the way that he is in, albeit the way, he said, descended from Rome, yet he hath ever since in publicke and private, laboured to make me and others, odious in the eyes of the people, albeit formerly I was well accounted of him, yet now he reviles me and others almost where ever he comes.[36]

That Burch and her husband, along with other evangelically minded parishioners, would have rejected Mann's claims of Roman precedent is unsurprising. Clark describes the situation across Kent: "Lay anger was aroused not only by the new found aloofness and arrogance of Laudian clergy ... but by a feeling that while clerical pretension was on the increase, the ecclesiastical order was cutting back on its responsibilities and duties in the wider society." Doctrinal disputes seem to have been aggravated by class-based prejudices. As Smetham remarks, Mann's chief offense seems to have been his comment that "Parliament-men were not gentlemen of quality." Such prejudices reflect cultural divisions throughout the 1640s and 1650s between the (largely) aristocratic Royalists and the (largely) working- and middle-class Parliamentarians.[37] Burch seems to be as disturbed by Mann's remarks about the poverty and parochialism of Strood's oyster-dredgers and fishermen as she is by his theological views. Emphasizing her personal knowledge, Burch writes, "My selfe heard him say, that wee were poore, ignorant, simple people, and as concerning God wee knew nothing, (which thing I desire God to pardon in him)."[38] Mann's accusation was a common slur on lower-class evangelicals, but Burch's outrage is manifest: whatever else they were, she and her husband were committed Christians who possessed a thoroughgoing knowledge of scripture and the Protestant faith.

Burch draws upon this scriptural knowledge in crafting her catechism, which she conceives of as her defense against Mann's claims concerning her poverty and ignorance. Although she does not deny her poverty, Burch insists that scriptural truth is available to all believers, rich or poor, male or female. Such availability was a central tenet of early modern Protestant theology; Burch contends that it falsifies Mann's insults. The Lord, writes Burch, "hath promised to teach his with the teachings of his own Spirit, and will not let them be so ignorant, that they shall know nothing of him."[39] She cites Hebrews 8:10 as support: "For this is the Testament that I will make with the house of Israel, After those days Saith the Lord, I will put my Lawes in their minde, and in their heart I wil write them, and I will be their God and they shall be my people." Crucially, this passage represents God's promise to teach his people as a sign of his testament (or covenant) with them: it is precisely because they enjoy this unique relationship that the Israelites have knowledge of God's laws. Thus, when Mann claimed that the parishioners of St. Nicholas were "poor, ignorant, and simple people" who knew nothing about God, he attacked Burch's sense of herself and her community as committed Christians, "God's people."

Burch's "Letter" conveys her sense of herself as a spokeswoman for this small community of fishermen, oyster-dredgers, and mariners, the majority of whom would have been less literate than she was. She insists that she is not personally offended by Mann's remarks, which, she explains, "much grieved mee to heare, not in respect of my selfe, for I thinke my selfe not worthy to be one of them which he so vilifies, which are a knowing people and precious in the sight of God."[40] While we find in this passage evidence of Burch's piety, it also underscores her rhetorical skill: against Mann's claim that the parishioners of St. Nicholas were "a poor ignorant, and simple people," Burch counters that they are "a knowing people." Her linkage between this knowledge and their status before the Lord (they are "precious in the sight of God") emphasizes her awareness of the covenantal relationship between God and his chosen people depicted in Hebrews 8:10. It also accords with her insistence elsewhere in this prefatory letter that all Christians should be able "in some measure to answer every one which shall demand a reason of the faith and hope that it is in us."[41] In support, she cites 1 Peter 3:15, demonstrating her intimate knowledge of scripture and thus providing an additional counter to Mann's claims concerning her lack of learning. The verse reads, "But sanctifie the Lord God in your hearts: and bee ready always to give an answere to every man that asketh you a reason of the hope that is in you with meekenesse and reverence." According to Peter, Christians have a responsibility to be "readie" to provide an articulate defense of their faith.

Burch explains that she composed her catechism to provide just such a defense: it offers a public witness of her scriptural knowledge. "The Lord has promised to teach his people," writes Burch, "although not all alike, it came into my minde to see what God hath taught me, I set pen to paper and asking myself questions and answering of them."[42] Burch here describes her decision to compose as catechism as artless: it simply "came into her minde" one day to discover what God had taught her. Such a statement is, of course, an instance of the humility topos: while it declares Burch as the author of the catechism, it cautions the reader not to expect erudition or artistry in her text. But this statement also affirms Burch's commitment to her community. By acknowledging that the Lord does not teach all of his people "alike," Burch implies that perhaps not everyone in Strood enjoys her high degree of scriptural literacy; nonetheless, they are all "his people." Thus, Burch's "Letter" recognizes both that political and religious differences are at the center of the disagreement between herself and Mann and that these differences were compounded by Mann's disdainful views about working-class poverty and illiteracy. Burch intends her catechism as a challenge to these views.

The Full, Free, and Eternall Love of God

A Catechisme of the Severall Heads does not address the usual catechetical subjects: there is no discussion of the creed, the Decalogue, or the sacraments. It is, however, strongly reliant upon Scripture. For example, in response to the question, "Can none be saved without this new birth?" Burch replies, "No. John. 3.3.5.6.7."[43] Burch's terse answer expects that her auditor (or reader) knows at least the first of these verses – "Verily, Verily, I say unto thee, Except a man be born againe, he cannot see the kingdome of God" – and that he or she is able it to perceive its relevance to the question posed. In this, she resembles Katherine Fitzwilliam, whose catechisms were considered in Chapter 2. Moreover, *A Catechisme of the Severall Heads* demonstrates Burch's thoroughgoing knowledge of Calvinist doctrine, articulating, for example, the differences between sanctification, justification, satisfaction, and glorification. She explains the Calvinist understanding of election as a consequence of divine grace: "It is the great mercy of God before the world was made, to choose some to be saved by Jesus Christ" and cites Ephesians 1.4 in support of this claim: "As hee hath chosen us in him, before the foundation of the world that wee should bee holy and without blame before him in love."[44]

Although doctrinally advanced, *A Catechisme of the Severall Heads* is very much a text designed to teach others. It is tempting to attribute this to Burch's experience catechizing her children. Throughout, she displays a developed understanding of the practical implications of abstract religious doctrines, often raising possible objections to her claims. As we have seen in Chapter 1, this is a characteristic feature of the most popular maternally directed catechisms. So, for example, after explaining that Christ allowed himself to be crucified so that he "could give his graces to us by imputation," she imaginatively recreates an auditor's question: "Could not God have pardoned the sinnes of his people, if Christ had not come and paid what their sinnes had deserved?" Burch's answer, "God is a God of justice as well as of mercy," encapsulates the *quid pro quo* at the heart of the doctrine of atonement in such a way that a child might be able to understand. Similarly, after explaining that "good works" do not "justify" sinners, Burch voices a commonsensical question: "Why doe the people of God doe good workes, seeing they justifie not?" She then provides six reasons why the godly should do good works even though these contribute nothing to a person's salvation. Two of the reasons underscore the importance of such works for the godly community. We should do good works, she explains, "for the edification, benefit, and comfort of others."[45] Burch's question-and-answer exposition also reveals a commonsensical appreciation of human psychology. In response to a question concerning God's preparation of the godly during their lifetime, she acknowledges that ordinary people, until they are saved, are often bored by godly practices: "Take one that hath not this new birth in him, and let him be with people that performe holy duties, it will be so tedious unto him, that he cannot indure it; then thinke what he would doe if he were in heaven, where there is nothing but holinesse and praising God day and night."[46]

Perhaps most distinctive in Burch's presentation of religious doctrine in *A Catechisme of Severall Heads* is her repeated insistence on God's love in question-and-answer sequences:

Q. What is the true love of God in us?
A. It is when wee have brought our hearts to this frame, that wee can doe all that wee doe in the service of God onely in love to his Majestie.

Q. What causeth a soule to Love God?
A. Nothing more then the apprehension of God's love to his soule.[47]

Q. What is faith?
A. This is a mightie worke of God upon his people, making the soule so to believe

this, and to rest upon Christ in his full, free, and eternall love of God to their soules.[48]

In such exchanges, Burch depicts God's love as the impetus for faith and the love of humans for God. Burch describes prayer as an intimate conversation, a "powring out of the soule unto God."[49] Once a person is made new by the love of Christ, earthly "priviledges" become devoid of meaning; those "that have their life in Christ," Burch declares, gain "the greatest and happiest priviledge in the world, all other priviledges are but as shadows to this great substance."[50] Her emphasis on an all-encompassing divine love, together with her discussion of earthly life as a shadow of divine glory, reflects what Janice Knight has described as an Augustinian, affective strain of Puritan piety associated with "the spiritual brethren," a group of London theologians and ministers that included William Gouge, John Preston, and Richard Sibbes.[51] It is no surprise to discover connections between the theology of the spiritual brethren and *A Catechisme of the Severall Heads*, since, as we have seen, the parish of St. Nicholas of Strood was demonstrably connected to Gouge and Davenport's London churches. By stressing the importance of God's love to faith, Burch reveals her awareness and embrace of a vibrant strain of seventeenth-century London Puritan piety.

Burch imaginatively draws upon her experience as a mother to extend and elaborate the theology of the Spiritual Brethren. *A Catechisme of the Severall Heads* is admittedly not a "maternally directed" catechism, since it does not contain the usual features of such works: "mother" is not a character; it does not provide advice on recitation or aids to a child's memory. As we have seen, however, Burch does include maternal love, among other motives, for her publication. Burch's catechism differs from most seventeenth-century catechisms, even those expressly designed for children, in the degree to which it applies her experience as a mother of young children to elucidate theological points. She uses her intimate understanding of women's reproductive experience to illustrate the Protestant belief that a person can be saved by faith alone. Burch writes, "our best workes are as menstrous clothes; they are so far from justifying us, that if we trust them, they will condemn us."[52] Such a comparison is common in early modern catechisms and is based upon Isaiah 64:6: "But we have all bene as an uncleane thing and all our righteousnes is as filthy cloutes." But where male catechists often speak in general terms about "filthy rags," Burch activates a second (more literal) interpretation of the Hebrew included in a marginal notation in the Geneva Bible: "We are justly punished and brought into captivitie, because we have provoked thee to anger, and though we would excuse our selves, yet our rightousnes, and best vertues are before thee as vile clouts, or (as some reade) like menstrous clothes of a woman."[53]

Not one of the catechisms I included in *Catechisms Written for Mothers* uses the experience of motherhood as insistently as Burch's work as a means of understanding God's relationship with humankind. To take one example: Vavasor Powell's *The Scripture's Concord* (1646), a catechism to be discussed in more detail subsequently, was published in the same year and by the same printer as Burch's work. Burch's maternal imagery is more consistent and far-reaching than Powell's, such as when she applies her knowledge of a newborn's hunger to convey the desire of the newly born-again: God "fits his people for heaven in this life, by working in them this new birth, and this new birth desires new food, and not old."[54] She cites Isaiah 54:13 in her prefatory letter: "And all thy children shalbe taught of the Lord, and much peace shalbe to thy children." Like Powell, she illustrates divine mercy with the parable of the prodigal son, urging her readers to "consider the prodigal, when he returned to his Father how joyfully he received him."[55] But where Powell simply paraphrases the biblical passage (Luke 15:21) to illustrate how one should acknowledge one's sins, Burch offers the parent-child relationship in this parable as a model for human-divine relations. Gesturing to Galatians 4:7 ("Wherefore, thou art no more a servant, but a sonne: now if thou be a sonne, thou art also the heire of God through Christ"), Burch claims that a true Christian loves God not as a slave or a servant, but as a son. A "sonne" writes Burch, "workes not for feare of punishment, nor yet for wages, for he knows he is free from all punishment and heaven is given him for an inheritance, as a father gives an inheritance to his son, not because he hath served him, but because he is his sonne, which causeth him to serve with abundance of joy and delight."[56] More poignantly, since we know that several of her children died before the age of six, Burch gestures to Zechariah 12:10 ("And they shall lament for him, as one mourneth for his onely sonne, and be sorry for him as one is sorry for his first borne") to evoke the true repentance a Christian feels for her sin, comparing it to the sorrow of a parent who "mourneth for his first born."[57] I am not arguing that such references to maternity constitute a deliberate strategy. Rather, I suggest that Burch's experience as a mother seems to have provided her with a habit of thought that informed her theological belief in the transforming power of Divine love. As a wife and mother writing in a small village in Kent, Burch drew upon what she knew best to understand, scripturally, humankind's relationship to God. As Caroline Walker Bynum has noted, it is not uncommon for theological writers to use metaphors drawn from everyday experience to elucidate fine theological points; what is interesting about Burch's understanding of humankind's relationship with God is that it is so clearly linked to her experience as a mother.[58]

Printers, Preachers, and Mothers: The Seventeenth-Century Godly Community

When Dorothy Burch composed her catechism, she did not originally intend to publish it. In this, she resembles other female catechists we have examined. In her letter, "To the Christian Reader," Burch states that although she has "propounded many very necessary questions with their answers, necessary to be knowne and learned by every good Christian, when I first collected them together, I had no thought of putting them in print."[59] She recounts how she was convinced by "one of neere relation to me, [who] seeing them desired they might be put into print, which I held not necessary, because I feare the weaknesse of the worke, yet through their perswasion I was contented for three causes."[60] While authorial reluctance is conventional in early modern women's writing, I see little reason to doubt its veracity here, since it accords so closely with Burch's account of the composition of the catechism as responding to a theological dispute in her local parish community.

Because of gaps in the historical and archival record, we may never know with certainty how Burch's catechism came to be published. But I take seriously her claim that she was induced to publish her text "by one of neere relation to me." As we have seen, Burch's husband Peeter shared not only her religious beliefs but her evangelicalism. We know as well that Peeter Burch took repeated trips to London on parish business and that St. Nicholas' parish had connections to the London evangelical community. It is not unlikely that, while in London, Peeter Burch would have been in contact with like-minded evangelical Christians, such as Matthew Simmons (1608–54), the printer who published *A Catechisme of the Severall Heads*. Together with his wife, Mary (d. 1688) and son Samuel, Simmons operated one of the more successful seventeenth-century printing businesses. D. F. McKenzie records that in 1637, Simmons was in the Netherlands meeting with Dutch booksellers, where he "noted the large number of English books printed there." But Simmons is perhaps best known for his longstanding association with Milton. He published or played a role in the publication of the majority of Milton's pamphlets throughout the 1640s.[61]

Simmons' motive for printing *A Catechisme of the Severall Heads* may have been largely financial. Catechisms were traditionally good money-makers; they provided a steady revenue stream for printers like Simmons. This might have been especially important for Simmons in 1646, his most prolific year in terms of output, when he printed or had a part in printing fifty-four works.[62] But it is equally possible that Simmons was motivated by Civil War politics. Early modern printers often shared the political and religious viewpoints of their authors; Simmons was the preferred printer of the Independents. As I have indicated, the same year that he published Burch's work, Simmons printed another catechism originating from Kent, Vavasor Powell's *The Scripture's Concord*.[63] Powell would eventually play a central role in Civil War politics, but in the early 1640s, he was an orthodox Calvinist preacher and minister residing in Dartford, a small village fourteen miles from Strood.[64] (A "Mr. Powell" preached at St. Nicholas in 1639. In 1639, Vavasor Powell was working as an itinerant preacher; Peeter Burch was churchwarden at St. Nicholas, so Powell and the Peeter Burch may well have known one another.) Like Burch's text, *The Scripture's Concord* offers evidence of Protestant evangelism in the Kentish countryside, which could have provided a powerful contrast with the machinations of the government and the Laudian clergy. Simmons' publication of these catechisms may plausibly reflect ongoing tensions in the struggle to define the national church.[65]

There is evidence of the intent to forefront a local evangelical piety on the title page of Burch's catechism. In early modern England, title pages were typically the responsibility of the printer, not the author. Here, Simmons echoes Burch's claim in "The Letter" that she did not compose her catechism for publication. Only now, he states, is it to be "published for the good and benefit of others, by the importunitie of some friends."[66] Equally significantly, Simmons places on the title page a quotation of Romans 14:13. "Let us not therefore judge one another any more: but judge this rather, that no man put a stumbling block, or an occasion to fall in his brothers way."[67] This passage seems to refer to the conflict between Burch and John Mann, which Burch narrates on the very next page of her work. This indicates that one of the implications that Simmons took from Burch's catechism – and one of the implications that he wanted readers to take from it – was that a working-class shopkeeper's wife could be a match for an educated clergyman in articulating her faith. Such an implication could serve as a powerful counterargument to Laudian attempts to regulate the lay reading of scripture. While I do not contend that Simmons published Burch's catechism as part of a programmatic attack on Royalist clergy, I do suggest that he published it at least in part because its message resonated with his own religious and political beliefs.

When these diverse particulars are assembled, a picture begins to emerge of some previously unrecognized communities that supported not only Dorothy Burch's composition of her catechism, but her entrance into early modern print culture. Burch and her husband Peeter were literate Christians living in a small but well-located village in the Kentish countryside. In the early 1640s, a Royalist minister arrived at her local parish church and insulted the local parishioners, the majority of whom worked as fisherman, oyster-dredgers, and mariners. Dorothy Burch composed her catechism to demonstrate her – and her community's – knowledge of the Protestant faith. She chose this genre in part because of the importance accorded to catechizing within evangelical Protestantism, but also because catechisms were a genre traditionally associated with women and mothers. When, at the urging of "one of near relation," Burch decided to publish her catechism, she was supported by a printer who shared her religious commitments.

Dorothy Burch was a working-class wife and mother. But the image that emerges from a close reading of her text is not that of a pious alabaster figure kneeling at her husband's tomb. It is of a woman, who, despite her poverty, has confidence in her scriptural knowledge and in her ability to serve as a spokesperson for her small fishing community. This confidence emerged in part from Burch's active engagement in a vibrant parish church led by a godly minister. But her self-assurance also developed from her experience as a mother responsible for the religious instruction of her children. Throughout her catechism, Burch draws upon her understanding of motherhood as a way of conceptualizing humankind's relationship to God.

Notes

1. George Herbert, *A Priest to the Temple* (London, 1671), 72.
2. Dorothy Burch, *A Catechisme of the Severall Heads of the Christian Religion* (London, 1646), in *Catechisms Written for Mothers, Schoolmistresses, and Children*, 1575–1750, ed. Paula McQuade (Aldershot: Ashgate, 2008), Sig. A3.
3. Sylvia Browne briefly discusses Burch in "The Eloquence of the Word and the Spirit," in *Women and Religion in Old and New Worlds*, ed. Susan Dinan and Debra Meyers (New York: Routledge, 2001), 187–212, especially 193–4; as do I: see "Introduction," in *Catechisms Written for Mothers, Schoolmistresses, and Children*, xvi–xix. Phyllis Mack devotes a paragraph to Burch's authorship in

Visionary Women: Ecstatic Prophecy in Seventeenth-Century England (Berkeley: University of California Press, 1992), 121. Burch's *A Catechisme* is not cited in any of the printed bibliographies of early modern women writers, but it is included in *Renaissance Women Writers' Online* database as of 2010.

4. The absence of non-elite voices is, at least in part, a function of generally low levels of literacy for women throughout the first half of the seventeenth century. According to David Cressy, "women were almost universally unable to write their own names for most of the sixteenth and seventeenth centuries." *Literacy and Social Order* (Cambridge: Cambridge University Press, 1980), 145. Cressy's analysis has been critiqued for its overemphasis on the ability to sign one's name as a manifestation of literacy, as well as its under-acknowledgment of the link between scripturalism and improved literacy for both women and men. I agree with Tessa Watt: Cressy's "literary statistics should be taken as minimum figures, not certainties." *Cheap Print and Popular Piety* (Cambridge: Cambridge University Press, 1991), 7.

5. On the role of working-class women in seventeenth-century English separatism, see Margaret Ezell, *Writing Women's Literary History* (Baltimore: John Hopkins University Press, 1993), 132–60; Katharine Gillespie, *Domesticity and Dissent in the Seventeenth Century* (Cambridge: Cambridge University Press, 2004), 25–61. See also Richard Greaves, "Foundation Builders: The Role of Women in Early English Non-Conformity," 75–92, and Dorothy Ludlow, "Shaking Patriarchy's Foundations," 93–123, both in *Triumph Over Silence: Women in Protestant History*, ed. Richard Greaves (London: Longwood Press, 1985). Greaves remarks, "of the twenty-eight separatists living in Great Yarmouth, Norfolk, in 1630, twenty or twenty-one were women. Eight were described as poor" (76).

6. I am grateful to Catherina Clement for her analysis of local text records and their implications concerning the occupation of Peeter Burch. She concludes, "a process sort of analysis would suggest [that Peeter Burch was] a tradesman, which also fits [his] middling sort of status, literacy, and tax rating." Clement, personal communication, May 23, 2012.

7. Nigel Smith declares "in that all but the poorest now had the possibility of authorship, we can say that the English Revolution was more thoroughgoing in its extension of the possession and use of words than it was in property distribution." *Literature and Revolution in England, 1640–1660* (New Haven: Yale University Press, 1994), 6.

8. *The Elizabethan Puritan Movement* (Berkeley: University of California Press, 1967), 26–7.

9. Concerning the higher degree of female literacy in London, Cressy remarks, "Women in London were not bound by this gradual secular evolution. Under Elizabeth and the early Stuarts they were not much better than women anywhere else, but in the last decades of the seventeenth century their writing ability was transformed ... Literacy may have been an important factor in internal migration, especially if it was better rewarded in the capital than in provincial England." *Literacy and Social Order*, 149.

10. "Introduction," in *Religion in Revolutionary England*, ed. Christopher Durston and Judith Maltby (Manchester: Manchester University Press, 2006), 1–18, 3.
11. For a detailed study of responses to Laud in Kent, see Jacqueline Eales, "So Many Sects and Schisms: Religious Diversity in Revolutionary Kent," in *Religion in Revolutionary England*, 226–48. Eales writes, "in particular, the altar policy instigated in 1633 by the new Archbishop of Canterbury, William Laud, was widely interpreted as a return to pre-Reformation and Roman Catholic practices. In the winter of 1640–41 the link between the newly railed altars and Catholic 'superstition' was explicitly made by the laity in a number of parishes across Kent" (228).
12. Elizabeth Clarke argues analogously regarding the publication of Elizabeth Richardson's *A Mother's Legacy* in 1645. Clarke notes that although Richardson composed her text earlier, when she published it in 1645, it was as "an intervention in contemporary liturgical debates." "The Legacy of Mothers and Others," in *Religion in Revolutionary England*, 69–90, 70.
13. On the usefulness of "history from below" to early modern women's writing, see Jim Sharpe, "History from Below," in *New Perspectives on Historical Writing* (University Park, PA: Penn State University Press, 1992), 25–42. Also, Lena Cowen Orlin, "A Case for Anecdotalism in Women's History," *English Literary Renaissance*, 31 (2001): 52–77.
14. On the county's longstanding reputation for Protestant evangelicalism and religious diversity, see Peter Clark, *English Provincial Society from the Reformation to the Revolution: Religion, Politics, and Society in Kent, 1500–1640* (Rutherford: Farleigh Dickinson Press, 1977), 151–2. Also Eales, "So Many Sects and Schisms," 227. The population figures for Strood are my own estimate based upon a 1598 poor relief survey.
15. According to Clark in *English Provincial Society*, Kent probably had more "medium sized, well-established communities" than any other county. He estimates that Rochester, like Faversham, Dover, and Maidstone "had populations of between 1,000 and 2,000 people" (9).
16. *The Churchwardens' Accounts of Saint Nicholas, Strood*, ed. Henry Plomer (Kent Archeological Society: Kent, 1927), 182–6.
17. Clement, personal communication.
18. Clark, *English Provincial Society*, 355. The eighteenth-century historian Edward Hasted described Strood as "consisting in great measure of seafaring men, fishermen, and oyster-dredgers." *The History and Topographical Survey of Kent*, Vol. 3 (Canterbury, 1797), 547. Cressy, in *Literacy and Social Order*, suggests that fishermen were among the least literate of seventeenth-century laborers: "the most illiterate cluster of trades included building workers like bricklayers, masons, and thatchers ... and all-weather workmen like fishermen and shepherds" (134). His analysis suggests that at least 81 percent of fishermen were unable to sign their name. This does not tally with my estimation of literacy rates in Strood. See endnote 27 for a more complete discussion. Margaret Spufford provides anecdotal evidence that usefully supplements Cressy's conclusions concerning the literacy of fisherman. She

notes an "Anne Gwin of Falmouth, daughter of a fisherman and fish merchant, born in 1692," who "took to learning very Young, and soon became a good reader viz, when she was but about Three yeares and a half old; she wrote tolerably well before five." *Small Books and Pleasant Histories* (Athens, GA: University of Georgia Press, 1981), 25.

19. Plomer, *The Churchwardens' Accounts*, 185; Clark, *English Provincial Society*, 11.
20. Hasted, *The History*, 557; Plomer, *The Churchwardens' Accounts*, 184.
21. Plomer, *The Churchwardens' Accounts*, 159; Margo Todd, *Christian Humanism and the Puritan Social Order* (Cambridge: Cambridge University Press, 1987), 168–9.
22. Patrick Collinson, "England and International Calvinism," in *From Cranmer to Sancroft* (London: Hambledon Continuum, 2006), 75–100, 86. On Sibbes and Gouge, see Janice Knight, *Orthodoxies in Massachusetts* (Harvard: Harvard University Press, 1994), 111–13.
23. Plomer, *The Churchwardens' Accounts*, 159.
24. I thank Kate Herron for obtaining these baptismal and death records for me through the International Genealogical Index Database (www.familysearch.org) and the England and Wales Christening Records, 1530–1906 (www.ancestry.com).
25. One resident was taxed at 6 d (pence); seven residents at 8 d; fourteen residents at 1 s (shilling); ten residents at 2 s; four residents at 3 s; five residents at 4 s; five residents at 5 s; two residents at 6 s; and one resident at 10 s. Plomer, *The Churchwardens' Accounts*, 102. These taxation rates confirm the working class status of the majority of St. Nicholas' parishioners. Catherine Clement (personal communication) notes that Peeter Burch seems to have been consistently assessed in the upper middle of St. Nicholas' parishioners.
26. *Calendar of the Proceedings of the Committee for Advance of Money*, Part 3, 1650–55, ed. Mary Anne Everett Green (Her Majesty's Stationary Office: London, 1888; reprint: Kraus reprint Ltd., Lichtenstein, 1967), 1228–35.
27. I calculated this rate from the number of men who were able to sign the 1629 petition at St. Nicholas: out of twenty-one men, nine signed with a mark. I could find additional information concerning literacy rates in Strood by examining how many men were able to sign the yearly churchwardens' accounts, but the data vary considerably from year to year, with some years omitted. Moreover, the number of men who sign these accounts is considerably smaller and, accordingly, less representative. I have therefore based my calculation on the largest available sample.
28. Watt, *Cheap Print*, 7. Cressy, *Literacy and Social Order*, 91.
29. Plomer, *The Churchwardens' Accounts*, xxviii.
30. Plomer, *The Churchwardens' Accounts*, 183–4 (the table appears on p. 184 of the source).
31. The link between Protestantism and increased literacy is well established. See, for example, Margaret Hannay, *Silent But for the Word* (Kent: Kent State University Press, 1985). Spufford provides considerable evidence that connects evangelical Protestantism and literacy in *Small Books*, 1–44, as does Cressy,

Literacy and Social Order, 3–6. See also Margaret Spufford and Kenneth Charlton, "Literacy, Society, and Education," in *The Cambridge History of Early Modern English Literature*, ed. David Lowenstein and Janel Mueller (Cambridge: Cambridge University Press, 2002), 15–55.

32. Quoted in Henry Smetham, *A History of Strood* (Rochester: Parrett and Neves, 1899), 107.
33. Plomer, *The Churchwardens' Accounts*, xxvii.
34. Quoted in Smetham, *A History*, 107.
35. Plomer, *The Churchwardens' Accounts*, 189.
36. Burch, *A Catechisme*, Sig. A2r–A3v.
37. Clark, *English Provincial Society*, 367; Smetham, *A History*, 107. On these cultural divisions and their relation to genre, see Smith, *Literature and Revolution*, 1–21.
38. Burch, *A Catechisme*, Sig. A3v.
39. Burch, *A Catechisme*, Sig. A3v–r.
40. Burch, *A Catechisme*, Sig. A3v.
41. Burch, *A Catechisme*, Sig. A3r.
42. Burch, *A Catechisme*, Sig. A3v.
43. Burch, *A Catechisme*, Sig. B1r.
44. Burch, *A Catechisme*, Sig. A8r.
45. Burch, *A Catechisme*, Sig. A6r–A7v.
46. Burch, *A Catechisme*, Sig. B2r.
47. Burch, *A Catechisme*, Sig. B3v.
48. Burch, *A Catechisme*, Sig. B1v.
49. Burch, *A Catechisme*, Sig. B3v.
50. Burch, *A Catechisme*, Sig. A5r.
51. Knight, *Orthodoxies*, 3–4.
52. Burch, *A Catechisme*, Sig. A6r.
53. John Willison explains that works cannot justify us because "all our righteousness is as filthy rags before God." *The Mother's Catechism* in *Catechisms for Mothers, Schoolmistresses, and Children*, 17. Vavasor Powell writes that he sees "all my righteousness as filthy ragges." *Scripture's Concord* (London, 1646), 22. Thanks to Janel Mueller (personal communication, February 19, 2015) for pointing out that Burch draws upon the second, more literal interpretation.
54. Burch, *A Catechisme*, Sig. B2v.
55. Burch, *A Catechisme*, Sig. A7r.
56. Burch, *A Catechisme*, Sig. B3v.
57. Burch, *A Catechisme*, Sig. B2r.
58. Bynum writes that she "assumes that the linguistic trappings of texts are often more telling than the explicit arguments ... the technical arguments of philosophical and theological treatises frequently betray the problems they cannot solve – social and psychological as well as intellectual problems – in the limiting cases, examples, and metaphors they use and in the ways they distort or misread conventional images." *The Resurrection of the Body in Western*

Christianity (New York: Columbia University Press, 1995), xvi. On the use of maternity to conceptualize humankind's relation to God, see Bynum's *Jesus as Mother* (Berkeley: University of California Press, 1982).

59. Burch, *A Catechisme*, Sig. A2r.
60. Burch, *A Catechisme*, Sig. A3v.
61. D. F. McKenzie, "The Economies of Print, 1550–1750," in *Produzione e Commercio della Carta e del Libro secc. XIII–XVIII: atti della "Ventriteesima Settimana di Studi, 15 Aprile, 1991"* (Firenze: le Monnier, 1992), 399, 422. Stephen Dobranski remarks that Milton "maintained a life-long relationship with the Simmons family." *Milton, Authorship, and the Book Trade* (Cambridge: Cambridge University Press, 1991), 106.
62. McKenzie, "Economies," 422.
63. *The Scripture's Concord* was printed by M. S. for Hanna Allen, at the Crown in Pope's Head Alley; *A Catechisme of the Severall Heads* was printed by Matthew Simmons for J. H. in Pope's Head Alley. The only printer with the initials M. S. working in Pope's Head Alley in the 1640s was Matthew Simmons.
64. Powell, *The Scripture's Concord*, Sig. A3; see also, Edward Bagshaw, *The Life and Death of Vavasor Powell* (London, 1671), 14–15.
65. For more on the various religious factions of the 1640s within Kent and their relation to the established church, see Eales, "So Many Sects and Schisms," 240–4. St. Nicholas parish continued to play an active role in religious politics in Kent throughout the 1650s. Eales remarks that in 1655, Daniel French, curate of St. Nicholas in Strood, engaged Richard Coppin, a suspected Ranter, in a "four day disputation," during which he (along with other clergy) attacked Coppin as a "heretic and a blasphemer" (240–1). Eales characterizes this debate as "the most high profile disputation to take place in Kent in the revolutionary period" (241).
66. Burch, *A Catechisme*, Sig. A1.
67. Simmons quotes from the *Authorized Version of the Holy Bible, 1611 Edition: King James Version* (Peabody, MA: Hendrickson Publishers, 2011). Femke Molekamp urges against reading too much into a person's preference for the Geneva or AV: "Again, the similarity between the appearance of the AV and Genevean quartos is so strong it begs the question of whether an early seventeenth-century reader would immediately recognize which quarto she had before her. This should warn us against constructing a narrative of the repudiation by the AV of the Geneva Bible. Rather, the two Bibles were very often read interchangeably." *Women and the Bible in Early Modern England* (Oxford: Oxford University Press, 2013), 33.

CHAPTER 6

Prophecy, Catechesis, and Community in Mary Cary's The Resurrection of the Witnesses *(1653)*

Introduction

In 1648, Mary Cary, a twenty-seven-year-old London woman, wrote and first published *The Resurrection of the Witnesses*, an exegesis of Revelation 11: 1–14 that predicts the success of Oliver Cromwell's New Model Army. Several seventeenth-century sources identify Mary Cary as a gentlewoman and, as Bernard Capp remarks, "her fluid and confident style points in the same direction."[1] Cary was closely associated with the Fifth Monarchists, a millenarian political group, and several contemporary scholars have remarked upon her authorial prowess and political engagements.[2] She was also skilled at maneuvering in the seventeenth-century print marketplace, republishing *The Resurrection of the Witnesses* in 1653, adding a postscript as well as a long "Preface to the Reader" in which she discusses herself and her work within the tradition of biblical female prophets.[3] One might suppose that Cary added this preface in 1653 because she had experienced resistance to her earlier publication. By placing her writing within a tradition of visionary female prophecy, the argument might go, Cary sought to authorize her entrance into masculine print culture.

But, as Erica Longfellow observes, such a supposition would be incorrect: Cary discusses other female prophets to assert her independence from them. "Here let me not be mistaken," Cary insists, "as though I made any comparison with the Prophets or with those women in the Gospel, I say not that I have any immediate revelation that the Witnesses are risen or that I have been told it by an Angel or the like."[4] As Cary surely recognized, this disavowal is significant: by insisting that she is not recording an immediate revelation from God, she repudiates the usual means by which female (and sometimes male) visionaries authorized their public pronouncements. Prophecy has a privilege.[5] But Cary refuses it.

Cary instead bases her authority in her domestic study of scripture: "But this only I do assert, that I have from my child-hood, but especially since I was fifteen years of age, been (I doubt not but I may say) by the spirit of God, set upon a serious and continual study of the Scriptures in general, and more particularly, of the Book of Revelation." She concludes: "This, I say, is all that I assert concerning this, and I have no other grounds but these for these things."[6] Cary's claim regarding her composition is unusual in seventeenth-century English women's writing. It counters more than a millennium of religious tradition, deriving from Paul, which prohibited women from teaching outside the home unless inspired by a direct revelation from God. Cary thus sets herself a twofold task: to interpret Revelation 11 as a commentary on contemporary political events, a task which requires considerable exegetical skill, and to establish her interpretation as authoritative even though she does not claim divine inspiration.

To accomplish this twofold task, Cary adapts the catechetical genre. As *The Orlando Project* notes, "At several points in her text Mary Cary uses questions and answers in the style of a catechism."[7] In employing questions and answers to address topics of a religious nature, *The Resurrection of the Witnesses* satisfies Ian Green's two-part definition of a catechism.[8] I am less interested in reclassifying Cary's text, however, than I am in understanding the usefulness of catechesis to her argument. Although she was not formally educated, Cary was a talented writer. Even her opponents acknowledge her "good colour for the phrase of the context." "There are many things in that book," admits the author of *The Account Audited*, "which are good and of which a Christian improvement may be made."[9] So why does Cary intersperse her prose exegesis with question-and-answer sequences? I will maintain that Cary inserts these brief catechisms in order to activate the power and authority accorded to women within the home. Like Dorothy Burch, Mary Cary adapts a genre associated with domestic religious instruction to legitimate her politically significant publication.

But Cary is also interested in the implications of catechesis for church structure. Traditionally located within the home, by the mid-seventeenth century, a form of catechesis was also practiced in godly assemblies where men and women sought to discover the meaning of scripture by asking one another questions and answering them. Such exchanges were an extension of the power and authority invested in domestic catechesis. In *The Resurrection of the Witnesses*, Cary juxtaposes prose scriptural exegesis with instances of communal oral catechesis, thus placing the latter at the center of her imaginative re-visioning of Christian community. Implicitly engaging with contemporary debates over the lawfulness of women's public teaching, Cary elaborates a vision of godly assembly in which all of the "saints" are called to serve as "prophets, teachers, and evangelists."[10]

This interpretation allows us to see continuities between *The Resurrection of the Witnesses* and Mary Cary's other works. Contemporary scholars have written admiringly of Cary's "visionary utopianism." David Lowenstein writes that Cary envisions a world where "spiritual glories enjoyed by the saints will be accompanied by material ones" including "commodious houses," gold and silver, and "apparel in great abundance." James Holstun recounts Cary's proposals "to end tithes, nurture voluntary religion ... new-model the universities to encourage poor scholars, establish work-houses, simplify law codes, [and] favor the poor in law suits ...."[11] I suggest that Cary's radically communitarian vision of church government reflects and shapes her sociopolitical convictions; this potentially subversive vision, in turn, is shaped by her experience with domestic and group catechesis. Underpinning this vision is Cary's commitment to shared scriptural study as a process through which the saints both enact and experience divine love.

Prophecy: Infused Knowledge and Scriptural Exegesis

Christian theology contains several competing (not necessarily contradictory) conceptions of prophecy. This results in part because prophecy was not defined categorically, but instead was allowed to evolve over time; as different understandings of prophecy emerged, they were incorporated into older models. The oldest understanding of prophet is that of a person selected by God to proclaim his message, exemplified in various calls to men and women in the Hebrew Scriptures. So, for example, Jonah is a prophet primarily because God calls him to urge the Ninevites to reform, not because he possesses any special knowledge of the future (Jonah 3:1–3). This conception of prophecy typically characterizes what the prophet knows as *scientia infusa*, or infused knowledge – awareness of God's will by supra-rational means. Narratively, this awareness is often represented as a divine vision or inspired dream.[12] Unlike rational perception, *scientia infusa* was instantaneous, complete, and overwhelming; it came to be associated with mystical experience. John Donne equated the prophetic office with this mode of apprehension, remarking that John the Baptist "knew, by *scientiam infusam*, by infused knowledge, for he was a prophet."[13] Over time, the conception of prophecy as divine inspiration became increasingly identified with a divinely given ability to predict the future. Inspired prophecy-as-prediction became increasingly linked to eschatology, so that a prophet was understood to be a person who, inspired by God, revealed the coming of God's kingdom on earth. Underpinning this understanding of inspired prophecy was the belief in divine omnipotence: by revealing God's plans, the prophet affirms God's power.[14]

At least from the patristic period, however, some theologians held a more complex understanding of a prophetic office. According to this understanding, a prophet need not rely upon infused knowledge to predict God's future plans. Instead, a prophet uses his reason to interpret the scriptures in a way that reveals God's will. In this connection, the depiction of the risen Christ in Luke 24:27 is paradigmatic: he meets two unnamed disciples on the road to Emmaus and "he beganne at Moses, and at all the Prophets, and interpreted unto them in all the Scriptures the things which were written of him."[15] This understanding of prophecy takes account both of the importance of reason and of Divine omnipotence: God can choose to reveal his will for the future either through infused knowledge or through rational scriptural interpretation. Like inspired prophecy more generally, rational prophecy was often, although again not exclusively, linked with eschatology. Thus, while inspired prophecy and rational prophecy converge in their understanding of the prophet as a person who predicts the future, they differ in the means they identify by which the prophet is able to make such predictions.

The distinction has gendered implications. As one might expect, inspired prophecy is gender-neutral. The omnipotent God can choose to inspire anyone to speak for him, however "weak the vessel." As Erica Longfellow explains, "The spirit could speak through anyone, and when the spirit spoke, the normal order was suspended, and the 'Weaknes & Subjection' of a woman's speech were subsumed in the (male) authority of the spirit speaking in her."[16] Both the Hebrew Scriptures and the New Testament testify to this: Deborah (Judges 4:4), Anna (Luke 2:36) and the daughters of Phillip the Deacon are prophetesses (Acts 21.9). While some seventeenth-century Englishwomen drew upon this understanding of prophecy to justify their intervention in contemporary political events, they do so nearly always by emphasizing their powerlessness. Longfellow observes that when Anna Trapnel was questioned on the charge that she made a public disturbance during her "prophetic tour of Cornwall," she defended her actions by denying her agency: "the Lord moved me, and gave me leave."[17] Elizabeth Avery claims that she published her visions only to affirm Divine omnipotence: "I do here present it to the view of all; and the rather, because the power of God doth appear in it in respect of the weaknesse and contemptibleness of the instrument whom he doth here employ."[18]

Why doesn't Cary similarly claim divine inspiration for her prophetic exegesis of Revelation? In all likelihood, the reason is that she does not believe herself to have experienced it: "I say not," she confesses, that "I have any immediate revelation."[19] Instead Cary identifies herself as a prophet who will draw upon her knowledge of scripture, gained from seventeen years' study, to reveal what God's plans are for the future. The problem for Cary, however, is the lack of a tradition of female prophetic exegetes. As Phyllis Mack remarks, ". . . a woman who interrupted a Parliamentary meeting by babbling or singing, her eyes glazed, would probably have seemed less of an anomaly than one who tried to appear as a concerned citizen or minister engaging in public theological debates or rational biblical exegesis."[20] This is in part because the mode of rational prophecy closely resembled public religious teaching, which nearly all Christians held that women could not do. This prohibition was upheld even in most radical sectarian communities, where ministers often pointed to 1 Corinthians 14:34, "Let your women keepe silence in the Churches: for it is not permitted unto them to speake." As a female member of one such sectarian community, Cary confronts a difficult problem: she believes that her many years of scriptural study have equipped her to discern God's will for the saints. On the other hand, she does not claim that her prophecy results from a direct communication from God; she does not see herself as a mere nothing creature but as an active interpreter who uses her knowledge to declare God's will to others. Thus, by asserting that her predictions are solely based upon her "serious and continual study of the scriptures" and by publishing them, Cary is advancing an ambitious claim for a woman's ability to teach, one which challenges a longstanding Pauline prohibition.

Some Might Say

In 1651, the Baptist minister Thomas Tillam matter-of-factly described encountering a people "daily exercised in reading his word and opening the same in order." On the day that he met them, they were studying Revelation 11. Tillam describes how they invited him to participate:

> They desired my help in Expounding this Mysterious piece, which sudden and unexpected motion, did somewhat surprize me, as knowing that it hath been accounted one of the hardest knots in the revealed will of God: and

withall, considering how various the Opinions of Writers are upon the subject matter thereof, and how little satisfaction I had ever received from any of them.[21]

Tillam's narrative attests to the diffusion of interpretative authority within communal scriptural study in Civil War London. Perhaps recognizing that Tillam was a minister, the group asks for his assistance, but there is little indication that they rely overmuch upon his authority. One gets the sense that if they not been gratified by his interpretation, these "judicious hearers" would have resumed their previous discussion, asking one another questions and answering them. Arnold Hunt has suggested that such groups were an extension of the power and authority accorded to laymen and women in domestic religious instruction. However much ministers might urge parishioners to stick to the written sermon or catechism, oral repetition encouraged amplification and even independent analysis. "The paradox of repetition," remarks Hunt, "was that while it might join the godly laity closer to their preachers, it might also have the effect of emancipating them from parish ministry and giving them the freedom and confidence to expound scripture on their own."[22]

I suggest that Cary's use of the catechetical form in her written text reflects and elaborates upon her experience with domestic and communal catechesis and scriptural study. She first uses the form to address a common problem among the seventeenth-century godly – the inability to pray.

> OBJECT. But perhaps some might say, when I go about to pray, I find much deadness, fleshliness, carnality, and coldness in myself, both when I am to pray publiquely with other Saints, and when I am privately retired; and I look upon this as an effect of Babylonian darkness. I question therefore, whether I may pray, until it be wholly done away.
>
> ANSW. The Apostle, when he bids us, in all things to make known our requests to God, and to pray without ceasing, and to continue in prayer, and to pray continually, Philippians 4. 6, 1 Thessalonians 5.17, Colossians 4.2, did very well know That Saints did carry flesh about them which would be opposing the spirit.[23]

Alec Ryrie provides multiple examples of seventeenth-century ministers reassuring worried parishioners that such feelings were common, so Cary here emulates ministerial authority.[24] She supports her answer with scriptural citations that provide proof for her claims and reveal the extent of her scriptural knowledge, reinforcing her credibility as one who speaks knowledgeably to men and women within a community. She subsequently expands upon this answer with another series of imagined questions and answers that originate from members of this community: "But another may say ... and therefore I question whether it be not sinful for me to continue praying untill I am fully come out of Babylon." Cary's confident answers draw upon her scriptural knowledge to speak authoritatively: "First, if thou wert in Babylon as thou supposes, yet that the Saints while they have been under the bondage of Babylon have had a spirit of prayer and have had their petitions heard, is evident." "Second ... Let me tell thee, That if in those things, in which though hast no confidence, thou do pray for them with the submission of thy will unto the will of the Father, it may be no sin for thee so to pray."[25]

At another point, Cary pauses her exegesis to address another imagined question from her community:

> QUERY. But now, before I proceed any further, the Query will be, What those Gentiles are in particular, to whom the Temple and the holy City was to be given and by whom they were to be troden under foot? For as Jerusalem and the Temple of old were given to the Babylonians in particular, so the question is now, Who the particular enemies are to whom the Temple, and the holy City, now are delivered? For though the holy City hath many enemies, yet she is not given to them all.
> ANSWER. I answer, Though in this Chapter there be no other description of them, but only this, the Gentiles; yet we have a large description of them, in three several Chapters of this prophecy, which descriptions as they lie, I shall here insert.[26]

A skilled teacher, Cary anticipates possible moments of textual confusion and responds to them. She pauses to address a question that she knows her readers "will" have. But in this exchange, she takes the role of reporting the question and the role of answering it. She states, for example, that the first answer can be found in Revelation 12:3–4 and the second in Revelation 13: 1–8, but she still places her answer within communal scriptural analysis and thus mitigates the potential threat posed by her public teaching.

To "open" the "very mysterious" images of Revelation 11:2, Cary turns to Revelation 17:3–18. She includes this passage in its entirety in her text, a decision that may reflect her desire for her readers to compare her exegesis with the scriptural text, as well as her recognition that not all of her readers have access to a Bible. It also reveals her (or her printer's) reliance upon the Authorized Version of the Bible.[27] Perhaps because this passage is rhetorically complex, Cary inserts into her exegesis a four-page catechism, consisting of five interlocking questions and answers, in which she methodically "unveils" its images. I'll first quote the questions without their answers, so that we can see the progression of her analysis:

1. First, If it be queried, What is the Beast?
2. But secondly, If it be queried, What that Woman is, that is said Chapter 17.3 to sit upon this beast?
3. But thirdly, If the Question be, What the seven heads of the Beast are?
4. Fourthly, If it should be enquired, What the ten horns are, mentioned in Chap 12.3 and 13.1 and 17.3?
5. But fifthly, If it should be queried, What the many waters are upon which the Woman sitteth, mentioned in Chapt 17. 1 and 12.1?[28]

Each of these questions isolates a particular "mysterious image" in Revelation 17:7–18 that needs explication before she can return to Revelation 11:2: the beast, the woman, the beast's seven heads, ten horns, and the waters. Cary explains that this method of interpretation, which assumes that a reader can use other passages as exegetical keys to preceding obscure ones, generally applies to eschatological dream visions like Revelation and Daniel.[29] She thus follows the advice of Puritan divines like Josias Nichols, who urged home catechists to unlock confusing scriptural passages by reading subsequent ones, an interpretive decision that arguably suggests the influence of domestic catechesis upon her writings.[30]

We can get a sense of how Cary uses the catechetical form to structure her exposition by looking at her response to her second question: "What that woman is, that is said Chapter 17.3 to sit upon this beast?"

> We have an Answer to this, in the 18 verse of this 17 Chapter in these words: And the woman which thou sawest, is that great city which reigneth over the Kings of the Earth. Now what that great City was, that did then reign over the Kings of the earth . . . Yet the Scripture could sufficiently inform us . . . it is clear in Scripture (and all histories do acknowledge it) that Rome was the great City that reigned over the Kings of Earth. Then it appears, That Rome is that woman that is said to sit upon the Beast.[31]

Perhaps the most interesting feature of this serial exchange is Cary's use of the plural pronoun: she phrases the question as a passive conditional, "if it be queried" and then inserts herself as one of those who seek to answer the question through scriptural citation and analysis: "We have an answer" and "Scripture could sufficiently inform us," a diffusion of interpretive authority that arguably links Cary's analysis to the type of group scriptural study witnessed by Tillam. Throughout *The Resurrection of the Witnesses*, where

Cary adapts the catechetical form, it is made to serve a dual purpose. On the one hand, it allows Cary to activate the authority of domestic catechesis to authorize her public teaching; on the other, it enables Cary to represent herself simultaneously as instructor and student, thus highlighting the utility of oral catechesis within godly community.

To Maintain a Communion among the Saints

Catechesis is central to Cary's understanding of Christian community. She describes the book of Revelation as "a Revelation, Declaration or Manifestation of the mind of God about the things which were come to pass shortly after the revealing of it." Like Milton, she emphasizes the beauty of divine condescension, remarking that God does not need to reveal himself to his servants; instead, his decision to reveal his plans for us is a deliberate choice which reflects his love.[32] "It is the pleasure of God," she writes, "to have his Servants acquainted with his secrets, and to know what is his mind concerning things to come." Although we can never really know why he chooses this, admits Cary, we can surmise that he reveals himself in part to demonstrate his omnipotence. The only appropriate human response to divine condescension is gratitude. Because God has revealed himself to us in scripture, "it teaches Saints to admire, and magnify the love of the Father, that doth express Himself so graciously to them as to afford them that honour to be as his friends in revealing his secrets to them."[33]

Cary explains that God invites human beings "to observe how God hath brought to pass the things which he did pre-declare he would bring to pass," an activity which leads human beings to "experience" both divine omnipotence and divine love. To attain this "experience" humans must study scripture to perceive how the events that God has predicted in earlier scriptural books are subsequently fulfilled: "But how can Saints have experience of this, but by comparing his word and works together?" Cary uses various personifications to evoke this process of revelation as an unmerited act of love. God is "our dear friend" but also a "tender Husband" who "unbosomes himself, and discovers his secrets to his beloved Wife, and cannot with-hold them from her: So the Lord God doth express his tender love unto his Servants, in revealing his secrets to them and he will do nothing but he will discover it unto them."[34] Like Dorothy Burch, Cary portrays God's revelation of himself through scripture as an act of intimacy; it is an "unbosoming," a "discovering," of his "tender love."

Cary further explains that if God chooses to reveal himself to humans through scripture, these humans must be committed readers who avidly compare "his words and his works together." "Doth the Lord reveal his secrets to his Servants?" asks Cary, "Then ought they to be diligent observers of what he reveals unto them." Not to do so would break the friendship between humankind and God by rejecting his proffered intimacy: if "a man reveals his secret unto his dear friend, if his friend should slight him in it, and take no notice of what he discovers to him, he were a very unkind, and a very unworthy friend."[35] For Cary, then, scriptural exegesis is fundamental not because it reveals an authoritative interpretation of a passage but rather because it is a process whereby a believer enacts and nourishes a personal relationship with God. This understanding of exegesis resembles what we saw in Chapter 1 concerning the importance of catechesis as an enactment of love between mother and child.

Cary describes God's revealing of his will in scripture as a deliberate choice made to solidify the Christian community. A thoroughgoing Calvinist, Cary believes that the omnipotent God has other options for revealing his will, but he choses "rather to do it by instruments, by Apostles, and Prophets, and Evangelists, and Pastors, and Teachers which he hath appointed." Cary concludes that God chooses to reveal himself through "instruments" for three reasons. The first two reasons reflect her emphasis upon divine omnipotence and sovereignty. The third reason is to foster a sense of community, or as Cary says, "to maintain a communion among Saints." By revealing himself in scripture, God encourages men and women to interpret scripture with one another: "For if God should reveal himself to all alike, then would not his people have such communion one with another, as they have, to the end they may partake one of another's gifts."[36] Cary's careful phrasing carries the implication that communal catechesis and scriptural study, not the Eucharist, is the foundation of Christian community.

Giving Vent to the "Bublings" of Christ

Near the end of *The Resurrection of the Witnesses*, Cary returns to the question she broached in her preface: how can a woman speak publically about religion if she is not a prophet? At the time, London congregations were actively debating the role of women within the church. Erica Longfellow has described the extensive debate occasioned in one church community when a woman insisted that "she could not walk where she had not liberty to speak." In *Rome Ruined*, the Fifth Monarchist John

Spittlehouse voices the traditional view that although a woman may teach in the home (like Aquila) or prophesy ("if they be so gifted") under ordinary circumstances she is not permitted to preach or speak in Church. Writing of his Dublin congregation, John Rogers remarks that this question has caused "bitter contentions" and was "one thing that helped to set at a distance the two societies" there. Perhaps because of his personal experience with this issue, Rogers' view is more liberal than many: he concludes that although women may not teach "as Officers or Ministers do," they may avail themselves of the "common, ordinary liberty due to them as members of the church. Viz. To speak, object, offer, or vote with the rest."[37]

For her part, Cary draws upon the authority accorded to women within domestic catechesis to argue for a broadened understanding of prophecy to include all of the godly. "And indeed every true Saint is a Prophet," affirms Cary, " because the Lord revealing his secrets to a soul, as it maketh it a Saint, so it maketh it a Prophet, and so the Lord looks upon his Saints as his Witnesses and Prophets. Ephesians 4:10–13." Again adopting the question-and-answer form, Cary asks and responds:

> OBJECT. But how could all the Witnesses of Christ be said to prophesy?
> I ANSWER. Every Saint in a sense may be said to be a Prophet. For they are Prophets to whom God discovers his secrets; and there are no true Saints, but the secrets of God are discovered to them.

Cary inverts the syntax, which conflates God's active discovery of his secrets with saints who have secrets "discovered." This phrase echoes Thomas Tillam's more conventional description of communal catechesis as the "opening" of the divine will revealed through the study of Scripture. Like the prophets, saints can have the secrets of God "dis-covered" or "opened" to them. "You that are Saints," Cary urges, returning to the topic of group scriptural study, "have Communion with one another."[38]

Cary also invokes catechesis to advocate an expansion of the prophetic office. Just as "every true Saint is a Prophet," so all of the godly are called to teach and minister to one another. "A man that is a true Prophet of Jesus Christ may be, and in some degree truly is, an Evangelist, and Pastour, and Teacher also." For,

> First, to be an Evangelist, is to be able to hold forth the Gospel, in the grace and sweetnesse of it, and he that is so, in an Evangelist. And
> Secondly, to be a Pastour, is to be able to feed the flock of Christ, both the sheep and the tender Lambs, with the wholesome saving truths of Christ, to the nourishing, and strengthening of their Souls. And

> Thirdly, to be a Teacher, is to be able to unfold the mysteries of the Gospel, and clearly to hold forth the truths of Christ, to the instruction of the ignorant, and increasing of knowledge. And he that is so is a Teacher. Now he that is a Prophet, may be all these.[39]

According to Cary, the prophet is not exclusively a divinely chosen mouthpiece infused with heavenly knowledge (although she may be that); a prophet is also an evangelist, pastor, and, perhaps most importantly, teacher, a person who relies upon reason to "unfold the mysteries of the Gospel" to instruct the ignorant – which is, of course, precisely what Cary does in *Resurrection of the Witnesses*. Her understanding of prophecy reflects a shift in emphasis: whereas previous understandings emphasize the prophet's relation to God, Cary defines a prophet relationally – a person is a prophet when they "feed" and instruct" a community. "It cannot be said of a Prophet," concludes Cary, "that he is no Evangelist, nor Pastor, nor Teacher."[40]

Cary recognizes the challenge inherent in her redefinition of prophecy. Against those who claim that the offices of teaching and preaching belong exclusively to ministers, Cary insists that educational status and gender are irrelevant to one's ability to serve as a prophet; what matters is the speaker's intent: "He that speaketh to edification, exhortation, and consolation, though with much weakness, doth as truly prophesy as he that has the greatest abilities." "Prophesying, and Evangelizing, and feeding, and teaching, and building up one another" declares Cary, "were common to all in the Church, as everyone had received the gift so as to minister as good stewards of the Grace they had received." "It is hereby clear," Cary concludes, "That they may be Prophets, Evangelists, Pastors, and Teachers, that were never ordained by the laying on of hands." A marginal note defiantly concludes that "to confine this speaking or prophesying to such only as are ordained Bishops or Presbyters is a principle derived from Babylonian darkness and hath not the least footing in the Scripture."[41]

Cary acknowledges that the gift of prophecy is not given equally to all: some saints have a larger share of prophetic gifts. To explain this, Cary draws upon 1 Corinthians 12:8–10:

> For to one is given by the Spirit the word of wisedome, to another the word of knowledge, by the same Spirit, to another faith, by the same Spirit, to another, the gift of healing, by the same Spirit, to another the working of miracles, to another prophecie, to another discerning spirits, to another divers kinds of tongues, to another the interpretation of tongues.

For Cary, the significance of this passage is that the disposition of gifts takes place within community. It is certainly possible for one person to possess all of these gifts; Cary acknowledges this to have been the case with Paul. "I say a Prophet may be, an Evangelist, a Pastor, and a Teacher, and so was Paul." But in most communities the gifts are distributed among its members. "Here the Apostle speaks of severall gifts, and saith that one is given to one, and another to another and a third to a third, etc. And his meaning is, That one saint is more eminent for one gift and another for another . . . ."[42] Just as divine truths "are discovered" and "opened" to the saints through communal scriptural study, so the gifts of the spirit are commonly experienced in community.

Cary explains that her understanding of Christian community prevents her from remaining silent, even though her public teaching violates religious restrictions on female teaching. "It is not possible for Instruments to be silent, nor to sit still, when God hath spoken to them and given them commission to do his work." Cary describes the workings of God in her heart with an analogy to human anatomy: A real saint cannot "but give vent to the bublings of Christ upon his heart." Implicit in the image is a sense of irresistible dynamism: just as pent up fluid requires release, so a saint must "hold forth the truths of Christ" to others. Cary does not seek to advance herself through her writings, but to support the spiritual life of the entire godly community. As a person who has been given the gift of teaching, she believes that she has the responsibility to share what she has learned about God's plans from her scriptural study. She concludes by urging those who are skeptical to attend communal gatherings, where they can witness for themselves the disposition of spiritual gifts: "Now do you desired to be edifyed? Do you desire to press forward toward perfection, that you may not be as children, carried about with every wind of doctrine? Then frequent assemblies of the Saints that you may partake of their gifts."[43]

As Say Historians

One year after *The Resurrection of the Witnesses* was published, an anonymous author responded to it, making Cary the only one of the six female catechists we have considered in the present study whose work was acknowledged in print. *The Account Audited* (1649) does not base its response on Cary's gender, although the author does contemptuously refer to her as "this female minister."[44] Instead, *The Account Audited* criticizes Cary's reliance upon oral exegesis. *The Resurrection of the Witnesses* has two key claims: that Revelation 11:7, which narrates the slaying of the two witnesses, refers to the Irish Rising of 1641 and that Revelation 11:11, which relates the resurrection of the witnesses, prefigures the revitalization of the New Model Army in 1645. In the 1648 text, Cary supports these claims with intricate computations:[45]

> that tearm of time which the Beast was to continue, and the Saints to be trodden under foot and to prophesie in sackcloth, is a thousand two hundred and threescore years as appears page 62. Now this 1260 years, being added to the year wherein the Beast received his devilish power, and feat, and great authority, in the rain of Phocus the Emperour: which was, as say Historians, in the year 404. I say adding to this, 1260, it makes up, 1664. And this year, 1664, should be the year wherein the Witnesses should finish giving their Testimony, Clothed in sackcloth, If this 1260 years should be computed according to the rule of Astronomers, allowing 365 daies to a year, and to every fourth year adding a day more. But we find that the holy Ghost in this prophesie, not observing that rule, doth allow but 360 daies to a year, and according to that rule, 1260 daies to three years and a half.[46]

Cary concludes that if one assumes that a year contains 365 days, then the resurrection of the witnesses will occur in 1664, but if one calculates according to the way "the holy Ghost here laies down," "the time of the Witnesses prophesying in sackcloth, is to expire eighteen years and almost a half, sooner then as by the other account: and so the beginning of the year 1645," the date that a newly invigorated New Model Army "began to march against the enemy."[47]

We might expect the author of *The Account Audited* to take issue with Cary's determination that a year consists of 360 days. But he does not. Instead, he claims that Cary errs in her knowledge of history:

> The author tels us on page 81 and 82 'That Historians say, the yeare 404 was the yeare wherein the Beast received his devilish power and seat in the reign of Phocas the Emperor.'
> ... I shall therefore debate it fully, wherein we might have made a more short cut, if the author had told us who are those Historians and where they say so. I have upon this occasion perused a variety of Historians, but all that I have met with do make the History of Phocas at least 200 y. later.[48]

The Account Audited argues that Cary misdates the reign of the emperor Phocas by 200 years and hence errs in her calculation. More significantly, Cary has not cited written (and thus verifiable) sources to support her calculation. By contrast, the author of *The Account Audited* conscientiously cites pages from Cary's text and examines "a variety of Historians" to check the validity of Cary's date. The author concludes by listing a number of published books, with precise page references, that Cary might have consulted to determine the precise date of the reign of Phocas: Szegedin's *Looking Glasse of Popes*, Barnes' *Treatise of the Lives of the Popes*, Morney's *Mysterie of Iniquity*, Cyprian Valera's *Treatise of the Lives of the Popes*, and Heylin's *Microcosmus*.[49]

This list suggests the vibrancy of religious print culture in mid seventeenth-century England, but it also exposes the basis for *The Account Audited*'s objection: *The Resurrection of the Witnesses* is the product of a communal scriptural study that attempts to compete with the learned and literate exegesis produced by Protestant ministers. In his preface to Cary's *The Little Horn's Doom and Downfall* (1651), the Fifth Monarchist Christopher Feake suggests that this distinction underpins contemporary objections to many of Cary's publications: "Many wise men after the flesh have been (and now are) much offended, that a company of illiterate men, and silly women, should pretend to any skill in dark prophecies and to a foresight of future events, which the most learned Rabbies, and the most knowing Politicians, have not presumed to hope for."[50] Thomas Tillam, the Baptist minister that we considered earlier, understood this difference and sought to bridge it, explaining his supra-rational vision with references to published authorities.[51]

Insisting that he does not object in principle to the work of an untrained (and admittedly talented) amateur, the author of *The Account Audited* labors to understand how Cary could have made such an error:

> I have cast about in my thoughts to see how a mistake of this nature could, in an Author of such abilities, be interpreted more favorably than a willful misreckoning, and two ways I doe apprehend that possibly the mistake might be entertained unawares.
> 1. Peradventure the author might have read in some History book, they year 404 misprinted for 604 ... though I have not yet met with that misprint in any one of those Treatises or in any of those Editions, which I have sought out and diligently compared on set purpose.
> 2. Peradventure the author might not have read the history of Phocas, but only received it upon hearsay, and so she might have mistook the Relator or swallowed down the relators mistake; and this later conjecture I look upon as the most probable in that it suits best with her own words, for shee does not say, "as historians write" but "as say historians."[52]

The author of *The Account Audited* criticizes Cary because she has based her analysis upon "hearsay," a term that he uses in a quasi-juridical sense to describe the act of erroneously obtaining evidence based upon a secondhand report. She does not say, "as historians write," he pointedly concludes, but, "as say historians." Because she has relied upon hearsay, Cary has "swallowed down the relators mistake" – wording that stresses the unreliability of oral communication.

The critique in *The Account Audited* turns on an implicit binary that associates educated evangelical male Protestants with sound exegesis and radical non-conformist women like Cary (and perhaps uneducated men) with communal hearsay. It concludes that her exegesis is necessarily unsound – a "pretended demonstration," "no more than a partial fansie."[53] Cary, however, seems not to have heeded such criticism, probably due to the importance she placed upon oral, communal, scriptural catechesis. In the 1653 edition, Cary alters her historical referents, associating the year 404 with the installation of Innocentius as Bishop of Rome and the beginning of the persecution of the Saints.[54] But she did not retract her reasoning. Instead, Cary doubles down, lodging a critique of an exclusively masculine ministerial authority by invoking Gospel accounts of the female resurrection witnesses. Just as the apostles rejected the women's authentic report, Cary suggests, so male authorities like the anonymous author of *The Account Audited* refuse to credit her teachings:

> When Jesus Christ himself was raised from the dead, his own disciples were in the dark concerning it, and scarce expected any such thing, and when it was told them they believed it not, then it is no wonder if now that his witnesses are raised, some of his own people are altogether in the dark, and see so little of it ... and with the rest of the disciples that when they were told by the women that had been at the sepulcre, that the Lord was risen, their words seemed unto them as idle tales and they believed them not.

"O fools," Cary exclaims, drawing upon Christ's words in Luke 24:25 to condemn her critics, "and slow of heart to believe all that the Prophets have spoken."[55]

Conclusion

Against those who hold that only an ordained male minister or divinely inspired female prophet can teach others, Cary asserts the importance of experiencing God's will through group scriptural study, insisting that all who are called to serve as God's instruments ought to teach – no matter what their gender. Cary conceives group scriptural catechesis as a central means by which human beings come to experience God's love, a conception that accords with my claims in Chapter 1 that maternal catechesis enacts and affirms maternal love. The importance of community leads to a redefinition of prophetic office; for Cary, a prophet is anyone who teaches or edifies the community; all saints are prophets; each has a responsibility to the other. Her contemporaries recognized the egalitarian implications of her exegesis and responded by faulting her reliance upon oral instruction, but Cary was undaunted; her 1653 title page proclaims that "all objections [have been] answered by the Author." In *The Resurrection of the Witnesses*, Cary adapts the catechetical genre to evoke her vision of Christian community, a vision that insists that all saints – male or female, rich or poor – cannot only be prophets but evangelists, pastors, and teachers.

Notes

1. Bernard Capp, 'Cary, Mary (b. 1620/21)', rev. *Oxford Dictionary of National Biography*, Oxford University Press, 2004: (www.oxforddnb.com.ezproxy.depaul.edu/view/article/37266). Christopher Feake describes Cary's work as "being a Gentlewoman's thoughts put into form and order by her self." "Letter," in Mary Cary, *The Little Horns Doom and Downfall* (London, 1651), Early English Books Online, (172:e.1274 [1]), Sig. A6r. I have also consulted a (presumably earlier) variant of *The Little Horns Doom and Downfall* (London, 1651), held by the Huntington library, that lacks Feake's letter. See also the anonymous author of *The Account Audited*, 2, who writes of Cary that it is a pity that "a woman of her parts" should have written such a text (London, 1649). Erica Longfellow, *Women and Religious Writing in Early Modern England* (Cambridge: Cambridge University Press, 2004), 154, notes Cary's status and the "social intimacy" it afforded her "with the men in power."

2. Bernard Capp, *The Fifth Monarchy Men* (Faber & Faber, 1972); David Lowenstein, "Scriptural Exegesis, Female Prophecy, and Radical Politics in Mary Cary," *Studies in English Literature, 1500–1900* 46.1 (Winter, 2006): 133–53; Jane Baston, "History, Prophecy, and Interpretation: Mary Cary and Fifth Monarchism," *Prose Studies* 3 (1998): 1–18; Katharine Gillespie, *Domesticity and Dissent in the Seventeenth Century: English Women Writers and the Public Sphere* (Cambridge: Cambridge University Press, 2004), 215–61; Susan Wiseman, *Conspiracy and Virtue: Women, Writing, and Politics in Seventeenth-Century England* (Oxford: Oxford University Press, 2006), 132–4.

3. Mary Cary, *The Resurrection of the Witnesses* (London, 1648). The revised edition of the text is *The Resurrection of the Witnesses* (London, 1653), Early English Books Online (111:E.719 [2]). All subsequent references will be to the 1653 edition unless otherwise noted. Cary lists "Books already published by this Author" in the 1653 edition and informs readers where they can purchase them (Sig. B1v).

4. Longfellow, *Women and Religious Writing*, 154. Cary, *The Resurrection of the Witnesses*, Sig. D1v. James Holstun remarks that Mary Cary "never claimed divine illumination and practiced methodical, scriptural exegesis," which he terms "rational prophecy." *Ehud's Dagger: Class Struggle in the English Revolution* (London: Verso, 2000), 265.
5. On female prophets, see Phyllis Mack, *Visionary Women: Ecstatic Prophecy in Seventeenth-Century England* (Los Angeles: University of California Press, 1992); Erica Longfellow, "Anna Trapnel Sings of Her Lover," in *Women and Religious Writing*, 149–79. Diane Watt, *Secretaries of God: Women Prophets in Late Medieval and Early Modern England* (Woodbridge: D.S. Brewer, 1997); Dianne Purkiss, "Producing the Voice, Consuming the Body: Women Prophets of the Seventeenth Century," in *Women, Writing, and History*, ed. Isobel Grundy and Susan Wiseman (Athens, Georgia: University of Georgia Press, 1992), 139–58; Susan Wiseman, "Unsilent Instruments and the Devil's Cushions: Authority in Seventeenth-Century Women's Prophetic Discourse," in *New Feminist Discourses: Critical Essays on Theories and Texts*, ed. Isobel Armstrong (London: Routledge, 1992), 176–96; Hilary Hinds, *God's Englishwomen: Seventeenth-Century Radical Sectarian Writing and Feminist Criticism* (Manchester: Manchester University Press, 1996), 10–12.
6. Cary, *The Resurrection of the Witnesses*, Sig. D1v.
7. "Mary Cary," in *The Orlando Project: Women's Writing in the British Isles from the Beginnings to the Present*: (orlando.cambridge.org/The Orlando Project).
8. Ian Green, *The Christian's ABC: Catechisms and Catechizing in England* (Oxford: Oxford University Press, 1996), 52.
9. *The Account Audited*, 1, 2.
10. Cary, *The Resurrection of the Witnesses*, 72–3.
11. The phrase, "visionary utopianism," is from Lowenstein, "Scriptural Exegesis and Female Prophecy," 142–3. Holstun, *Ehud's Dagger*, 275.
12. McCarthy, D. J. "Prophecy in the Bible," *New Catholic Encyclopedia* 11 (Detroit: Gale, 2003), 758–759. Gale Virtual Reference Library (CX3407709149).
13. Donne, John, "Sermon Preached at St. Paul's Midsommer Day, 1622," in *Sermons*, ed. George Reuben Potter and Evelyn Mary Spearing Simpson, Vol. 4 (Berkeley: University of California Press, 1959), 147.
14. Redmond, R. X. "Theology of Prophecy," *New Catholic Encyclopedia* 11 (Detroit: Gale, 2003), 759–764, 760. Gale Virtual Reference Library (CX3407709150).
15. Redmond, "Theology of Prophecy," 761.
16. Longfellow, *Women and Religious Writing*, 161.
17. Quoted in Longfellow, *Women and Religious Writing*, 162.
18. Elizabeth Avery, *Scripture-Prophecies Opened* (London, 1647), Sig. A3r.
19. Cary, *The Resurrection of the Witnesses*, Sig. D1v.
20. Mack, *Visionary Women*, 107–8.

21. Thomas Tillam, *The Two Witnesses: Their Prophecy, Slaughter, Resurrection and Ascention* (London, 1651), 1–2.
22. Arnold Hunt, *The Art of Hearing: English Preachers and Their Audiences, 1590–1640* (Cambridge: Cambridge University Press, 2010), 76–7.
23. Cary, *The Resurrection of the Witnesses*, 81–2.
24. Alec Ryrie, *Being Protestant in Reformation Britain* (Oxford: Oxford University Press, 2013), 102–8.
25. Cary, *The Resurrection of the Witnesses*, 84.
26. Cary, *The Resurrection of the Witnesses*, 24.
27. Cary quotes here from the Authorized Version: "And upon her forehead was a name written, Mystery, Babylon the Great, the Mother of Harlots, and abominations of the Earth … And when I saw her, I wondred with great admiration" (Revelation 17:5–6). The same passage in the Geneva Bible is as follows: "And in her forehead was a name written, A mysterie, that great Babylon that mother of whoredoms and abomination of the earth … And when I saw her, I wondred with great marvell." The extended quote from Revelation 11:1–14 similarly confirms her reliance upon the Authorized Version (2–3). See my more extensive discussion of this issue in Chapter 5, endnote 67.
28. Cary, *The Resurrection of the Witnesses*, 26–30.
29. Cary, *The Resurrection of the Witnesses*, 26–7.
30. Josias Nichols, *An Order of Houshold Instruction* (London, 1596), Sig. D2r.
31. Cary, *The Resurrection of the Witnesses*, 28.
32. Cary, *The Resurrection of the Witnesses*, 4. Adam thanks Raphael for "this friendly condescension to relate / Things else by me unsearchable." *Paradise Lost*, in *Milton: Complete Poems and Major Prose*, ed. Merritt Hughes (Indianapolis: Hackett Publishing, 2003), 8:9–10.
33. Cary, *The Resurrection of the Witnesses*, 6–7, 9, 7.
34. Cary, *The Resurrection of the Witnesses*, 4, 5, 7.
35. Cary, *The Resurrection of the Witnesses*, 7.
36. Cary, *The Resurrection of the Witnesses*, 8, 9.
37. Longfellow, *Women and Religious Writing*, 159. John Spittlehouse, *Rome Ruined* (London, 1649), 314. John Rogers, *Ohel or Beth-Shemesh* (London, 1653), 463, 475. See also Capp, *The Fifth Monarchy Men*, 174.
38. Cary, *The Resurrection of the Witnesses*, 72, 36, 80.
39. Cary, *The Resurrection of the Witnesses*, 72, 73.
40. Cary, *The Resurrection of the Witnesses*, 75.
41. Cary, *The Resurrection of the Witnesses*, 37, 76, 79, 81.
42. Cary, *The Resurrection of the Witnesses*, 74, 73, 74.
43. Cary, *The Resurrection of the Witnesses*, 11, 37, 80.
44. *The Account Audited*, 2.
45. Although we know that Cary (or her printer) quotes from the Authorized Version of the Bible in *The Resurrection of the Witnesses* (1653), it is tempting to consider whether such calculations may have been encouraged by her (perhaps earlier) use of the Geneva Bible, which included in post 1599 editions

a table prefacing Franciscus Junius' annotations to Revelation. As Femke Molekamp describes it, "the table provides in one column a chronological list of events described in Revelation; the other column dates these events but . . . there is a blank space in the second column for some phenomena: the church's defeat of the whore of Babylon, the two beasts, the dragon, and death. The reader can fill in these details, and thus is invited by this table to be a historiographer of the apocalypse." *Women and the Bible in Early Modern England* (Cambridge: Cambridge University Press, 2013), 66–7.

46. Cary, *The Resurrection of the Witnesses* (London, 1648), 81–2.
47. Cary, *The Resurrection of the Witnesses* (London, 1648), 81–2, 99.
48. *The Account Audited*, 5–6.
49. *The Account Audited*, 6–7.
50. Cary, *The Little Horn's Doom and Downfall*, Sig. A6r.
51. Tillam, *The Two Witnesses*, 2.
52. *The Account Audited*, 9.
53. *The Account Audited*, 14.
54. Cary, *The Resurrection of the Witnesses*, 46.
55. Cary, *The Resurrection of the Witnesses*, Sig. C4r, Sig. C3r.

Epilogue
Catechisms and the History of Women's Writing

> Untaught and simple, can you hope to find,
> Candor so prevalent in human kind,
> As from a female lessons to receive,
> Must Woman dictate – and must Man believe?
>   Judith Singer Sargent, "Upon Printing My Little Catechism" (1782)[1]

Catechisms and Women's Writing has sought to recover a body of women's writing hidden in plain sight. It grew out of my conviction that scholars, partly because of their preference for literary genres as well as for politically subversive texts, had severely underestimated the importance of maternal catechesis in early modern England and thus failed to analyze these early modern female-authored texts. It was not difficult to find the six female catechists that I have discussed in this study. Moreover, there are at least three additional early modern female catechists – Dorcas Martin (1536/7–99), Anna Cromwell Williams (1623–88), and Sarah Henry Savage (1664–1752) – whose work I have discussed only briefly in this study but whose catechisms merit further consideration.[2] Further archival work will undoubtedly reveal additional female catechists, as well as numerous anonymous catechisms that may very well have been written by women. There are also multiple catechisms of unknown authorship that have been written in the margins of printed catechisms – the work of men and women who, following ministerial instructions, were expanding and amplifying the formal catechetical instruction.[3] These original catechisms, which remain unexplored, offer valuable insight into the lay practice of catechesis and, more broadly, the relation between print and manuscript composition in early modern England.

    Throughout, I have relied upon the work of scholars who have demonstrated the importance of attending to non-literary genres in the study of early modern women's textual production. This growing body of work, which has examined women's writings on monuments and sculptures as well as women's recipes, medicinal writings, and trial narratives, has turned scholarly attention to the many ways in which such writing reveals women's creativity, insight, and awareness of generic conventions.[4] At the same time, I have drawn upon scholarly work arguing for a broadened understanding of authorship that includes women's manuscript composition, compilation, and transcription.[5] I have also been influenced by scholars who have emphasized the centrality of religion to early modern women's writing, especially those who have urged that we pay attention to writing that does not directly challenge orthodox belief.[6] Underpinning these disparate scholarly approaches is a belief I share: if we are to understand early modern women's textual production, we need to put aside contemporary understandings of literary value and Romantic and post-Romantic understandings of authorship to consider instead the genres, forms, and compositional practices relied upon by the majority of early modern women.

By focusing upon the genre of catechism, I have sought to attend to the features shared across texts as well as the originality of individual catechisms. This method has allowed me to account for the variety of female catechisms while attending to the complexity of the genre's engagement with early modern culture. *Catechisms and Women's Writing* has explored catechisms written by gentlewomen, such as Lady Fitzwilliam and Lady Montagu, and tradeswomen like Dorothy Burch. It has studied female-authored catechisms displaying a range of religious beliefs within seventeenth-century Protestantism, from the Church of England loyalist Katherine Thomas to the evangelically minded Dorothy Burch. It has demonstrated that early modern women adapted the catechetical form for a variety of literate purposes, including redacting complex devotional treatises and copying published catechisms into manuscript devotionals. By remaining attentive to these disparate uses, *Catechisms and Women's Writing* has discovered two early modern women who used the catechetical form to engage with prohibited Catholic devotional texts. These chapters enlarge our understanding of the complex relationship between Catholicism and Church of England loyalism in seventeenth-century England.

Above all else, I have attempted in *Catechisms and Women's Writing* to convey not only the variety but also to account for the complexity and intelligence of early modern women's catechetical writing. Dorothy Burch, studied in Chapter 5, lived in in a small village in Kent. But she composed a catechism in order to display her – and her community's – scriptural knowledge and subsequently published it in order to intervene in a contemporary religious dispute. Katherine Thomas, studied in

Chapter 3, was a widow and mother who lived in a small agricultural community on the Welsh border who sympathetically read and commented upon a prohibited Catholic book. She was also deeply interested in the figure of Mary Magdalene and her role as the primary witness of Christ's resurrection, an interest she improbably shared with the religiously radical Fifth Monarchist Mary Cary. The household catechisms of Lady Katherine Fitzwilliam, discussed in Chapter 2, bear witness to her piercing intelligence and (arguably) her dry sense of humor. The image that emerges from close readings of these women's manuscript and print catechisms is not of silent and submissive subordinates. It is of flesh-and-blood women, from a variety of social classes, who have confidence in their ability to interpret scripture, teach religious doctrine, and serve as defenders of their religious communities. Their gender does not inhibit their creativity; it enables it.

Throughout this book I have tried to articulate a more nuanced understanding not only of gendered authorship but also of early modern motherhood. *Catechisms and Women's Writing* has demonstrated that in contrast to some scholarly representations of early modern maternity, print and manuscript catechisms represent mothers as religiously knowledgeable and capable women who enjoy spending time with their children. Early modern mothers saw catechesis as an enactment of their love for their children that also potentially contributed to the mother's own spiritual growth. I have argued further that catechesis provided early modern women with generic awareness and experience in argumentation and textual analysis – training that I have suggested was fundamental to their emergence as authors. *Catechisms and Women's Writing* has also demonstrated that two early modern women used the cultural authority afforded to them as maternal religious instructors to compose catechisms intervening in Civil War politics. By showing that motherhood could fuel intellectual activity and political action, *Catechisms and Women's Writing* joins recent work urging a reconsideration of maternal authority in early modern England.[7]

I have focused primarily on the seventeenth century, but this period is but the beginning of a long tradition of female catechists who asserted their authority in both the home and public spheres. Motivating their compositions, moreover, are many of the same factors that we have seen impelled seventeenth-century female catechetical composition. The American Judith Singer Sargent (1751–1820) wrote a catechism, *Some Deductions from the System Promulgated in the Page of Divine Revelation*, for her stepdaughters explaining Universalist doctrine. Hannah More (1745–1833) wrote a catechism to be used in the education of poor children, *Questions and*

Answers for the Mendip and Sunday Schools, which combined basic religious instruction with literacy lessons. The Norfolk gentlewoman Ann Fellowes carefully copied two catechisms in manuscript, likely in an effort to provide a textual representation of her pious maternity.[8] In the nineteenth century, Hannah Killiam (1774–1832), Mary Martha Sherwood (1775–1851), and Sarah Flowers Adams (1805–48) published catechisms as well.[9] These examples suggest that the catechism's association with virtuous womanhood and maternity continued to be used to authorize women's interventions in contemporary political and religious controversies. Singer Sargent's catechism, for example, provided a lively, scripturally based defense of Universalist belief; when, at the urging of her mother, she agreed to publish it, it became one of the Universalist Church's official articulations of its beliefs.[10] Hannah More's catechism was used as part of a wide-ranging effort at social and educational reform.[11] Our understanding of women's literary history changes when we think of it not as a fractured narrative of misunderstood, solitary literary geniuses but as a continuous tradition of composition in genres like the catechism. Conceptualized in this way, we discover a continuum of women's writing, one that spans generations and includes England and America.

There is, however, a difference between these women and their seventeenth-century predecessors: many of the eighteenth- and nineteenth-century women wrote in multiple genres. Ambivalent about entering into public religious debate by printing her catechism, Judith Singer Sargent described its publication as "crossing the Rubicon." She went on to become a published poet, playwright, and essayist, as well as an early advocate for women's education, publishing an essay, "On the Equality of the Sexes," in 1790.[12] Hannah More was an essayist, playwright, and friend of Samuel Johnson and Edmund Burke.[13] Ann Fellowes transcribed or composed a work of educational theory, which urges parents to encourage children's intellectual freedom. She also wrote poetry.[14] Whether these later writers viewed their catechetical compositions as stepping stones to their other compositions or, as I might argue, as one genre among many in which they could exercise their discursive and imaginative talents, they testify to the continued vitality of the genre whose origins I have studied in this book.

Notes

1. Sheila L. Skemp, *Judith Sargent Murray: A Brief Biography with Documents* (Boston: Bedford St. Martins, 1998), 132.

2. Dorcas Martin, *The Manner How to Examine*, in *Catechisms Written for Mothers, Schoolmistresses, and Children*, ed. Paula McQuade (Aldershot: Ashgate Publishing, 2008); Anna Cromwell Williams, MS Harleian 2311, Miscellany Compiled by Anna Cromwell Williams, British Library, London, UK; Sarah Henry, Bailey Collection A.2. 125, Commonplace Book and Catechetical Instructions on Sabbath Evenings, Chethams Library, Manchester, UK.
3. See, for example, the handwritten catechism composed within John Ball's *A Short Treatise* (London, 1631), held by the Union Theological Seminary, Early English Books Online (1226:22). An entire catechism has been written in the margins of *The ABC with the Catechism* (London, 1687), held by Cambridge University Library, Early English Books Online (2281:02). A copy of John Mayer's *The English Catechisme Explained* (London, 1635), held by the University of Illinois, Urbana-Champaign, contains extensive penciled cross-referencing and concludes with several handwritten prayers.
4. See Patricia Phillippy, ed. *The Writings of an English Sappho*, trans. Jaime Goodrich (Toronto: Centre for Reformation and Renaissance Studies, 2011). Phillippy observes that Elizabeth Russell's voice was conveyed through "her unpublished correspondence, manuscript poems, monumental inscriptions and elegies, sculptural images, legal transcripts, ceremonial performances, and a single printed translation" (5). See also Susan Frye, *Pens and Needles: Women's Textualities in Early Modern England* (Philadelphia: University of Pennsylvania Press, 2010); Rebecca Laroche, *Medical Authority and Englishwomen's Herbal Texts, 1550–1650* (Aldershot: Ashgate, 2009) and Wendy Wall, "Literacy and the Domestic Arts," *Huntington Library Quarterly*, Special Issue, "The Textuality and Materiality of Reading in Early Modern England," ed. Jennifer Richards and Fred Schurink 73:3 (2010): 383–412. Genelle Gertz discusses early modern women's trial narratives in *Heresy Trials and English Women Writers, 1400–1670* (Cambridge: Cambridge University Press, 2012).
5. Margaret Ezell has been a consistent advocate for the importance of early modern women's authorship in manuscript. See, for example, her *Social Authorship and the Advent of Print* (Baltimore: John Hopkins University Press, 1999). Victoria Burke makes a strong case for considering compilation as a form of female authorship: "Anne Bowyer's Commonplace Book (Bodleian Library, Ashmole MS 51): Reading and Writing among the 'Middling Sort,'" *Early Modern Literary Studies* 6.3 (2001): 1–28. Janel Mueller discusses the religious and political implications of Katherine Parr's compilation of her prayer book in *Katherine Parr: Complete Works and Correspondence*, ed. Janel Mueller (Chicago: University of Chicago Press, 2011), 489–510. Jaime Goodrich urges that we consider translation a form of female authorship in *Faithful Translators: Authorship, Gender, and Religion in Early Modern England* (Evanston, IL: Northwestern University Press, 2013).
6. See the groundbreaking essays in *Silent But for the Word: Tudor Women As Patrons, Translators, and Writers of Religious Works*, ed. Margaret Hannay

(Kent State University Press, 1985). I have been especially influenced by Janel Mueller, "A Tudor Queen Finds Voice: Katherine Parr's *Lamentation of a Sinner*," in *The Historical Renaissance: New Essays on Tudor and Stuart Literature and Culture*, ed. Heather Dubrow and Richard Strier (Chicago: University of Chicago Press, 1988), 15–47; and Erica Longfellow, *Women and Religious Writing in Early Modern England* (Cambridge: Cambridge University Press, 2004), 10–11, who argues powerfully for the importance of paying attention to what twenty-first-century critics sometimes dismiss as women's "private," and therefore "less transgressive" and "less interesting," religious writings.

7. I discuss these works in the introduction to this volume, 3.
8. Judith Singer Sargent, *Some Deductions from the System Promulgated in the Page of Divine Revelation* (Norwich, 1782); Hannah More, *Questions and Answers for the Mendip and Sunday Schools* (Bath, 1795), Eighteenth Century Collections Online (CW3321994724); Ann Fellowes, *A Short Catechism for the Instruction of Children*, Norfolk Record Office, Fel. 628, 554x2.
9. "Catechism," in *The Orlando Project: Women's Writing in the British Isles from the Beginnings to the Present* (orlando.cambridge.org/The Orlando Project).
10. Sheila L. Skemp, *First Lady of Letters: Judith Sargent Murray and the Struggle for Female Independence* (Philadelphia: University of Pennsylvania Press, 2009), 61–6.
11. Patricia Demers, *The World of Hannah More* (Lexington: University of Kentucky Press, 1996), 100–1.
12. Skemp, *First Lady of Letters*, 215. Skemp, 216, observes a connection between the views expressed in "On the Equality of the Sexes" and those presented in the introduction to Sargent Murray's catechism.
13. Demers, *The World of Hannah More*, 6.
14. Ann Fellowes, *Some Rules to Observe Respecting the Children*, Norfolk Record Office, Fel., 625, 554X2. The poem is contained within a Family Commonplace Book, Fel., 738, 555X2.

Select Bibliography

MANUSCRIPTS

British Library, London, UK
MS Harleian 2311. Miscellany Compiled by Anna Cromwell Williams.
Chethams Library, Manchester, UK
Bailey Collection A.2.125. Commonplace Book and Catechetical Instructions on Sabbath Evenings.
Bailey Collection A.2.126. Commonplace Book; Scriptural Questions.
The Huntington Library, San Marino, CA
HM 43213. An Introduction to the Christian Faith.
National Library of Wales, Aberystwyth
MS 4340A. Katherine Thomas' Commonplace Book.
Norfolk Record Office, Norfolk, UK
Fel. 628, 554X2. A Short Catechism for the Instruction of Children.
Fel. 625, 554X2. Some Rules to Observe Respecting the Children.
Fel. 738, 555X2. Commonplace Book.
Northamptonshire Record Office, Northampton, UK
FH 246. Devotional Notebook of Lady Katherine Fitzwilliam.
Montagu Vol.3, Folio 241. The Loose Papers of Lady Ann Montagu.
Warwickshire County Record Office, Warwickshire, UK
CR 1368 Vol.1/99. The Upbringing of Penelope and Kate Mordaunt.
William Andrews Clark Library, University of California
MS 20009.13. Manuscript Notebook Containing Transcriptions of Several Different Works by Joseph Hall.

EARLY PRINTED BOOKS

The ABC with the Catechism. London, 1687.
The ABC with the Catechism of the Church of England. Philadelphia, 1788.
Abbot, Robert. *Milk for Babes; Or, a Mother's Catechism for Her Children (1646).* In *Catechisms Written for Mothers, Schoolmistresses, and Children, 1575–1750,* edited by Paula McQuade. Aldershot: Ashgate Publishing, 2008.
The Account Audited. London, 1649.

Avery, Elizabeth. *Scripture-Prophecies Opened Which Are to Be Accomplished in These Last Times*. London, 1647.
B., W. *The Farmer's Catechize*. London, 1657.
Bagshaw, Edward. *The Life and Death of Mr. Vavasor Powell, That Faithful Minister and Confessor of Jesus*. London, 1671.
Ball, John. *A Short Treatise Contayning All the Principall Grounds of Christian Religion By Way of Questions and Answers*. London, 1617.
Ball, John. *A Treatise of Faith Divided into Two Parts*. London, 1637.
Baxter, Richard. *The Mother's Catechism*. In *The Practical Works of the Late Reverend and Pious Mr. Richard Baxter*, 29–56. London, 1707.
Baxter, Richard. *Reliquiae Baxterianae, or, Mr. Richard Baxter's Narrative of the Most Memorable Passages of His Life and Times*. London, 1696.
Bentham, Joseph. *The Society of the Saints: Or a Treatise of Good Fellowship*. London, n.d.
Bernard, Richard. *Two Twinnes: or Two Parts of One Portion of Scripture*. London, 1613.
The Bible: That Is, the Holy Scriptures. London, 1610.
Blount, Thomas. *Kalendarium Catholicum for the Year 1686*. London, 1686.
Bunyan, John. *Grace Abounding With Other Spiritual Autobiographies*, edited by John Stachniewski and Anita Pacheo. Oxford: Oxford University Press, 1998.
Bunyan, John. *Instruction for the Ignorant* (1675). In *The Complete Works of John Bunyan*, edited by John Gulliver. Vol. 4, 926–43. Philadelphia, 1874.
Bunyan, John. *The Pilgrim's Progress*, edited by Roger Lundin. New York: Penguin, 2002.
Burch, Dorothy. *A Catechisme of the Severall Heads of Christian Religion* (1646). In *Catechisms Written for Mothers, Schoolmistresses, and Children, 1575–1750*, edited by Paula McQuade. Aldershot: Ashgate Publishing, 2008.
Canisius, Peter. *An Introduction to the Catholick Faith* (1633). In *English Recusant Literature, 1558–1640*. Vol. 134. Ilkley: Scolar Press, 1973.
C., E. *An A.B.C. or Holy Alphabet, Conteyning Some Plaine Lessons Gathered Out of the Word*. London, 1626. Early English Books Online (E3:4[4]).
C. J., Mrs. *The Mother's Catechism in an Explication of Some Questions of the Assemblies Shorter Catechism* (1734). In *Catechisms Written for Mothers, Schoolmistresses, and Children, 1575–1750*, edited by Paula McQuade. Aldershot: Ashgate Publishing, 2008.
Calendar of the Proceedings of the Committee for Advance of Money, Part 3, 1650–55, edited by Mary Anne Everett Green. Her Majesty's Stationary Office: London, 1888; reprint: Kraus reprint Ltd., Lichtenstein, 1967.
Cary, Mary. *The Little Horns Doom and Downfall or A Scripture-Prophesie of King James, and King Charles, and of This Present Parliament, Unfolded*. London, 1651.
Cary, Mary. *The Resurrection of the Witnesses and England's Fall from (the Mystical Babylon) Rome Clearly Demonstrated to Be Accomplished*. London, 1648.
Cary, Mary. *The Resurrection of the Witnesses and England's Fall from (the Mystical Babylon) Rome Clearly Demonstrated to Be Accomplished*. London, 1653. Early English Books Online (111:E719[2]).

Castlemaine, Roger Palmer. *To All the Royalists That Suffered for His Majesty, and to the Rest of the Good People of England the Humble Apology of the English Catholicks.* London, 1666.

Cawdry, Robert. *A Short and Fruitfull Treatise, of the Profit and Necessitie of Catechising.* London, 1604. Early English Books Online (1599:12).

Clark, Samuel. *The Blessed Life and Meritorious Death of Our Lord and Saviour Jesus Christ.* London, 1664.

Clark, Samuel. *The Lives of Sundry Eminent Persons in this Later Age in Two Parts.* London, 1683.

The Confession of Faith and the Longer and Shorter Catechism. Glasgow, 1675.

Cooper, Thomas. *The Christian's Daily Sacrifice Containing a Daily Direction for a Setled Course of Sa[n]ctification.* London, 1608.

Coote, Edmund. *The English Schoolmaster Teaching All His Scholars.* London, 1670.

Craig, John. *The Mother and the Child: A Short Catechisme or Briefe Summe of Religion, Gathered Out of Mr. Cragges Catechisme* (1611). In *Catechisms Written for Mothers, Schoolmistresses, and Children, 1575–1750*, edited by Paula McQuade. Aldershot: Ashgate Publishing, 2008.

Craig, John. *A Short Summe of the Whole Catechisme Wherin the Question Is Propounded, and Answered in Few Words.* London, 1632.

Croft, Herbert. *A Short Narrative of the Discovery of a College of Jesuits at a Place Called the Come in the County of Hereford.* London, 1679.

Culverwell, Ezekiel. *A Treatise of Faith Wherein Is Declared How a Man May Live by Faith and Finde Releefe in All His Necessities.* London, 1623.

Donne, John. "Sermon Preached at St. Paul's Midsommer Day, 1622." In *Sermons*, edited by George Reuben Potter and Evelyn Mary Spearing Simpson. Vol. 4, 145–62. Berkeley: University of California Press, 1959.

Donne, John. "To Mrs. Magdalen Herbert: Of Saint Mary Magdalene." In *The Complete Poems of John Donne*, edited by Robin Robbins, 489–90. London: Longman, 2010.

Downame, John. *A Guide to Godlynesse or a Treatise of a Christian Life Shewing the Duties Wherein It Consisteth.* London, 1622.

Dugdale, William. *The History of St. Pauls Cathedral in London from Its Foundation Untill These Times.* London, 1658.

Egerton, Stephen. *The Practice of Christianitie. Or, An Epitomie of Seven Treatises.* London, 1618. Early English Books Online (1609:13).

Egerton, Stephen. *The Practice of Christianitie. Or, An Epitomie of Seven Treatises.* London, 1623.

The First Book for Children: or, the Compleat School-Mistress (1705). In *Catechisms Written for Mothers, Schoolmistresses, and Children, 1575–1750*, edited by Paula McQuade. Aldershot: Ashgate Publishing, 2008.

Fiske, John. *The Watering of the Olive Plant in Christ's Garden. Or A Short Catechism for the First Entrance of Our Chelmesford Children.* Cambridge, Massachusetts Bay Colony, 1657.

Foley, Henry. *Records of the English Province of the Society of Jesus.* London: Burns & Oates, 1878.

Gouge, William. *Of Domesticall Duties*. London, 1622.
Gouge, William. "To the Christian Reader." In *The Practice of Christianitie, or, An Epitomie of Seven Treatises*, Sig. a4v–a6v. London, 1623.
The Grounds and Principles of Religion Contained in a Shorter Catechism. London, 1708.
Hall, Joseph. "A Brief Summe." In *The Works of Joseph Hall Doctor in Divinitie, and Deane of Worcester*, 799–800. London, 1625.
Hall, Joseph. *Contemplations Upon the Remarkable Passages in the Life of the Holy Jesus*. London, 1679.
Hasted, Edward. *The History and Topographical Survey of Kent*. Canterbury, 1797.
Heigham, John, ed. *The Life of Our Lord and Savior Jesus Christ*. St. Omer, 1634.
Herbert, George. *A Priest to the Temple, or, The Country Parson, His Character, and Rule of Holy Life*. London, 1671.
Hieron, Samuel. *The Doctrine of the Beginning of Christ Short for Memory, Plaine for Capacitie*. London, 1620.
Hoffman, John. *The Principles of Christian Religion in Twenty Questions and Answers*. Oxford, 1653. Early English Books Online (1880:08).
The Holy Bible, 1611 edition. King James Version. Peabody, MA: Hendrickson Publishers, 2010.
Hunter, Father Thomas, ed. *An English Carmelite: The Life of Catharine Burton, Mother Mary Xaveria of the Angels... Collected from Her Own Writings and Other Sources*. London, 1883.
The Key of Paradise (1623). In *English Recusant Literature, 1558–1640*, Vol. 394. Ilkley: Scolar Press, 1979.
The Key of Paradise Opening the Gate to Eternal Salvation. St. Omer, 1675. Early English Books Online (944:08).
Leslie, Henry. *A Full Confutation of the Covenant Lately Sworne and Subscribed By Many in Scotland*. London, 1639.
Martin, Dorcas. *The Manner How to Examine (1582)*. In *Catechisms Written for Mothers, Schoolmistresses, and Children, 1575–1750*, edited by Paula McQuade. Aldershot: Ashgate Publishing, 2008.
Mayer, John. *The English Catechisme Explained*. London, 1635.
Milton, John. *Paradise Lost*. In *Milton: Complete Poems and Major Prose*, edited by Merritt Hughes, 173–470. Indianapolis: Hackett Publishing, 2003.
More, Hannah. *Questions and Answers for the Mendip and Sunday Schools*. Bath, 1795. Eighteenth Century Collections Online (CW3321994724).
Nichols, Josias. *An Order of Houshold Instruction*. London, 1596.
Noble, Mark. *Memoirs of the Protectoral-House of Cromwell; Deduced from an Early Period, and Continued Down to the Present Time*. London, 1787.
Nowell, Alexander. *A Catechisme, or First Instruction and Learning of Christian Religion*. London, 1571.
Pagit, Eusebius. *The Historie of the Bible Briefly Collected by Way of Question and Answer*. London, 1628.
Parsons, Daniel, ed. *The Diary of Sir Henry Slingsby, of Scriven, Bart*. London, 1836.

Perkins, William. *An Exposition of the Symbole or Creed of the Apostles According to the Tenour of the Scriptures.* London, 1595.

Perkins, William. *The Foundation of Christian Religion Gathered into Sixe Principles.* London, 1597.

Plomer, Henry, ed. *The Churchwardens' Accounts of Saint Nicholas, Strood.* Kent Archeological Society: Kent, 1927.

Powell, Vavasor. *The Scriptures Concord or a Catechisme, Compiled out of the Words of Scripture.* London, 1646.

Powell, Vavasor. *Spirituall Experiences of Sundry Beleevers Held forth by Them at Severall Solemne Meetings, and Conferences to that End.* London, 1653. Early English Books Online (180:E1389[1]).

Priestly, Joseph, ed. *Dr. Watts' Historical Catechisms.* Dublin, 1793.

Rigge, Ambrose. *A Scripture-Catechism for Children Collected Out of the Whole Body of the Scriptures for the Instructing of Youth.* London, 1672.

Rogers, John. *Ohel or Beth-Shemesh A Tabernacle for the Sun.* London, 1653.

Rogers, Richard. *Seven Treatises Containing Such Direction as is Gathered out of the Holie Scriptures.* London, 1603.

Sargent, Judith Singer. *Some Deductions from the System Promulgated in the Page of Divine Revelation: Ranged in the Order and Form of a Catechism: Intended as an Assistant to the Christian Parent or Teacher.* Norwich, 1782.

Slingsby, Henry, Sir. *A Father's Legacy. Sir Henry Slingsbey's Instructions to His Sonnes.* York, 1706. In Daniel Parsons, ed. *The Diary of Sir Henry Slingsby, of Scriven, Bart,* 195–236. London, 1836.

Spittlehouse, John. *Rome Ruin'd by White Hall, or, The Papall Crown Demolisht.* London, 1649.

Taffin, Jean. *Of the Markes of the Children of God, and of Their Comforts in Affliction (1590),* translated by Anne Prowse. In *The Collected Works of Anne Vaughn Lock,* edited by Susan M. Felch, 74–190. Tempe, AZ: Renaissance English Text Society, 1999.

Taylor, Jeremy. *Antiquitates Christianae, or, The History of the Life and Death of the Holy Jesus.* London, 1678.

Taylor, Jeremy. *Unum Necessarium. Or, The Doctrine and Practice of Repentance.* London, 1655.

Tillam, Thomas. *The Two Witnesses: Their Prophecy, Slaughter, Resurrection and Ascention: or, An Exposition of the Eleventh Chapter of the Revelation.* London, 1651.

The Way to True Happiness. London, 1642.

"To Our Beloved in the Lord." In *The Geneva Bible: A Facsimile of the 1560 Edition.* Peabody, MA: Hendrickson Publishing, 2007.

Watts, Isaac. *A Discourse on the Way of Instruction by Catechisms.* London, 1786.

Webber, George. "A Short Exercise." In *A Garden of Spiritual Flowers.* London, 1687.

Wilson, John. *The English Martyrologe.* St. Omer, 1608.

Wilson, John. *The Treasury of Devotion Contayning Divers Pious Prayers and Exercises Both Practicall, and Speculative (1622).* In *English Recusant Literature, 1558–1640.* Vol. 346. Ilkley: Scolar Press, 1977.

Willison, John. *The Mother's Catechism for the Young Child* (1735). In *Catechisms Written for Mothers, Schoolmistresses, and Children, 1575–1750*, edited by Paula McQuade. Aldershot: Ashgate Publishing, 2008.

SECONDARY SOURCES

Adelman, Janet. *Suffocating Mothers: Fantasies of Maternal Origin in Shakespeare*. London: Routledge, 1992.

Allison, A.F. "John Heigham of St. Omer." *Recusant History* 4 (1959): 226–42.

Archibold, W.A. "John Kemble." In *Oxford Dictionary of National Biography*. Oxford: Oxford University Press, 2004. http://www.oxforddnb.com.ezproxy.depaul.edu/view/article/15320.

Baston, Jane. "History, Prophecy, and Interpretation: Mary Cary and Fifth Monarchism." *Prose Studies* 3 (1998): 1–18.

Blom, J.M. *The Post-Tridentine English Primer*. The Netherlands: Catholic Record Society, 1982.

Brown, Raymond. *An Introduction to the New Testament*. New Haven: Yale University Press, 1997.

Brown, Raymond. *The Community of the Beloved Disciple*. New York: Paulist Press, 1979.

Brown, Raymond. "Roles of Women in the Fourth Gospel." In *The Community of the Beloved Disciple*, 183–98. New York: Paulist Press, 1979.

Brown, Sylvia. "The Eloquence of the Word and the Spirit." In *Women and Religion in Old and New Worlds*, edited by Susan Dinan and Debora Meyers, 187–212. New York: Routledge, 2001.

Brown, Sylvia. "'Over Her Dead Body': Feminism, Post Structuralism, and the Mother's Legacy." In *Discontinuities: New Essays on Renaissance Literature and Criticism*, edited by Paul Stevens and Viviana Comensoli, 3–26. Toronto: University of Toronto Press, 1998.

Burke, Victoria. "Anne Bowyer's Commonplace Book (Bodleian Library, Ashmole MS 51): Reading and Writing among the 'Middling Sort'." *Early Modern Literary Studies* 6, no. 3 (2001): 1–28.

Burke, Victoria. "Manuscript Miscellanies." In *The Cambridge Companion to Early Modern Women's Writing*, edited by Laura Lunger Knoppers, 54–67. Cambridge: Cambridge University Press, 2009.

Burke, Victoria. "'My Poor Returns': Devotional Manuscripts by Seventeenth-Century Women." *Parergon: Journal of the Australian and New Zealand Association for Medieval and Early Modern Studies* 29, no. 2 (2012): 47–68.

Burke, Victoria. "Seventeenth-Century Women's Manuscript Writing." In *The History of Women's Writing, 1610–1690*, edited by Mihoko Suzuki, 99–112. Basingstoke: Palgrave Macmillan, 2011.

Bynum, Caroline. *Jesus as Mother*. Berkeley: University of California Press, 1982.

Bynum, Caroline. *The Resurrection of the Body in Western Christianity*. New York: Columbia University Press, 1995.

Cambers, Andrew. "Reading, the Godly, and Self Writing in England, circa 1580–1720." *Journal of British Studies* 46 (2007): 796–825.
Cambers, Andrew and Michelle Wolfe. "Reading, Family Religion, and Evangelical Identity." *The Historical Journal* 47 (2004): 875–96.
Capp, Bernard. "Cary, Mary (b. 1620/21)." In *The Oxford Dictionary of National Biography*. Oxford: Oxford University Press, 2004. http://www.oxforddnb.com.ezproxy.depaul.edu/view/article/37266.
Capp, Bernard. *The Fifth Monarchy Men*. New York: Faber & Faber, 1972.
Cannon, Charles Dale, ed. *A Warning for Fair Women*. The Hague: Mouton, 1975.
Charlton, Kenneth. *Women, Religion, and Education in Early Modern England*. London: Routledge, 1999.
Chartier, Roger. "Laborers and Voyagers: From the Text to the Reader." *Diacritics* 22, no.2 (1992): 49–61.
Chedgzoy, Kate. *Women's Writing in the British Atlantic World: Memory, Place, History, 1550–1700*. Cambridge: Cambridge University Press, 2007.
Clark, Peter. *English Provincial Society from the Reformation to the Revolution: Religion, Politics, and Society in Kent, 1500–1640*. Rutherford: Farleigh Dickinson Press, 1977.
Clarke, Elizabeth. "The Legacy of Mothers and Others." In *Religion in Revolutionary England*, edited by Christopher Durston and Judith Maltby, 69–90. Manchester: Manchester University Press, 2006.
Cliffe, J.T. *The Puritan Gentry*. London: Routledge, 1984.
Coles, Kimberly Ann. *Religion, Reform, and Women's Writing in Early Modern England*. Cambridge: Cambridge University Press, 2008.
Collinson, Patrick. "A Comment Concerning the Name Puritan." *Journal of Ecclesiastical History* 31 (1980): 483–88.
Collinson, Patrick. *The Elizabethan Puritan Movement*. Berkeley: University of California Press, 1967.
Collinson, Patrick. "England and International Calvinism," in *From Cranmer to Sancroft*, 75–100. London: Hambledon Continuum, 2006.
Collinson, Patrick. "The English Coventicle," in *From Cranmer to Sancroft*, 145–72. London: Hambledon Continuum, 2006.
Crawford, Julie. "Literary Circles and Communities." In *The History of British Women's Writing, 1500–1610*, edited by Caroline Bicks and Jennifer Summit, 34–59. Basingtoke: Palgrave Macmillan, 2010.
Cressy, David. *Literacy and Social Order*. Cambridge: Cambridge University Press, 1980.
Cust, Richard. "Montagu, Edward, 1562/3–1644." In *The Oxford Dictionary of National Biography*. Oxford: Oxford University Press, 2004. http://www.oxforddnb.com.ezproxy.depaul.edu/view/article/19007.
D. P. "Priory of Robert Knaresborough and Sir Henry Slingsby." *Notes and Queries* SXI (Jan. 19, 1867): 53–4.
Danielson, Dennis. "Catechism, *The Pilgrim's Progress* and the Pilgrim's Progress." *Journal of English and Germanic Philology* 94, no. 1 (1995): 42–58.

de Letter, P., "Two Concepts of Attrition and Contrition." *Theological Studies* (March 1950): 3–33.
Demers, Patricia. *The World of Hannah More*. Lexington: University of Kentucky Press, 1996.
Dobranski, Stephen. *Milton, Authorship, and the Book Trade*. Cambridge: Cambridge University Press, 1991.
Dolan, Frances. *Dangerous Familiars*. Ithaca, NY: Cornell University Press, 1994.
Dowd, Michelle. "Genealogical Counter Narratives in the Writings of Mary Cary." *Modern Philology* 109, no. 4 (2012): 440–62.
Duffy, Eamon. "The Godly and the Multitude in Stuart England." *Seventeenth Century* 1, no. 1 (1986): 31–55.
Duffy, Eamon. "The Long Reformation: Catholicism, Protestantism, and the Multitude." In *England's Long Reformation, 1500–1800*, edited by Nicholas Tyacke, 33–70. London: University College London Press, 1998.
Duffy, Eamon. *Marking the Hours*. New Haven: Yale University Press, 2006.
Durston, Christopher, ed., and Judith Maltby, ed. "Introduction," in *Religion in Revolutionary England*, 1–18. Manchester: Manchester University Press, 2006.
Eales, Jacqueline. *Puritans and Roundheads: The Harleys of Brampton Bryan*. Cambridge: Cambridge University Press, 1991.
Eales, Jacqueline. "So Many Sects and Schisms: Religious Diversity in Revolutionary Kent." In *Religion in Revolutionary England*, edited by Christopher Durston and Judith Maltby, 226–48. Manchester: Manchester University Press, 2006.
Everett Green, Mary Anne, ed. *Calendar, Committee for the Advance of Money*, Part 3, 1650–55. Her Majesty's Stationary Office: London, 1888.
Ezell, Margaret. "Elizabeth Isham's Book of Remembrance and Forgetting." *Modern Philology* (2009): 71–84.
Ezell, Margaret. *Social Authorship and the Advent of Print*. Baltimore: John Hopkins University Press, 1999.
Ezell, Margaret. *Writing Women's Literary History*. Baltimore: John Hopkins University Press, 1993.
F. C. H., "Sir Henry Slingsby." *Notes and Queries* SXI (March 2, 1867): 183.
Felch, Susan. "'Halff a Scripture Woman': Heteroglossia and Female Authorial Agency in Prayers by Lady Elizabeth Tyrwhit, Anne Lock, and Anne Wheathill." In *English Women, Religion, and Textual Production, 1500–1635*, edited by Micheline White, 147–66. Aldershot: Ashgate, 2011.
Finch, Mary. *Five Northamptonshire Families*. Winchester: Wykeham Press, 1966.
Fish, Stanley. *The Living Temple: George Herbert and Catechizing*. Berkeley: University of California Press, 1978.
Fitzmyer, Joseph. *The Gospel According to Luke (X-XXIV)*. Garden City, NJ: Doubleday, 1985.
Fowler, Alastair. *Kinds of Literature: An Introduction to the Theory of Genres and Modes*. Cambridge: Harvard University Press, 1982.
Frye, Susan. *Pens and Needles: Women's Textualities in Early Modern England*. Philadelphia: University of Pennsylvania Press, 2010.

Gertz, Genelle. *Heresy Trials and English Women Writers, 1400–1670*. Cambridge: Cambridge University Press, 2012.

Gillespie, Katharine. *Domesticity and Dissent in the Seventeenth Century: English Women Writers and the Public Sphere*. Cambridge: Cambridge University Press, 2004.

Goodrich, Jaime. "'Ensigne-Bearers of Saint Claire': Elizabeth Evelinge's Early Translations and the Restoration of English Franciscanism." In *English Women, Religion, and Textual Production, 1500–1625*, edited by Micheline White, 83–101. Aldershot: Ashgate Press, 2011.

Goodrich, Jaime. *Faithful Translators: Authorship, Gender, and Religion in Early Modern England*. Evanston, IL: Northwestern University Press, 2013.

Gordis, Lisa. *Opening Scripture: Bible Reading and Interpretive Authority in Puritan New England*. Chicago: University of Chicago Press, 2003.

Greaves, Richard. "Foundation Builders: the Role of Women in Early English Non- Conformity." In *Triumph Over Silence: Women in Protestant History*, edited by Richard Greaves, 75–92. London: Longwood Press, 1985.

Green, Ian. *The Christian's ABC: Catechisms and Catechizing in England, 1530–1740*. Oxford: Oxford University Press, 1996.

Green, Ian. "A Finding List of English Catechisms." In *The Christian's ABC: Catechisms and Catechizing in England, 1530–1740*. Oxford: Oxford University Press, 1996.

Green, Ian. *Print and Protestantism in Early Modern England*. Oxford: Oxford University Press, 2000.

Green, Ian. "Varieties of Domestic Devotion in Protestantism." In *Private and Domestic Devotion in Early Modern Britain*, edited by Jessica Martin and Alec Ryrie, 10–31. Aldershot: Ashgate, 2012.

Gregory, Brad S. "The True and Zealous Service of God: Robert Parsons, Edmund Bunny, and the First Book of Christian Exercises." *The Journal of Ecclesiastical History*, 45 no. 2 (1994): 238–68.

Groot, Jerome de. "Coteries, Complications, and the Question of Female Agency." In *The 1630's: Interdisciplinary Essays on Culture and Politics in the Caroline Era*, edited by Ian Atherton and Julie Sanders, 189–209. Manchester: Manchester University Press, 2006.

Groot, Jerome de. "Every One Teacheth After Thyr Own Fantasie." In *Performing Pedagogy in Early Modern England: Gender, Instruction, and Performance*, edited by Kathryn Moncrief and Kathryn McPherson, 33–52. Aldershot: Ashgate, 2011.

Hackel, Heidi Brayman. *Reading Material in Early Modern England: Print, Gender, and Literacy*. Cambridge: Cambridge University Press, 2005.

Hall, David. *World of Wonders, Days of Judgment*. New York: Knopf, 1989.

Hannay, Margaret, ed. *Silent But for the Word: Tudor Women as Patrons, Translators, and Writers of Religious Works*. Kent: Kent State University Press, 1985.

Heller, Jennifer Louise. *The Mother's Legacy in Early Modern England*. Aldershot: Ashgate, 2011.

Select Bibliography

Henry E. Huntington Library and Art Gallery. *Guide to British Historical Manuscripts in the Huntington Library*. San Marino: Huntington Library, 1982.

Hill, Christopher. *The World Turned Upside Down*. New York: Viking Press, 1972.

Hinds, Hilary. *God's Englishwomen: Seventeenth-Century Radical Sectarian Writing and Feminist Criticism*. Manchester: Manchester University Press, 1996.

Holstun, James. *Ehud's Dagger: Class Struggle in the English Revolution*. London: Verso, 2000.

Hopper, Andrew J. "Belasyse, John, first Baron Belasyse of Worlaby." In *The Oxford Dictionary of National Biography*. Oxford: Oxford University Press, 2004. http://www.oxforddnb.com.ezproxy.depaul.edu/view/article/1977.

Hunt, Arnold. *The Art of Hearing: English Preachers and Their Audiences, 1590–1640*. Cambridge: Cambridge University Press, 2010.

Jansen, Katherine Ludwig. "Maria Magdalena: Apostolorum Apostola." In *Women Preachers and Prophets through Two Millennia of Christianity*, edited by Beverly Kienzle and Pamela Walker, 57–96. Berkeley: University of California Press, 1998.

Kahn, Coppelia. "The Absent Mother in King Lear." In *Rewriting the Renaissance: The Discourses of Sexual Difference in Early Modern Europe*, edited by Margaret Ferguson, Maureen Quilligan, and Nancy Vickers, 33–49. Chicago: University of Chicago Press, 1985.

Keenan, Siobhan. "Embracing Submission? Motherhood, Marriage, and Mourning in Katherine Thomas's Seventeenth-Century Commonplace Book." *Women's Writing* 15, no. 1 (2008): 69–85.

King, Karen L. "Prophetic Power and Women's Authority: The Case of the Gospel of Mary (Magdalene)." In *Women Preachers and Prophets*, edited by Beverly Kienzle and Pamela J. Walker, 21–41. Berkeley: University of California Press, 1998.

King, Karen L. *The Gospel of Mary of Magdala: Jesus and the First Woman Apostle*. Santa Rosa, California: Polebridge Press, 2003.

Knight, Janice. *Orthodoxies in Massachusetts*. Harvard: Harvard University Press, 1994.

Knights, Mark. *Representation and Misrepresentation in Later Stuart Britain: Partisanship and Political Culture*. Oxford: Oxford University Press, 2005.

Lake, Peter and Michael Questier. "Prisons, Priests and People." In *England's Long Reformation 1500–1800*, edited by Nicholas Tyacke, 195–235. London: University College London Press, 1998.

Laroche, Rebecca. *Medical Authority and Englishwomen's Herbal Texts, 1550–1650*. Aldershot: Ashgate, 2009.

Lierheimer, Linda. "Preaching or Teaching, Defining the Ursuline Mission in Seventeenth-Century France." In *Women Preachers and Prophets through Two Millennia of Christianity*, edited by Beverly M. Kienzle and Pamela J. Walker, 212–26. Berkeley: University of California Press, 1998.

Longfellow, Erica. *Women and Religious Writing in Early Modern England*. Cambridge: Cambridge University Press, 2004.

Love, Harold. *Scribal Publication in Seventeenth-Century England*. Oxford: Oxford University Press, 1993.

Lowenstein, David. "Scriptural Exegesis, Female Prophecy, and Radical Politics in Mary Cary." *Studies in English Literature, 1500–1900* 46, no. 1 (2006): 133–53.

Ludlow, Dorothy. "Shaking Patriarchy's Foundations." In *Triumph Over Silence: Women in Protestant History*, edited by Richard Greaves, 93–123. London: Longwood Press, 1985.

Mack, Phyllis. "In a Female Voice: Preaching and Politics in Eighteenth-Century British Quakerism." In *Women Preachers and Prophets through Two Millennia of Christianity*, edited by Beverly M. Kienzle and Pamela J. Walker, 248–63. Berkeley: University of California Press, 1998.

Mack, Phyllis. *Visionary Women: Ecstatic Prophecy in Seventeenth-Century England*. Berkeley: University of California Press, 1992.

Marotti, Arthur. *Manuscript, Print, and the English Renaissance Lyric*. Ithaca: Cornell University Press, 1995.

Maltby, Judith. "Suffering and Surviving: The Civil Wars, the Commonwealth, and the Formation of 'Anglicanism,' 1642–1660." In *Religion in Revolutionary England*, edited by Christopher Durston and Judith Maltby, 158–80. Manchester: Manchester University Press, 2006.

Mathias, Roland. *Whitsun Riot: An Account of a Commotion amongst Catholics in Herefordshire and Monmouthshire in 1605*. London: Bowes and Bowes, 1963.

McCarthy, D. J. "Prophecy in the Bible." *New Catholic Encyclopedia* 11 (2003): 758–59. Gale Virtual Reference Library (CX3407709149).

McGiffert, Michael. *God's Plot: Puritan Spirituality in Thomas Shepard's Cambridge*. Amherst: University of Massachusetts Press, 1994.

McKenzie, D. F. "The Economies of Print, 1550–1750." In *Produzione e Commercio della Carta e del Libro secc. XIII-XVIII: atti della "Ventriteesima Settimana di Studi, 15 Aprile, 1991,"* 389–425. Firenze: le Monnier, 1992.

McKenzie, D. F. "Speech-Manuscript-Print." In *Making Meaning: Printers of the Mind and Other Essays*, edited by Peter D. McDonald and Michael F. Suarez, 237–58. Amherst: University of Massachusetts Press, 2003.

McPherson, Kathryn and Kathryn Moncrief. *Performing Maternity in Early Modern England*. Aldershot: Ashgate, 2008.

McPherson, Kathryn and Kathryn Moncrief. *Performing Pedagogy in Early Modern England: Gender, Instruction, and Performance*. Aldershot: Ashgate, 2011.

McQuade, Paula. "Household Religious Instruction in Seventeenth-Century England and America: The Case of Sarah Symmes Fiske's *A Confession of Faith* (Composed 1672)." *ANQ* 24 (2011): 108–17.

McQuade, Paula. "Introductory Note." In *Catechisms Written for Mothers, Schoolmistresses, and Children, 1575–1750*. Aldershot: Ashgate, 2008.

Molekamp, Femke. "Reading Christ the Book in Aemilia Lanyer's *Salve Deus Rex Judaeorum* (1611)." *Studies in Philology*. 109.3 (2012): 311–322.

Molekamp, Femke. *Women and the Bible in Early Modern England*. Oxford: Oxford University Press, 2013.

Monta, Susannah. "Uncommon Prayer? Robert Southwell's *Short Rule for a Good Life* and Catholic Domestic Devotion in Post-Reformation England." In *Redrawing the Map of Early Modern English Catholicism*, edited by Lowell Gallagher, 245–72. Toronto: University of Toronto Press, 2012.

Morgan, John. *Godly Learning: Puritan Attitudes towards Reason, Learning, and Education, 1560–1640*. Cambridge: Cambridge University Press, 1986.

Mueller, Janel. "Devotion as Difference: Intertextuality in Queen Katherine Parr's *Prayers or Meditations*." *Huntington Library Quarterly* 53, no. 3 (1990): 171–97.

Mueller, Janel. "The Feminist Poetics of *Salve Deus Rex Judaeorum*." *Aemilia Layner: Gender, Genre, and the Canon*, 99–127. Lexington, KY: University of Kentucky Press, 1998.

Mueller, Janel, ed. *Katherine Parr: Complete Works and Correspondence*. Chicago: University of Chicago Press, 2011.

Mueller, Janel. *The Native Tongue and the Word*. Chicago: University of Chicago Press, 1984.

Mueller, Janel. "A Tudor Queen Finds Voice: Katherine Parr's *Lamentation of a Sinner*." In *The Historical Renaissance: New Essays on Tudor and Stuart Literature and Culture*, edited by Heather Dubrow and Richard Strier, 15–47. Chicago: University of Chicago Press, 1988.

Narveson, Katherine. *Bible Readers and Lay Writers in Early Modern England*. Aldershot: Ashgate Press, 2012.

O'Collins, Gerald, and Daniel Kendall. "Mary Magdalene as Major Witness to Jesus' Resurrection." *Theological Studies* 48 (1987): 631–46.

Orlin, Lena Cowen. "A Case for Anecdotalism in Women's History." *English Literary Renaissance* 31 (2001): 52–77.

Pagels, Elaine. "Visions, Appearances, and Apostolic Authority." In *Gnosis: Fetzschrift for Hans Jonas*, edited by Barbara Aland, 416–27. Gottingen: Vandenhoeck and Ruprecht, 1978.

Phillippy, Patricia. "Living Stones: Lady Elizabeth Russell and the Art of Sacred Conversation." In *English Women, Religion, and Textual Production, 1500–1625*, edited by Micheline White, 17–37. Aldershot: Ashgate, 2011.

Phillippy, Patricia, ed. *The Writings of an English Sappho*, translated by Jaime Goodrich. Toronto: Centre for Reformation and Renaissance Studies, 2011.

Pincus, Steven. *1688: The First Modern Revolution*. New Haven: Yale University Press, 2009.

Poole, Kristen. "'The Fittest Closet for All Goodness': Authorial Strategies of Jacobean Mothers' Manuals." *Studies in English Literature* 35, no. 1 (1995): 69–88.

Purkiss, Diane. "Producing the Voice, Consuming the Body: Women Prophets of the Seventeenth Century." In *Women, Writing, and History*, edited by Isobel Grundy and Susan Wiseman, 139–58. Athens, GA: University of Georgia Press, 1992.

Ragusa, Isa, ed. *Meditations on the Life of Christ, An Illustrated Manuscript of the Fourteenth Century*, translated by Rosalie B. Green. Princeton: Princeton University Press, 1961.
Redmond, R. X. "Theology of Prophecy." In *New Catholic Encyclopedia* 11 (2003): 759–64. *Gale Virtual Reference Library* (CX3407709150).
Richards, Jennifer and Fred Schurink. "The Textuality and Materiality of Reading in Early Modern England." *Huntington Library Quarterly* 73, no. 3 (2010): 345–61.
Rose, Mary Beth. "Where Are the Mothers in Shakespeare: Options for Gender Representation in the English Renaissance." *Shakespeare Quarterly* 42, no. 3 (1991): 291–314.
Ross, Sarah C.E. "Early Modern Women and the Apparatus of Authorship." *Parergon* 29, no. 2 (2012): 1–8.
Ross, Trevor. "The Emergence of 'Literature': Making and Reading the English Canon in the Eighteenth Century." *ELH* 63, no. 2 (1996): 397–422.
Ryrie, Alec. *Being Protestant in Reformation Britain*. Oxford: Oxford University Press, 2013.
Sasek, Lawrence. *Images of English Puritanism*. Baton Rouge: Louisiana State University Press, 1989.
Schussler-Fiorenza, Elizabeth. "Patriarchal Household of God and the Ekklesia of Women." In *In Memory of Her: A Feminist Theological Reconstruction of Christian Origins*, 285–333. New York: Crossroad Publishing, 1987.
Scodel, Joshua. *The English Poetic Epitaph: From Jonson to Wordsworth*. Ithaca: Cornell University Press, 1991.
Scott, David. "Slingsby, Sir Henry." In *The Oxford Dictionary of National Biography*. Oxford: Oxford University Press, 2004. http://www.oxforddnb.com.ezproxy.depaul.edu/view/article/25727?docPos=3
Sharpe, Jim. "History from Below." In *New Perspectives on Historical Writing*, edited by Peter Burke, 25–42. University Park, PA: Penn State University Press, 1992.
Shuger, Debora. *Habits of Thought: Religion, Politics, and the Dominant Culture*. Toronto: University of Toronto Press, 1997.
Shuger, Debora. *The Renaissance Bible: Scholarship, Sacrifice, and Subjectivity*. Berkeley: University of California Press, 1994.
Skemp, Sheila. *First Lady of Letters: Judith Sargent Murray and the Struggle for Female Independence*. Philadelphia: University of Pennsylvania Press, 2009.
Skemp, Sheila. *Judith Sargent Murray: A Brief Biography with Documents*. Boston: Bedford St. Martins, 1998.
Sleeper, Stephanie. "Ramist Logic." In *Puritans and Puritanism in Europe and America: A Comprehensive Encyclopedia*, edited by Francis Bremer and Tom Webster, 517–18. ABC-CLIO, 2006.
Smetham, Henry. *A History of Strood*. Rochester: Parrett and Neves, 1899.
Smith, Geoffrey Ridsdill. *Without Touch of Dishonour: The Life and Death of Henry Slingsby, 1602–1658*. Kineton: The Roundwood Press, 1968.
Smith, Helen. *Grossly Material Things: Women and Book Production in Early Modern England*. Oxford: Oxford University Press, 2012.

Smith, Nigel. *Literature and Revolution in England, 1640–1660*. New Haven: Yale University Press, 1994.
Spicksley, Judith, ed. *The Business and Household Accounts of Joyce Jeffreys, Spinster of Hereford, 1638–48*. Oxford: Oxford University Press, 2012.
Spufford, Margaret. "First Steps in Literacy: The Reading and Writing Experiences of the Humblest Seventeenth-Century Spiritual Autobiographers." *Social History* 4, no. 3 (1979): 407–45.
Spufford, Margaret. *Small Books and Pleasant Histories*. Athens: University of Georgia Press, 1981.
Spufford, Margaret and Kenneth Charlton. "Literacy, Society, and Education." In *The Cambridge History of Early Modern English Literature*, edited by David Lowenstein and Janel Mueller, 15–55. Cambridge: Cambridge University Press, 2002.
Spurr, John. "From Puritanism to Dissent, 1660–1700." In *The Culture of English Puritanism*, edited by Christopher Durston and Jacqueline Eales, 234–65. London: Palgrave, 1996.
Stevenson, Bill. "The Social Integration of Post-Restoration Dissenters, 1660–1725." In *The World of Rural Dissenters*, edited by Margaret Spufford, 360–87. Cambridge: Cambridge University Press, 1995.
Stone, Lawrence. *Love, Sex, Marriage, and the Family in England*. New York: Harper and Row, 1979.
Strier, Richard. *Resistant Structures: Particularity, Radicalism, and Renaissance Texts*. Berkeley: University of California Press, 1995.
Tentler, Thomas. *Sin and Confession on the Eve of the Reformation*. Princeton: Princeton University Press, 1977.
Tindall, William York. *Mechanick Preacher*. New York: Columbia University Press, 1934.
Todd, Margo. *Christian Humanism and the Puritan Social Order*. Cambridge: Cambridge University Press, 1987.
Voght, Peter. "A Voice for Themselves: Women as Participants in Congregational Discourse in the Eighteenth-Century Moravian Movement." In *Women Preachers and Prophets through Two Millennia of Christianity*, edited by Beverly M. Kienzle and Pamela J. Walker, 227–47. Berkeley: University of California Press, 1998.
Wall, Wendy. *The Imprint of Gender: Authorship and Publication in the English Renaissance*. Ithaca, NY: Cornell University Press, 1993.
Wall, Wendy. "The Textuality and Materiality of Reading in Early Modern England." *Huntington Library Quarterly* 73, no. 3 (2010): 383–412.
Walsham, Alexandra. *Charitable Hatred: Tolerance and Intolerance in England, 1500–1700*. Manchester: Manchester University Press, 2006.
Walsham, Alexandra. *Church Papists: Catholicism, Conformity, and Confessional Polemic in Early Modern England*. Woodbridge: Boydell and Brewer, 1999.
Walsham, Alexandra. "Domme Preachers: Post-Reformation Catholicism and the Culture of Print." *Past and Present* 168, no. 1 (2000): 72–123.

Warnicke, Retha. "Lady Mildmay's Journal: A Study in Autobiography." *Sixteenth Century Journal* 20 (1989): 55–68.
Watt, Diane. *Secretaries of God: Women Prophets in Late Medieval and Early Modern England.* Woodbridge: D.S. Brewer, 1997.
Watt, Tessa. *Cheap Print and Popular Piety, 1550–1640.* Cambridge: Cambridge University Press, 1991.
Western, J.R. *Monarchy and Revolution: The English State in the 1680's.* New Jersey: Rowan and Littlefield, 1972.
White, Micheline. "A Biographical Sketch of Dorcas Martin: Elizabethan Translator, Stationer, and Godly Matron." *Sixteenth-Century Journal* 30, no. 3 (1999): 775–92.
White, Micheline. "Power Couples and Women Writers in Elizabethan England: The Public Voices of Dorcas and Richard Martin and Ann and Hugh Dowriche." In *Framing the Family: Narrative and Representation in the Medieval and Early Modern Periods*, edited by Rosalynn Voaden and Diane Wolfhal, 120–38. Tempe, AZ: Arizona Center for Medieval and Renaissance Studies, 2005.
White, Micheline. "A Woman with St. Peter's Keys." *Criticism* 45, no. 3 (2003): 323–41.
White, Micheline. "Women Writers and Literary-Religious Circles in the Elizabethan West Country: Anne Dowriche, Anne Lock Prowse, Anne Lock Moyle, Elizabeth Rous, and Ursula Fulford." *Modern Philology* 103, no. 2 (2005): 187–214.
Wiseman, Susan. *Conspiracy and Virtue: Women, Writing, and Politics in Seventeenth-Century England.* Oxford: Oxford University Press, 2006.
Wiseman, Susan. "Unsilent Instruments and the Devil's Cushions: Authority in Seventeenth-Century Women's Prophetic Discourse." In *New Feminist Discourses: Critical Essays on Theories and Texts*, edited by Isobel Armstrong, 176–96. London: Routledge, 1992.
Woods, Susan, ed. *The Poems of Aemilia Lanyer: Salve Deus Rex Judaeorum.* Oxford: Oxford University Press, 1993.
Zagano, Phyllis. *Holy Saturday: An Argument for the Restoration of the Female Diaconate in the Catholic Church.* New York: Crossroads Publishing, 2000.

ONLINE RESOURCES

Early English Books Online: www.eebo.chadwyck.com.
Family Search: www.familysearch.org.
The History of Ewyas Lacy: An Ancient Hundred of South-West Herefordshire: www.ewyaslacy.org.uk.
History of Parliament: the House of Commons 1660–1690, edited by B.D. Henning. Suffolk: Boydell and Brewer, 1983: www.historyofparliamentonline.org.
Elizabeth Isham, *My Book of Rememberance*, edited by Elizabeth Clarke and Erica Longfellow. Coventry: University of Warwick Centre for the Study of the Renaissance: web.warwick.ac.uk/english/perdita/Isham.

Orlando: Women's Writing in the British Isles from the Beginnings to the Present. Cambridge: Cambridge University Press: www.orlando.cambridge.org /The Orlando Project.
Oxford Dictionary of National Biography: www.oxforddnb.com.
Oxford English Dictionary Online Oxford University Press: www.oed.com.
Perdita Manuscripts, 1500–1700: www.amdigital.co.uk.
Who Were the Nuns? Queen Mary University of London: wwtn.history.qmul.ac.uk.

Index

Abbot, Robert, 4, 31, 59, 65
The Account Audited, 174–7
Adams, Sarah Flowers, 185
Allison, A.F., 98
Apostolorum Apostola, 92
"arouse to faith," 3
Authorized Version of the Bible, 168
authorship and audience, 65–8
Avery, Elizabeth, 165

Bakere, Mary, 59
Ball, John, 28, 79
Baxter, Richard, 29, 30
Bellasis, John, 123
Bellasis, Margaret, 123
Bentham, Joseph, 43
Bernard, Richard, 37
Bible teachings, 19
Book of Common Prayer, 22, 59
Book of Remembrance (Isham), 29
Book of Revelation, 163, 170
Branch, Katherine, 24
Branford, James, 147–8
A Brief Catechisme of the Christian Religion (Fist), 59
A Briefe Summe of the Principles of Religion, Fit to be Knowne of Such as Would Addresse Themselves to Gods Table (Hall), 46–7, 49, 118
Brown, Raymond, 107
bublings of Christ, 171–4
bubonic plague, 143
Bunny, Edmund, 131
Bunyan, John, 24
Burch, Dorothy
    Burch, Peeter, 144, 145–7, 146t, 154
    A Catechisme of the Severall Heads of Christian Religion, 34, 141, 142, 150–4
    composition of catechism, 147–50
    conclusion, 183
    Evangelical Protestantism, 145–7, 146t

    introduction, 2, 34, 141–3
    Mann, John, 147–50, 155
    national/international Protestantism, 143–5
    publication of catechism, 154–6
Burch, Peeter, 144, 145–7, 146t, 154
Burke, Edmund, 185
Burke, Victoria, 6
Burton, Catharine, 25
Bynum, Caroline Walker, 154

Calvinist theology, 76
Cambers, Andrew, 73, 96–7
Can It Be Otherwise (Fitzwilliam), 57, 65–6, 67, 78
Canisius, Peter, 125
Capp, Bernard, 162
Cary, Mary
    communion among saints, 170–1
    conclusion, 177–8
    infused knowledge and scriptural exegesis, 164–6
    interpretative authority within communal scriptural study, 166–70
    introduction, 2, 162–4
    response to catechism of, 174–7
    understanding of prophecy, 171–4
Catechism or The Manner How to Examine Children (Calvin), 59
A Catechisme of the Severall Heads of Christian Religion (Burch), 34, 141, 142, 150–4
catechisms and women's writing. *See also* maternal catechesis; Protestant devotional treatises; individual writers; specific catechisms
    childhood catechesis experiences, 37–8
    composition of catechism, 147–50
    domestic catechesis, 17, 21–2
    female authorship, 1–3, 182–5
    historical catechism, 32–4
    household publication, 61–3
    impact of, 3–5
    inter-confessional dialogue, 89

Index

introduction, 1–2
manuscript catechetical composition, 6, 7
memorizing catechisms, 25–9
methodology, 5–7
overview, 7–10
places of scripture, 39–43, 42t
print and polemic, 139
publication of catechism, 154–6
sermon notes and, 63–4
Westminster Shorter Catechism, 30
women as resurrection witnesses, 103–6
Catechisms Written for Mothers (McQuade, Travitsky, Prescott), 153
Cater, Francis, 121–2
Catholicism
conversions to, 121–2
devotional treatises, 2, 108–10
English Catholics, 5
importance of devotional works, 134
seventeenth-century Catholic lives, 97–100
Cawdry, Robert, 67
Chamberlaine, Robert, 144, 147
Chartier, Roger, 22
childhood catechesis experiences, 37–8
children's salvation concerns, 36
A Child's First Lesson (Fitzwilliam), 57, 65, 66
Christian Exercises (Parson), 76, 131
Christianity. *See also* catechisms and women's writing; God; Jesus Christ; Magdalin, Mary; Protestantism
"arouse to faith," 3
Authorized Version of the Bible, 168
Bible teachings, 19
children's salvation concerns, 36
communion among saints, 170–1
communitarian vision of church government, 164
Geneva Bible, 68, 72
Gospel of John, 101–2, 125, 126
Magdalin, Mary, 106–8, 183–4
male-dominated Christian ecclesiology, 91
New Testament, 33, 42, 107, 165
Old Testament, 33, 107
prodigal son parable, 77
religious eclecticism, 108–10
resurrection witnesses in the gospels, 100–3
righteousness in, 45
sacrament of the Lord's Supper, 47
sermon notes, 63–4
understanding of prophecy, 171–4
The Christian's Daily Sacrifice (Cooper), 74
Church History of England (Dodd), 120
Church of England loyalism, 119, 120
Church of England Protestant, 120

The Churchwardens' Accounts record, 147
Clark, Katherine, 63
Clark, Peter, 143
Coles, Kimberly Ann, 2
Collinson, Patrick, 142, 144
communion among saints, 170–1
communitarian vision of church government, 164
Confession of Faith (Fiske), 70
Cooper, Thomas, 74
Coote, Edmund, 23–4
copia technique, 72
Corinthian community, 2
Counter-Reformation biblical scholarship, 104
Craig, John, 29, 30–1
Cromwell, Oliver, 117, 119, 162
Crummes of Comfort, 96
Culverwell, Ezekiel, 79, 81
Cust, Richard, 44

de Groot, Jerome, 123–4
Dering, Unton, 59
A Dialogue of Mental Prayer (Talbot), 128, 130–1
Directions to Those That Have Attained Faith (Fitzwilliam), 60
Divine condescension, 170
Divine omnipotence, 165
Dodd, Charles, 120
domestic catechesis, 17, 21–2. *See also* Fitzwilliam, Katherine; maternal catechesis
Donne, John, 102, 107
Dowd, Michelle, 3
Downame, John, 28
Duffy, Eamon, 3, 33
Dugdale, William, 95
Durston, Christopher, 142

Egerton, Stephen, 74, 75
English Catholics, 5
English Civil War, 142, 143
English Protestant reformers, 3
English Puritanism, 142
English Reformation, 124
The English Schoolmaster (Coote), 23–4
Evangelical Protestantism, 145–7, 146t, 155
Evelinge, Elizabeth, 99
Ezell, Margaret, 6

A Father's Legacy. Sir Henry Slingsbey's Instructions to His Sonnes, 120, 122
Feake, Christopher, 176
Felch, Susan, 60
Fellowes, Ann, 185
female religious community, 99
Fenton, Robert, 59
FH246 devotional (Fitzwilliam), 57, 61–3, 79

The First Book for Children, 33
The First Treatise Teacheth (Fitzwilliam), 57, 73–4, 92
Fiske, John, 25, 69–70
Fiske, Sarah Symmes, 70
Fist, Martin, 59
Fitzmyer, Joseph, 101
Fitzwilliam, Katherine. *See also* domestic catechesis
  authorship and audience, 65–8
  Can It Be Otherwise, 57, 65–6, 67, 78
  catechisms and sermon notes, 63–4
  A Child's First Lesson, 57, 65, 66
  conclusion, 82–3, 183, 184
  FH246 devotional, 57, 61–3, 79
  The First Treatise Teacheth, 57, 73–4, 92
  household publication, 61–3
  influences on, 73–8
  introduction, 2, 56–8
  A Larger Unfoulding, 57, 58, 62, 78–80
  maternal catechesis, 78–82
  originality of, 58–61
  scripture phraseology, 68–73
Ford, William, 121
The Foundation of the Christian Religion (Perkins), 40
Fowler Alistair, 5
French, Daniel, 147

Garnet, Henry, 124
Geneva Bible, 68, 72
German Reformation, 3
God
  Divine condescension, 170
  Divine omnipotence, 165
  as good parent, 81
  love of, 150–4
  as mother, 82
  as physician, 81
  revelation through scripture, 170–1
A Godly Dialogue Between Contrition and Attrition (Talbot), 128, 129–30
Goldie, Mark, 132
Goodrich, Jaime, 118
Gordis, Lisa, 72
Gospel of John, 101–2, 125, 126
Gospel of Nicodemus, 103
Gouge, William, 26–7, 37, 74–5
Green, Ian, 4, 30, 58, 64, 74, 163
Gregory, Brad, 131
The Guide to British Historical Manuscripts in the Huntington Library, 117

Hall, Joseph, 21, 46, 49, 118
Harley, Brilliana, 22
Harris, Tim, 132

Hebrew Scriptures, 165
Heigham, John, 93, 98–100, 103–4, 108–9
Henry, Phillip, 60
Herbert, George, 21, 26, 37
Herbert, Magdalen, 107
Hieron, Samuel, 37
historical catechism, 32–4
Historie of the Bible (Pagit), 39–40
The History of St. Paul's Cathedral in London from Its Foundations Untill These Times (Dugdale), 95
Hoffman, John, 28
Holstun, James, 164
household publication, 61–3
A Humble Apology, 121
Hunt, Arnold, 27, 63–4

images of maternity, 34–6
infused knowledge, 164–6
inter-confessional dialogue, 89
international Protestantism, 143–5
interpretative authority within communal scriptural study, 166–70
An Introduction to the Catholick Faith (Canisius), 125
An Introduction to the Christian Faith (Talbot), 125
Isham, Elizabeth, 25–6, 29

James II, 131–2
Jeffries, Joyce, 41
Jesus Christ. *See also* Christianity; God
  bublings of Christ, 171–4
  death and resurrection, 72, 92–3, 177
  pascal supper, 106–8
  righteousness as saving grace, 70, 71, 142
  sacrifice as freedom, 70, 151
  understanding of prophecy and, 172–3
Johnson, Samuel, 185

Kalendarium Catholicum, 120–1
Keenan, Siobhan, 20, 94–5
Kemble, John, 109
Kempis, Thomas à, 130
Kendall, Daniel, 101
The Key of Paradise (Wilson), 118, 121, 124–31
Killiam, Hannah, 185
Knights, Mark, 133

Lake, Peter, 121
Lanyer, Amelia, 93, 106
A Larger Unfoulding (Fitzwilliam), 57, 58, 62, 78–80
Lely, Peter, 132
Life of Christ (Kempis), 130
The Life of our Lord and Savior Jesus Christ, Gathered Out of the Famous Doctor Bonaventure (Heigham), 93, 98–100, 103–4, 108–9

Index

literacy rates, 145–6
The Little Horn's Doom and Downfall (Feake), 176
Longfellow, Erica, 162, 165, 171
Lowenstein, David, 164
Luther, Martin, 3

Mack, Phyllis, 166
Magdalin, Mary, 106–8, 183–4
male-dominated Christian ecclesiology, 91
Maltby, Judith, 142
Man, Thomas, 75
Mann, John, 147–50, 155
The Manner How to Examine (Martin), 35–6
manuscript catechetical composition, 6, 7
Marianna, Clara, 99
Martin, Dorcas, 35, 36, 182
maternal catechesis. *See also* Fitzwilliam, Katherine; Montagu, Ann; Thomas, Katherine
  conclusion, 49–50, 184
  difficulties of, 30–1
  historical catechism, 32–4
  as household duties, 29–30
  images of maternity, 34–6
  introduction, 3, 19–21
  learning the alphabet, 22–4
  maternal love, 37–9, 78–82
  memorizing catechisms, 25–9, 124
  overview, 3–5
  places of scripture, 39–43, 42t
  print culture, 24–5
  role of mothers in, 21–2
  various ages and abilities, 31–2
maternal love, 37–9
maternity images, 34–6
McKenzie, D.F., 75
memorizing catechisms, 25–9
Mildmay, Grace, 62, 96
Mildmay, Walter, 61
Milk for Babes (Abbot), 4, 31, 59, 65
Molekamp, Femke, 63
Montagu, Ann
  as basis for catechisms, 58–9
  collection of texts, 43–7, 118
  conclusion, 183
  introduction, 2, 21
  poems of, 47–9
Montagu, Edward, 43
More, Hannah, 184–5
The Mother and The Child (Craig), 30–1, 34, 35
The Mother's Catechism (Baxter), 29, 30, 34, 35
The Mother's Catechism For the Young Child (Willison), 29–30, 40
Mueller, Janel, 71

Narveson, Kate, 62
national Protestantism, 143–5
New Model Army, 175
New Testament, 33, 42, 107, 165
Nichols, Josias, 26, 32, 37, 68–9, 169
Noble, Mark, 120
Norton, Honoria, 59

Oates, Titus, 109, 123
O'Collins, Gerald, 101
Of Domesticall Duties (Gouge), 26–7
Of the Markes of The Children of God (Taffin), 79
An Old Book (Thomas), 92, 93, 97, 98, 104–6, 110
Old Testament, 33, 107
oral repetition, 167
An Order of Houshold Instruction (Nichols), 68–9

Pagels, Elaine, 92
Pagit, Eusebius, 39–40
Parkhurst, Nathaniel, 63
Parsons, Robert, 76, 131
pascal supper, 106–8
Perkins, William, 28, 40
Phocas (Emperor), 175
places of scripture, 39–43, 42t
Places of Scripture (Thomas), 92, 97, 104–5
Powell, Vavasor, 24, 153, 155
The Practice of Christianitie (Egerton), 74
Prayer Book Protestantism, 120
Preston, John, 120
print culture, 24–5
prodigal son parable, 77
prophecy, understanding of, 171–4
Protestant devotional treatises, 2
  importance of, 128
  repentance and, 72
  righteousness and, 45
  sola scriptura, 19
Protestantism
  English Protestant reformers, 3
  Evangelical Protestantism, 145–7, 146t, 155
  national/international, 143–5
Puritan families, 21

Questier, Michael, 121
question-and-answer form of writing, 1
Questions and Answers for the Mendip and Sunday Schools (More), 184–5

Ramist rhetorical structure, 64
religious eclecticism, 108–10
repentance, 72
The Resurrection of the Witnesses (Cary), 162–4

resurrection witnesses in the gospels, 100–3
Rogers, Richard, 57, 58, 73–8
Rome Ruined (Spittlehouse), 171–2
A Room of Her Own (Woolf), 3
Ross, Sarah, 5
Rudd, Gaspard, 121
Ryrie, Alec, 167–8

sacrament of the Lord's Supper, 47
Salve Deus Rex Judaeorum (Lanyer), 93
Sanders, Ann, 36
Savage, Sarah Henry, 182
Schussler-Fiorenza, Elizabeth, 92, 101
scientia infusa. See infused knowledge
Scott, David, 120, 121
scriptural exegesis, 164–6
scripture phraseology, 68–73
The Scripture's Concord (Powell), 153, 155
The Second Part of Pilgrim's Progress, 19–20, 32
sermon notes, 63–4
Seven Treatises (Rogers), 57, 58, 73–8
seventeenth-century Catholic lives, 97–100, 184–5
Sherwood, Mary Martha, 185
A Short Catechism (Coote), 24
A Short Narrative of the Discovery of a College of Jesuits at a Place Called the Come in the County of Hereford, 109
A Short Summe of the Whole Catechisme (Craig), 29
Shuger, Debora, 1
Simmons, Matthew, 154
Singer Sargent, Judith, 184, 185
Slingsby, Barbara Bellasis, 117, 122–4
Slingsby, Henry, 117, 119–22
Smith, Nigel, 141–2
So Short a Catechism (Fenton), 59
The Society of Saints: or a Treatise of Good Fellowes and Their Good-Fellowship (Bentham), 43
sola scriptura, 19
Some Deductions from the System Promulgated in the Page of Divine Revelation (Sargent), 184
spiritual autobiographies, 22
spiritual freedom, 2
Spittlehouse, John, 171–2
Spufford, Margaret, 22, 24

Taffin, Jean, 79, 81
Talbot, Barbara Slingsby
conclusion, 133–4

A Dialogue of Mental Prayer, 128, 130–1
A Father's Legacy. Sir Henry Slingsbey's Instructions to His Sonnes, 120, 122
A Godly Dialogue Between Contrition and Attrition, 128, 129–30
introduction, 2, 22, 89, 117–19
An Introduction to the Christian Faith, 125
last legacy of, 131–3
Slingsby, Barbara Bellasis, 117, 122–4
Slingsby, Henry, 117, 119–22
Wilson, John, 118, 124–31
Taylor, Jeremy, 129
Thomas, Katherine
conclusion, 110, 183–4
introduction, 2, 20–1, 91–4
manuscript miscellany, 94–7
An Old Book, 92, 93, 97, 98, 104–6, 110
pascal supper, 106–8
places of scripture, 39–43, 42t
Places of Scripture, 92, 97, 104–5
religious eclecticism, 108–10
resurrection witnesses in the gospels, 100–3
scripture formatting, 49
seventeenth-century Catholic lives, 97–100
women as resurrection witnesses, 103–6
Tillam, Thomas, 166–7, 172
Todd, Margo, 144
Tomson, Lawrence, 73
Trapnel, Anna, 165
The Treasury of Devotion (Wilson), 125
A Treatise of Faith (Ball), 79
A Treatise of Faith (Culverwell), 79
Tyndale, Luther, 45

Udall, William, 98
understanding of prophecy, 171–4

Wallington, Nehemiah, 27
Walsham, Alexandra, 109, 110
A Warning for Fair Women (Sanders), 36
The Watering of the Olive Plant (Fiske), 25, 69–70
Watt, Teresa, 24
Watts, Isaac, 27, 29, 31, 42
The Way to True Happiness catechism, 33
Westminster Shorter Catechism, 30
White, Micheline, 6, 7
Williams, Anna Cromwell, 182
Willison, John, 21, 29–30, 36
Wilson, John, 118, 124–31
women as resurrection witnesses, 103–6
Woolf, Virginia, 3
working-class mothers, 4

CPSIA information can be obtained
at www.ICGtesting.com
Printed in the USA
LVHW052137250321
682479LV00016B/740